THE SETUP

The Setup

For more information, please contact:
Goat Books, LLC
6005 Las Vegas Blvd. South
Suite 7
Las Vegas, NV 89119
Info@danbilzerian.com

CPSIA Code: PSHER0921A
Paperback ISBN: 978-1-7375501-0-5
Hardcover ISBN: 978-1-7375501-1-2
Leatherbound Hardcover ISBN: 978-1-7375501-2-9

Printed in the United States

For my father,

Thank you for diligently proofreading this book.

Sorry I didn't take any of your suggestions.

"If you release this book as it is,

it will be an unmitigated disaster."

PAUL BILZERIAN

“Rather than love, than money, than fame, give me truth.”

HENRY DAVID THOREAU

CONTENTS

Foreword

Ten years ago, you would have never seen my ass writing a foreword for Dan Bilzerian. I would have said I had absolutely nothing in common with the guy. The guy's family was loaded; I grew up in poverty. He gambles, I don't. He takes drugs, I don't. He's had sex with thousands of women; I don't even have morning wood because I work out so much! I was guilty of judging someone like Dan. I saw his wealth as privilege, an unfair advantage and head start in life. The playing field was not level and odds were all stacked in his favor in my jaded eyes. My black ass had been judged my entire life, and here I was doing the exact same thing.

My biggest problem was that I always used to see life through a very small scope therefore my field of vision was very narrow. I didn't have the ability to see beyond my own insecurities and fucked up life. I saw a person like Dan and said, "Me and this motherfucker have nothing in common." It wasn't until I started gaining perspective that I learned no one is exempt from life fucking you up. Unless you have been them or been there, the appropriate thing to do is shut the fuck up and go on your way.

Where the rubber meets the road, I am truly no different than Dan. The biggest thing I found that we have most in common is the uncommon desire to change the very beings we were in our young lives. Regardless of how different our circumstances were, no matter how much he had, and I didn't have, we both ended up in the same exact spot- we both felt inadequate.

Like most of us, the crux of all of our problems in life came from the very things we didn't have. For me, I wasn't a tough kid, and I wanted to be tough, so my only goal in life was to be the hardest man that has ever lived. In Dan's case, he sought approval and affection from his father. He thought he was unattractive and unappealing to women. All of these things and more drove Dan to master what he calls "The Setup."

Neither of us should have ended up where we did. In my high school yearbook, you never would have seen my picture with the description "Most likely to become a Navy SEAL and *New York Times* bestselling author." More likely it would have said "Most likely to be repeating Senior Year." For Dan, no one would have ever predicted that by his mid-thirties he would become the modern-day Hugh Hefner...on steroids- literally and figuratively.

That is the beauty and power of the mind! There is great power in your insecurities, but you must have the courage to examine them in order to find it. You have to look at yourself in the mirror and accept what you see and know to be true,—internal and external, and still be willing to put yourself out there and go for it. You have to not give a fuck about your chances of success, falling flat on your face or what others may think or say...to look in that mirror and not see exactly what you want to see but still have the confidence to bet on yourself. For both Dan and I, our insecurities were the fuel for the drive. Our drive took us down different paths but we both ended up as extreme outliers.

As fucked up as it may be to some, Dan Bilzerian had a dream to fuck as many hot women as he could and become rich as shit and own the best of everything—cars, toys, houses, planes, and bongs (or whatever those things from which shit is smoked are called!). Like it or not, whatever game the motherfucker was playing, he won. "The Setup" has made Dan one of the world's biggest social media celebrities. There are tens of millions of guys all over the world living vicariously through Dan's shenanigans on social media and, on top of that, there are millions more silently following Dan while talking shit about him.

My "setup" was to take the souls of all those that doubted, made fun, and bullied me as well as those that called me nigger and ultimately, own real estate in their minds. One thing I respect most about people is their ability to be vulnerable and unapologetic about who they are. This motherfucker is not asking you to like him. He's not asking you to follow him on Instagram or other social media platforms. Look at how the motherfucker dresses—he wears the same shit every fucking day! He truly has gotten to a place in his life where he does not give a fuck what people think about him. He welcomes the criticism. If more people in this world could get to that place, more people could just be who they truly are and want to be. Whether people accept them or not, it doesn't matter. They accept themselves.

The cold hard truth is that we are all born to die. No one can debate that reality. In that timeframe, you better go after whatever it is that you are seeking to find with all of the ability that you have to find it. For Dan, that was perfecting "The Setup." Ultimately, it is your life to live and no one else's. Not everyone is going to approve of what you do with and in your life and that's ok. If you choose to be a puppet and allow those around you to control the strings, you will be that gray man. Some of us are fine with being that gray man and blending in with the crowd.

In my opinion, there are enough average motherfuckers in this world already. What makes this world unique are the people who are willing to go against the grain and say the things that no one else is willing to say. But, if you want to make a statement with your life, you will need to master your own personal "setup."

DAVID GOGGINS

Retired US Navy SEAL, *New York Times*
Best-selling Author, Endurance Athlete

Prologue

I was bullied as a kid, didn't have many friends, and believe it or not, I had a hard time getting laid. Given where I started, where I ended up might seem impossible, but I am going to take you on the journey and explain as we go.

From a young age I was breaking the rules and trying to find boundaries that didn't really exist. I've been through some pretty traumatic shit and the best way to describe my life would be a rollercoaster with the highest highs and the lowest lows. I've been rich, broke, and rich again. I've hung out with rock stars, rappers, movie stars, athletes, and DJs. I've been backstage at their shows, I've been to their parties, and it was cool. I'll tell you about it. But ultimately it paled in comparison to the circus that my life became.

I'm going to explain what I learned about women and how to get laid with significantly less effort. What works with women will surprise you, but once you understand their subconscious thought process, my counterintuitive strategies will make perfect sense.

I'm going to tell you how I went from flat broke to making over $10 million in a single day. Don't get your hopes up. This isn't a get rich quick book. What I did probably won't work for you, but the premise of *the setup* is universal.

I went from a guy who was made fun of relentlessly to "the most famous man in the world without a talent." I'll show you how I did that too, but once again, that probably isn't going to work for you because most people are too afraid of judgement to own who they are and accept the controversy.

I wrote this entire book myself. I didn't use a ghostwriter. I fact-checked everything, which meant going through thousands of pictures, and over a decade of text messages to verify it is one hundred percent authentic. This is the unvarnished truth, the good the bad and the ugly, not some highlight reel of my accomplishments.

I want all the people who said that I was their idol to understand exactly who they are looking up to. I am no hero. I've had more than my fair share of fuck ups, I've been selfish for the better part of my life, and the world might not be a better place for having me. But I am honest. From a young age, I wanted hot girls to like me, and I wanted to be rich so I wouldn't have to listen to anybody's bullshit. These are hardly lofty goals; I wasn't trying to save the manatees here. I wanted to get tons of pussy, and I wanted total freedom. I achieved those things and all of my other fucked up, hedonistic goals beyond what I ever dreamed was possible. Surprisingly, I did so without ending up in prison, and I've lived to tell you about it.

This book gets progressively crazier as you continue reading, and everything will make sense by the end. No one has lived a life like I have, and it's given me a unique understanding of how to attract women, the power of wealth and a look behind the curtain of fame. I learned how to get whatever I wanted, and I did it by mastering the art of the *setup*.

PART 1

Childhood

CHAPTER 1

Prison

The day started off so normal.

I was walking up to my mom's Jeep when, out of the corner of my eye, I noticed my dad was sitting in the front. I smiled as I opened the door and tossed my backpack under the seat. *Are we going on a vacation*, I wondered, *maybe to Disney World*? Dad never drove with us to school—ever. It was one week before my 11th birthday, so I figured *This had to be something cool,* I thought, *some kind of surprise*.

My mom hadn't even pulled out of the driveway when I asked what was going on.

No response.

I was right, I remember thinking as a smile crept over my face, *definitely a surprise*.

We drove in silence, which was nothing out of the ordinary. Conversations with my father were usually monologues or him reciting "classic" movie scenes. After thirty minutes of anticipation, right before we pulled into the elementary school parking lot, my dad turned around in his seat, facing my brother and me.

Here it comes, I thought.

"Boys, I'm going to prison."

I sat there in shock.

For two years, as news circulated about his conviction and kids made fun of me, he swore to us repeatedly that he wasn't going to prison, that there was no chance. He sounded so convinced, so *sure*, I never doubted him.

As words hung there, spoken so casually like it was some sort of weekend business trip—Boys, I'm going to prison—my brother and I burst into tears. A whirlwind of thoughts went through my head. Most of it wasn't about my dad but me: *I am going to look like an idiot for saying he wasn't going to jail. Everyone is going to make fun of me. I won't see him for years.*

After a couple minutes, he looked at his watch and said that we were gonna be late for school. *Late for school?* I didn't want to go anywhere near school. I wanted to stay in the Jeep. I knew what was waiting for me, but I didn't have a choice.

I wiped the tears away and tried to think about something else, anything else, but I couldn't. I was terrified and mortified, but I tried to be optimistic. *Maybe the kids don't know yet,* I thought as I opened the car door, *maybe I'll have a day to figure out a good comeback.*

As soon as I walked into my homeroom, reality set in—hard and fast. Everyone was laughing, fingers pointed. "Your dad is going to jail!" Since it was front page news, the kids all knew before I did. Everything they had been saying for the last two years was true and from that day on I was made fun of relentlessly.

People treated my family different after Dad went to prison. Some of the kids I used to hang out with in the neighborhood weren't allowed to come over anymore because their parents didn't want them "associating with criminals." I'd see adults whispering at the country club and I could tell they were talking about us by their reaction when I looked over. They'd avoid eye contact and keep their distance, acting like I had a contagious disease. Like the prison would rub off on them.

My father had lost the appeal, which shocked him. During the legal process, the feds offered my dad a plea agreement for a misdemeanor with no jail time and a small fine. He didn't listen to the attorney's advice to take it because he thought his innocence would prevail. In the past, he'd been right when everyone else was wrong, and he assumed the pattern would continue. His biggest strength was also his biggest shortcoming: thinking he could always win.

In the end, they sentenced Dad to four years in federal prison and ordered him to pay $62 million in penalties. He was a genius at valuing companies; taking them over; firing their pampered, poorly performing CEOs; and selling off the assets to make himself and the shareholders a big profit. However, those ousted CEOs had a habit of making big political campaign contributions. So when Rudy Giuliani was appointed US Attorney, he promised to crack down and did just that.

Looking back, Dad was a gambler, even with his own life. He had a clear path to no jail time and a small fine, but he rolled the dice on principle and risked a lot to win a little. It was a poorly calculated risk. When the government comes for their pound of flesh, they get it.

The lesson: Never gamble when the game is rigged...unless you rigged it.

CHAPTER 2

Time Is Money

When we first moved into a modest home in the neighborhood, several years before my father's conviction, people didn't think my parents had money. The ladies at the country club would pull up in their Mercedes-Benzes sporting designer bags and tilt their noses up at my mother because they thought she couldn't afford those things. I could never understand why she drove a Jeep instead of a Ferrari, and I told her so, but that was my mom.

My mother's name is Terri, a petite fair skinned Norwegian with a permanent smile and a positive attitude. Her standard uniform consisted of tennis outfits she bought on sale at Macy's and running shoes. My mother rarely wore makeup and even though my father gave her expensive jewelry she only wore fake gold clip on earrings and simple necklaces. She really didn't give a shit about money or impressing people and I think she got that from her father Harry.

My grandfather, Harry Steffen was a wealthy rancher who'd made it through World War II with everything except his hearing. He had permanently squinted eyes and a thick salt and pepper beard that covered his windburnt skin. Having grown up in the great depression, he took pride in doing hard work every day. Even in the dead of summer he'd sharpen his lawnmower blades and carry metal cans of diesel fuel to his tractor wearing a scratchy long sleeve wool shirt and polyester pants. I remember watching him perplexed, wondering, *what the fuck is the point of having money if you're gonna spend your time sweating your ass off doing bullshit work.*

Harry had a ranch in Northern California, and the family would go there for Thanksgiving and Christmas. There were moose heads on the wall and bear skin rugs, but what I was always fascinated with was his guns. Occasionally he would take me around on his four-wheeler to look for things to shoot. I remember him stopping after seeing a big hawk. He pointed up at it, and I looked at the majestic creature circling above us. Instead of saying, "Hey, look at that bird, it's beautiful," he said enthusiastically, "Look at that bird, let's see if you can bust him!" I was taught to kill animals, and if you didn't do that, you were a pussy, according to my uncles and cousins.

I felt bad shooting animals, but I thought it was just because I was a pussy. It wasn't until later that I realized it's actually the opposite, shooting animals for sport doesn't take courage, it's what insecure guys do to feel powerful, but at seven years old, all you know is what you're told.

One day, I saw a big rattlesnake slithering on the side of the road. Excited for the opportunity to kill something dangerous, I walked up behind it, quickly grabbed it by the tail and whipped it onto the pavement until it was dead. I was proud of my kill, because it was evidence that I wasn't a pussy, so I triumphantly draped it over the stop sign and continued on home. Some of the neighborhood kids saw this and immediately told their parents, who told my father.

"You killed a rattlesnake with your bare hands?" My father asked.

My brother and I.

I nodded, unsure how he was going to react.

"That's impressive, those are deadly!" he exclaimed. It was one of the first times I received his approval.

He told that story every time his friends visited, and I would just sit there and smile; he wasn't lying. But what I never had the heart to tell him was that that fucking snake must have been dying of cancer because I'd never seen anything move slower in my life. But I rarely got praise, and I certainly wasn't going to mention that small detail.

My dad, Paul, looked more like a PE coach than a businessman. He was an athletic six-foot, one-eighty-five with a bushy mustache and long sideburns. Whether it was a board meeting or a baseball game, my father always proudly wore his sweat-stained Boston Red Socks mesh back hat with his golf shirt neatly tucked into his swim trunks. He grew up in a poor family in Worcester, Massachusetts and enlisted in the military soon after dropping out of high school. After a tour in Vietnam, he aced the SATs and was accepted into Stanford where he would meet my mother.

Dad busted his ass and after four years got into Harvard Business school, which, as a high school dropout, was unheard of. My father was a machine, doing whatever it took to accomplish his objectives. And he was a complete maniac in the process. His work ethic was inexorable, but so was his temper. This most notably manifested itself in anything competitive like work or sports.

Growing up, I had very little interaction with my father because he would usually work around sixteen hours a day, seven days a week. The one exception was when he insisted on being my Little League coach. It sounded great, but sports with my father wasn't fun. It wasn't "Go out there and try your best"; it was "There are no points for second place." And if we lost, he would go crazy, which included everything from screaming at me and the other kids to throwing equipment at us in the dugout. He wouldn't speak for the entire ride home, and I could practically see the steam coming out of his ears.

Eventually, this doomed experiment in parenting resulted in my dad suing the Little League for slander.

Bilzerian Strikes Out*

Paul A. Bilzerian, the multimillionaire corporate raider and convicted felon, struck out again with his slander suit against a St. Petersburg Little League official. On Wednesday, a three-judge district appeals court panel in Tampa sided with a lower court order dismissing Bilzerian's suit against Rick Brannelly, vice president of the Northeast Little League.

Bilzerian sued Brannelly in May 1988 after the Little League official told the St. Petersburg Times that Bilzerian reneged on a pledge to give the league $5,000 if the 5-, 6-, and 7-year-old players raised an equal amount in a fund-raising drive. The league, selling household goods door-to-door, fell short by $52.25.

Bilzerian's suit was dismissed last August by Pinellas County Circuit Court Judge Fred L. Bryson Jr. after Bilzerian failed to prove he suffered damages from Brannelly's statements. Bilzerian, in fact, had a great year in 1988, buying Singer Co. for more than $1 billion and selling off most of its assets at a personal profit estimated at between $50 million and $100 million.

Meanwhile, Glenn Burton, the Little League's attorney, said the League "never got the $5,000...and both sides spent at least twice as much litigating this nonsense."

It started when the vice president of the Little League told the newspaper that Dad welched on an agreement. Pops said they lied about the accounting by over a thousand dollars and were trying to extort him, but either way, it was front page news.

By this point my father was worth hundreds of millions, but you'd never know looking at the guy. He'd pull up to the country club in a shitty Jeep wearing a Casio watch. It was very strange to me; I didn't

* James Greiff, "Bilzerian strikes out," *Tampa Bay Times*, October 17, 2005, https://www.tampabay.com/archive/1990/07/21/bilzerian-strikes-out/.

understand why he never bought nice things or what he even wanted all the money for.

Nothing about my father was normal and his parenting was no exception. The one thing I distinctly remember learning from my dad, other than to do whatever it takes to win, happened when my mother gave me shit about not making my bed at breakfast.

Mom was a genuinely good person who never had a bad word to say about anyone, and I remember her giving me a lot of insightful tips that, as a kid, I just laughed at. She said, "If someone talks bad about their friends when they aren't around, they will talk bad about you when you aren't around" and "The things people dislike the most in others are things they don't like about themselves." She was really smart, but I didn't realize it because my father would steamroll her any time there was a disagreement. She was too passive to fight back and I mistook her submissiveness for stupidity because she would effectively lose every argument.

"Dad doesn't make his bed!" I pointed out when she tried to get me to make mine.

Thinking she had a good life lesson all teed up, she turned to my father and said, "Honey, why don't you make the bed and be a good example?"

"I make ten thousand dollars an hour," he snapped back. "I pay the maid fifteen dollars an hour to clean this house. You want me to spend nine thousand, nine hundred, and eighty-five dollars to show your son how to make his bed? Think about how stupid that is. Time is money."

We sat there in the breakfast nook in shocked silence. It was such an unexpected response, but it made so much sense. The lesson was, *understand the value of your time and don't do work that is below your pay grade.* It instantly made me want to make a lot of money, so I wouldn't have to do bullshit work like make my bed. My father didn't act or think like everybody else, and the rebel in me liked that. That mentality made him rich, but it also made him stand out, and that made him a target.

CHAPTER 3

Ernie

You know the cliché "the grass is always greener"? Well, Ernie's grass really was fucking greener, but it wasn't his well-manicured lawn I was envious of.

Right before he was released from prison, my father's 36,000-square-foot flagship mansion was finished. After what seemed like four endless years of waiting, we moved in.

My dad's house.

All of a sudden, people were nicer, and everyone who had doubted me before, now wanted to visit. I proudly gave tours and spouted off the figures of the house. The twenty-one bathrooms stat was my favorite, along with the expression on people's faces when I opened the doors to the indoor basketball court, which was equipped with bleachers and a scoreboard. I found some identity in that house, and it felt good to finally be respected and have people admire me for something. This was probably the beginning of a lifelong pattern. The other part of that pattern was *wanting more.*

I stood on the balcony of our mansion and gazed over the wall at Ernie's 9,000-square-foot house that was only about a fourth the size of ours but seemed so much cooler. There was a Lamborghini and a Rolls in the garage, WaveRunners in the back, and a seemingly endless stream of beautiful women going and coming. He had everything we didn't have; he had everything I wanted. I remember thinking, *If I ever get rich and have my own money, I'm going to live like Ernie, not like my boring-ass parents.*

Our neighbor Ernie was a good-natured car dealer in his mid-thirties. He was tall with blond receding hair combed to the side and perpetually sunburnt, reddish skin. One summer Ernie came up to our lake house in Minnesota with an insanely hot, skinny college girl with big fake tits. I was shook. I didn't want to get caught staring at her, so I averted my eyes to Ernie. He was sporting a gold Rolex with a big diamond bezel, dress pants, and an expensive silk shirt. His friendship with my father was strange considering they were polar opposites. Dad was happily married, wore cheap clothes, and wasn't flashy. He worked all day and never smoked, cheated, did drugs, or drank alcohol. Ernie fucked around on his many girlfriends, partied, smoked cigars at strip clubs, got drunk, and took the dancers on vacation to the Bahamas.

He was a true inspiration, proof that money could buy happiness.

Ernest B. Haire the 3rd, "Ernie."

One Saturday, he pulled up, and I got in his new SUV for my first experience with paintball. I was nervous that it would hurt because I'd heard stories about the bloody welts and bruises, but I loved guns, and this was as close to combat as a little kid could get.

On our way to the paintball field, we stopped at a McDonald's drive-thru and I asked for my favorite breakfast item: beautiful deep fried, crispy hash browns. Three orders. As soon as Ernie yelled into the speaker, I heard a *whack, whack, whack*. The side windows of the cab seemed to explode in color. His redneck buddies were shooting paintballs at us while we were trapped in the fucking drive-thru. When the paint first hit the truck, I was scared. But that quickly turned to excitement. It felt like we were in an action movie shootout scene. I'd never been around adults who acted like this.

Ernie handed the girl a hundred-dollar bill, grabbed our food, and told her to keep the change as he peeled out. I couldn't believe it; he'd just given that girl an eighty-seven-dollar tip without a second thought. I'll never forget the look on her face as we sped off.

We pulled onto a state road, headed to the field when his fucking lunatic friends opened up on us again. The passenger was taking it seriously, shooting rapid-fire at us out of the truck's sliding back window like a machine gunner in a pillbox.

"Can I fire back?" I yelled to Ernie. For a minute, he tried to be responsible and told me no. But we were barreling down the road at seventy miles per hour with the wipers slinging paint off the windshield, and the dude in the other car was pummeling us.

"Okay, get the damn guns," Ernie ordered. I jumped over the seats and grabbed his state-of-the-art Automag paintball gun along with a Tippmann Pro Lite. Ernie leaned out his window with a gun in his left hand, and I had my right arm hanging out the passenger side as we started to unload.

I walked the stream of red paint closer to my target until I finally popped the shooter right in his mouth. His head dropped and he started gasping for air, which freaked the driver out because he didn't know if his buddy was spitting up blood or paint. My following paintballs continued into their cab and hit the *inside* of the windshield, rendering their wipers useless. As their vehicle swerved all over the road with the driver struggling to see where he was going, Ernie egged me on.

"Let those bastards have it!" he yelled. And I did.

That's what I liked about Ernie. He was rich, but he didn't act or think like the snooty country club guys in my neighborhood. While they were contemplating new golf clubs or what spoon to use for their caviar, Ernie was thinking about a new Cigarette boat or what girl he wanted to bring to a tropical island.

A couple months later, Ernie took me to a strip club for the first time. When we pulled up, the valets recognized him and rushed to open the doors of the car. "It's good to see you again Mr. Haire." Ernie nonchalantly slipped the doorman a hundred-dollar bill while the girl at the entry register smiled and flirted with him as he walked by. No one asked to see my ID as I strolled in, unbothered, behind Ernie, like the kid in the gangster movie *Goodfellas*.

Ernie and I were escorted to a private VIP section where he ordered a couple of bottles of Dom and lit a big Cuban cigar. Before he could say anything else, a barrage of topless women engulfed us. Blondes, brunettes, redheads. Their big tits bouncing as they walked had me mesmerized. Time stood still.

He bought me lap dances, while I sat there awkwardly, trying to figure out what to do with my hands. I didn't have any experience talking to hot girls, let alone having them grind on me naked.

Ernie smoked cigars and drank champagne while the dancers he was dating jockeyed for position and competed for his attention. I observed the interactions and sipped my club soda with lime until the club closed to the public. Then we proceeded to sit there for a few more hours while the manager hosted us privately.

They kept the thousand-dollar bottles of champagne coming until Ernie was good and hammered. He signed the bill around seven in the morning before stumbling out with a couple beautiful, scantily-clad strippers. I was put in a separate limo that dropped me off at my house. The sun was coming up as the iron gate slid open. I walked towards the house contemplating what I'd just witnessed.

Ernie was a very average looking guy, so *How did he do it?* I wondered. Up to this point, I'd only heard girls at my school talk about "hot guys." I remember thinking, *I'll never be a hot guy, but if Ernie could get girls like that, then maybe I could too.*

I had never seen women swoon over a guy before, and it started an obsession. In bed at night, I'd fantasize about having just one superhot girl flirt with me like that. In school, I'd imagine what it would be like if one of those women showed up in class and fawned all over me. What would everyone in school say if I walked out holding her hand? They could talk shit all they wanted, but they'd have to respect me if I pulled a girl like the ones they had posters of on their walls. That was my goal. Have a hot girl on my arm like Ernie. I couldn't even imagine having more than one like he did.

Meanwhile in reality, my classmates continued to make fun of me for having buck teeth or because my dad was in jail. Every morning, I hated going to school. I was in a rebellious stage—maybe not a "stage" since I'm still like that—but I didn't want to do what I was supposed to.

I had a hard time concentrating in class, so Mom took me to see a specialist. After running his tests, the doctor diagnosed me with attention deficit disorder. My parents weren't fans of medication, so my mind would be constantly going a million miles an hour. There were no smartphones providing endless hours of entertainment, so most of the time I was bored. My family encouraged me to be fearless, and the only guaranteed way I got attention was when I did something wrong...so the trouble started early.

After thirteen months, my dad returned from prison. I can't remember much about his return, but I do remember that one of the first things he had to do was meet with my principal Joe Merluzzi. The principal told my dad that I refused to respect authority and he had no choice but to expel me from the 7th grade.

"It will be interesting to watch Dan grow up," the headmaster said. "He will either become president of the United States or a master criminal."

CHAPTER 4

Big Dan

My father's world revolved around money. It was the lever he used to move the world and anyone in it. He liked the way money gave him power over others who wanted it, including my brother and me. He would give us money if we got up waterskiing or if we tried a new sport. It reached a point to where I was like an '80s supermodel—I didn't want to get out of bed if I wasn't being paid.

But being back home with an uncontrollable kid who'd just been expelled and a wife who didn't know how to discipline, however, soon wore my dad down. And he quickly decided that life might be better without me around. He also knew my brother would be much easier to deal with when I wasn't around to pick fights with him.

So Dad pawned me off on my mom's stoner brother Big Dan in Minnesota. My uncle, who weighed 130 pounds and was only 5'5", was referred to as "Big Dan" because compared to me, he was the bigger Dan. Pops pitched the whole adventure to Big Dan the only way he knew how: with money. He'd always curried favor with my mother's side of the family by buying them things. He bought my uncle new skis that year to butter him up for the big sale.

He offered Uncle Dan four grand a month to take care of me along with a weekly allowance to be doled out at my uncle's discretion. It was supposed to be tied to my good behavior, so if I got into trouble, then I lost the allowance that week. I only remember receiving the money twice, so I can only assume Big Dan pocketed the cash the rest of the time. He'd put his wallet in his pants, climb on a snowmobile, and spend my allowance at the bar.

One day, he was on his snowmobile run and my aunt was also out of the house. I found his bottle of Jack Daniels in the cupboard, and I wanted to see what it felt like to be drunk. I'd polished off a third of the bottle by the time my uncle got home. He stumbled in obviously hammered and put a chicken potpie in the microwave.

"You're way drunker than me," I declared.

He contested my accusation, which resulted in a wrestling match on the living room floor. After he bested me in what seemed to be a fair contest, he pulled his chicken pot pie from the microwave and headed to his room. He passed out in bed with half-defrosted, half-eaten pie oozing down his chest.

By that point, I couldn't stand upright, and I was crawling on the floor like a drunken sloth when Aunt Lisa came in the door. She started yelling, but I was too drunk to care. Lisa was getting more irate by the second, waking up Uncle Dan to yell at him, then yelling at me. "Either it's him or me!" She spit out the ultimatum to her husband.

I will never forget the shock on her face when he chose me. It wasn't through some sort of family bond or drunken loyalty, but practicality. Big Dan was a carpenter who lived well beyond his means, so wife or no wife, he wasn't giving up an extra four grand a month.

Unfortunately, Aunt Lisa was bluffing. She came back after a day or two, and it was uncomfortable living in the house after that. I felt unwelcome and out of place. I didn't have any friends, so I was constantly bored out of my mind with nothing to do and nobody to talk to. Life in wintery Minnesota was like living in a frozen circle of Hell.

I remember waiting for the bus in the snow when it was thirty degrees below zero. School was just as bad as home, only here they made fun of me for different things. I now received shit for not only my buck teeth—

"bucky"—but also for being a "city boy." The highpoint of my day came when the bus would stop to pick up Tanya, the Puerto Rican stepdaughter of Dan's best friend. She was a grade ahead of me, and even though she was only fourteen, she looked like she was twenty. Her waist was tiny, and she'd wear tight, low-cut tops to show off her big tits. I tried desperately to get her to like me by putting on my Cool Water cologne and asking her dumb questions. But she was banging high school guys and I was in seventh grade, so she wanted nothing to do with me. At least at the time.

My time in Minnesota came to an end when I was kicked out of 7th grade for the second time that year for leaving gym class on the back of a drug dealer's snowmobile. I didn't leave for any particular reason; I just figured fuck it, what are they gonna do? It's not like my life could get any worse. I was wrong.

CHAPTER 5

Losing My Virginity

For 8th grade, my parents sent me to a military boarding school called Admiral Farragut Academy, which the students lovingly referred to as Admiral Faggot Academy. The food was awful, and the barracks were even worse. I was crammed into a shoebox of a room with bunk beds and three other guys. The only thing I looked forward to was making a Cup O' Noodles every night with my illegal water heater. There wasn't a single hot girl in the whole school other than my blonde math teacher who wore blouses that were half-unbuttoned. I jerked off to her in the bathroom on a regular basis.

We had stupid fucking uniforms and marched in formation on the weekends. You'd have to really want your child to be miserable to send him to this shithole, but the structure and organization was probably better than the parenting I received at home. Another upside was there were exactly zero cool kids in the whole school, so there wasn't anyone to make fun of me.

One of my roommates was a Mexican kid we'll call Pedro. I hated my family at that point and was quite vocal about it, so when Thanksgiving break came, he invited me to spend it with him in Mexico.

"Why the fuck would I want to go to Mexico?" I asked.

"No, it's cool. I have my own house, a limousine, and we can do whatever we want."

"Can I buy a gun?"

"No, but we can buy dynamite."

I was sold. I was a sucker for limos and Mexican dynamite.

True to his word, we got picked up from the airport by a stretch limousine. Before even unpacking our bags, we procured the dynamite from a local flea market. It was really just gunpowder tightly wrapped in newspaper with a wick sticking out. And they were probably only about a quarter of the power of a legit stick of dynamite, but compared to the fireworks in the US, it might as well have been C-4.

Pedro had the driver pull over into a neighborhood, and we tested our newly acquired dynamite on some mailboxes. They blew completely apart, like vaporized. The explosion was strangely satisfying; however, the ringing in my ears that wouldn't stop was not.

We headed back to Pedro's house, throwing dynamite out the window of the limo along the way. I checked to make sure the road was empty the first few times, but then I got lazy and started just throwing them blindly into the street...until it happened.

I hurled one out the window, exactly as a car passed us. The dynamite went right in the driver's window. Time froze. I started to doubt what I'd seen. Maybe it didn't go into another car. Or maybe I was just hoping it didn't.

Suddenly, it looked like a light switch was flipped on and off inside the car. The light emitted was blinding, followed by pieces of newspaper blasting out the windows, then darkness. Horrified, I looked over at Pedro. *Did we just kill someone?* I wondered as I glanced back at the car, which was swerving all over the road. I was equal parts relieved and scared when the driver of the blown up car regained control, sped up and came to a screeching halt in front of our limo. The driver leapt out, screaming.

Our chauffer got out with a machete in his hand and started yelling at the driver, who shouted back at him. I couldn't understand what they were saying, but the machete went up into the air and that brought the conversation to an end. The guy got back into the car, managed to get it started, and rumbled off.

The chauffer calmly put his machete away and proceeded to shake us down. Pedro and I had to hand over every peso and centavo we had to prevent him from telling Pedro's father what we'd done. After fleecing us of our money, he then confiscated the dynamite. Fortunately, or unfortunately, depending on how you look at it, we had more cash back at the house.

A couple of days later, we were debating what we should do, when Pedro all of a sudden smiled. "Grab some cash," he said. "We're gonna get laid."

I thought he was just talking shit.

We climbed into the limo and headed out. Ten minutes later, we arrived at a bar where a string of hot women in lingerie marched out and lined up in front of us. Pedro told me to pick one. In my head, I wondered, *Pick one for what*? but I didn't want to act like I'd never done this before, so I pointed to the girl with the nicest tits in the place. She looked like a low rent, slightly out of shape Salma Hayek.

"How are you?" I asked her.

She ignored the question, took me by the hand, and led me to what looked like a dilapidated jail cell. There was no conversation because, despite taking Spanish since kindergarten, the only phrase I could remember was "*Donde esta la biblioteca*?" I'd never even kissed a girl, and before I could ask her the whereabouts of the library, she was sucking my dick.

That escalated quickly, I thought to myself. The gravity of the situation becoming more apparent by the minute. *Is she going to try and have sex with me? Where do I put it, what do I do?* I wondered. This was before the Internet, before little kids everywhere could go on Pornhub and see a chick with three dicks in her.

The hooker popped a condom in her mouth, slid it over my dick, and mounted me before I was fully sure of what was happening. After a minute or two of her riding me like Seabiscuit, I got my bearings and started to figure out how the whole sex thing worked. I got creative, bent her over, and after a couple of minutes, I wasn't a virgin anymore.

I strutted out of the room quite impressed with myself. Pedro came out five minutes later and told me to give her forty bucks. I was so naive that until that comment; I had no idea she was even a prostitute.

Forty bucks! Shit, that cost as much as the dynamite.

CHAPTER 6

Blackmail

Things only got worse in Utah.

Dad bought a computer robotics company based in Provo, Utah, so we moved there my freshman year. I still had zero identity and didn't know where I fit in. I was fourteen, no girls liked me, I didn't get along with my brother, and I barely spoke to my parents. So life in Provo mostly consisted of getting high, watching TV, and jerking off at night in the basement. There was no Internet, so there were no porn sites. The best you could hope for was late night Cinemax and Showtime topless sex scenes. I recorded the best parts on a VHS tape and then would slither downstairs to watch it.

I didn't have many friends, but there was a girl in my neighborhood named Chalet who was a year older than me. Her father was business partners with my dad, so I got to know her when our families would go on trips together. She drove four wheelers, she could snowboard, and she was hot—she was my dream girl. I reasoned that if we hung out enough, maybe she'd eventually like me too.

At first, things with Chalet actually seemed to be going well. I spent various weekends during the first few months of the school year hanging out with Chalet. Her dad would load their big race trailer full of custom Banshee four-wheelers, then haul it behind his dually truck to the sand dunes. After we warmed them up, Chalet and I would repeatedly drag race each other up the face of the biggest dune. She beat me every time, which was frustrating, but really just made me like her more.

Things only got better when I went with her family to lake Powel on a wakeboarding trip. One night after her parents went to bed, we snuck away and cliff jumped naked off some thirty-foot cliffs. After toweling off, we laid back on the rocks, and it seemed like we could see every star in the sky. I didn't try and hook up with her because I was nervous. I didn't want to screw it up. Still, I was excited because, for the first time in my life, it seemed like a hot girl liked me back.

On Sunday night, I was back home and had just finished unpacking from the trip. With nothing else to do, I crept downstairs to watch some Skinamax. I was in the middle of enjoying one of my favorite Provo pastimes when I heard a noise. I glanced up and saw something move by the basement window. Panicked, I turned off the TV and went to the window to get a better look outside. I didn't see anyone. *What could it have been?* I wondered. *A person?* After a second look, I convinced myself it was nothing, so I went upstairs and crawled into bed.

Ten minutes later, there was a knock at the front door. My heart pounded; my mind raced. I tried to tell myself, *it's probably not related.* But my mind raced until it settled on the haunting question: *Could someone have seen me jerking off in the basement?*

Downstairs, I heard my mom answer the door. "Dan it's for you," she called. *Fuck.* I wanted to hide, but my mom knew I was home. Peeking down the stairs, I saw it was some older thugs from my school. And they were smiling. Never in a million years would these guys just stop by my house. My heart sank, this was really bad. "Dan," my mom called again, "Come down! Your friends are at the door." Shit.

I did the walk of shame downstairs and they erupted in laughter like a pack of hyenas. I slunk towards the door as my mom stood there, beaming, looking proud I'd made "friends" in Provo. Thankfully she walked off when I made it to the door. After that, I don't remember exactly what happened or what was said because this was some traumatic shit my brain is still trying to block out. Still, I remember the gist of it. Not only did the thugs see me jerking off, but one of them recorded it.

They demanded I pay them a large sum of money or they were going to release the video to everyone, including my parents—*especially* my parents—then beat me up in front of the school. I didn't have the money, and I was scared shitless.

I couldn't sleep that night. I just laid in bed playing out the scenarios in my head. When you're fourteen, sexual humiliation is a fate worse than death. This is probably true when you're forty as well.

I went to school the next day in a daze, paralyzed with fear and anxiety. The worst part was I had no idea what to expect, wondering when—and how—they would strike. All I could do was try to keep my head down. I snuck into my first class without incident. The rest of the morning was also quiet. By lunch, I'd become somewhat optimistic, telling myself nothing was going to happen—at least not until school let out. As soon as the final bell rang, I booked it for my house while looking over my shoulder constantly. I burst through the front door and locked it behind me. I didn't know what was going on, confused why nothing had happened. I was about to get my answer.

CHALET DASTRUP

Family Friend/Dream Girl

Our fathers were friends and started doing business together, which lead the Bilzerian family to move to Utah. Our families spent a lot of time skiing, snowboarding, boating, going to the dunes, and traveling. Dan and I became best friends, always having a good time on some crazy adventure. We attended the same high school. I don't know the reasons certain people get singled out to get bullied, but I watched it happen to Dan. He was bullied.

I was at Will's Pit Stop, a gas station where everyone would meet up to hang out. There was a group of people watching a video and laughing. I heard them say TW's name. TW was a scary dude, known as a drug dealer and a local gang leader. He was someone you didn't mess with. I kept listening to their conversation about how TW was going to release this tape and humiliate the kid that was in it. Then a group of guys were going to jump him, beating him up in front of everyone at school.

Curious to see what was on this tape, I walked over, and as they replayed it, my heart dropped. It was a kid jerking off in his basement. It was Dan. I grabbed the camera, sprinted to my car and drove off. My adrenaline was pumping as I sped to TW's house.

I walked up to the kid who was sitting on the front porch and asked him where TW was. He pointed to the front door that was cracked open. I went into the house and walked straight up to TW. I told him I destroyed the tape and said they better not touch Dan. He yelled at me for walking into his house and said he'd do whatever the fuck he wanted.

As I walked away, I turned back to him and said, "Stop being a hypocrite. You jerk off in your basement too!" I couldn't sleep that night. I didn't care what they did to me; I just didn't want them to hurt Dan. I went to school the next day ready for anything to happen, but nothing did. Word of mouth was, TW was telling people to leave Dan alone.

My hopes with Chalet were dashed when I learned she'd come to my defense and somehow convinced the guys to not release the tape. In my mind, having her see it and stick up for me was almost as humiliating as if they'd just released it. My heart sank. I felt like a charity case, and I was too embarrassed to even be around her. Things were not going as planned.

I'm sure TW was scared of Chalet's older brother Jarom; he was a big guy who played football, had a lot of guns, and was even crazier than Chalet. If anyone touched Chalet, I honestly believe Jarom would've straight up murdered them. Either way, I dodged a bullet because TW was not fucking around; he would've released the tape, and they would've jumped me had it not been for Chalet. A bunch of kids saw the tape, and I was made fun of regularly, but it could've been much worse. TW ended up getting killed in a drug deal years later.

Thankfully we moved back to Florida soon afterward, and I started sophomore year at Tampa Preparatory School. Determined to end the cycle of bullying, I began lifting weights, and tried out for the baseball team. Dad's years of torturing me with hours of practice paid off, and I made the varsity team. I was the starting pitcher, and I was actually winning games. I made friends with the guys on the team and now all of a sudden, I wasn't a loser. The kids respected me, and girls weren't repulsed by me, so I hoped it would finally be a good year.

And it was...until I predictably fucked it up.

CHAPTER 7

Tampa Prep

My neighbor and I were getting hammered on a Sunday afternoon at my house when we decided to go to the mall to "pick up chicks." He'd just gotten a new Jeep Grand Cherokee for his sixteenth birthday, but he was in no condition to operate it. I was only fifteen, so I wasn't legal to drive or sober either, but I was less fucked up than him.

I smoked a joint as we passed a 40 of Schlitz back and forth on the way to the mall. We finished the beer and did a couple bong rips in the parking lot before walking into Nordstrom's. Unfortunately the mall was full of old ladies and middle school girls with braces, so instead of picking up girls, we grabbed a couple slices of Sbarro's pizza in the food court and took off.

It was pouring rain when we left. I took the freeway onramp too fast, and the Jeep fishtailed. Like an idiot, I stomped on the brakes and locked up the tires. The jeep slid sideways, a tire caught, and we started barrel rolling through the air. Everything happened so fast until the Jeep flipped. Then time slowed down. I glanced over at my buddy mid-tumble, and he was so fucked up that he was actually grinning from ear to ear.

The Jeep rolled three full times before coming to a stop upside down. A switch flipped in my head; I knew this was really bad, and I sobered up instantly. I pulled my buddy out of the window and immediately buried the bong, the weed, and the booze in one of the tire ruts while he sat on the ground in a daze. I was always good under pressure. In baseball, when the bases were loaded, and we needed to score, I would always come through. It was my one positive attribute. So I told him to be quiet and let me do the talking.

When the cops showed up, we were soaked, and the smell of smoke had been washed away. I told the officer we'd hydroplaned because of the rain, and when they asked my friend questions, I interjected quickly, answering and explained that he was a bit shook up. They didn't consider the possibility that two kids would be drunk and high at two in the afternoon on a Sunday, filed the report, and let us go.

The insurance company paid up and somehow, we walked away scot-free. I think his dad knew the truth, though, because he wasn't allowed to hang out with me ever again.

A few months later when I turned sixteen, my dad coincidentally leased me a Jeep Grand Cherokee. I'd clearly not learned my lesson because the first thing I did was put on two layers of limo tint so I could smoke weed while driving. Having my own ride was a big deal because now I could go to parties and feasibly pick-up girls.

My school was located conveniently close to the ghetto where it was easy to buy dime bags of schwag weed from the local drug dealers on the corner. I'd sit in the parking lot after school rolling joints to smoke on the way home. After smoking a blunt in the parking lot, I drove across the street to pick up my brother.

Upon pulling into school, I saw my math teacher. Good and stoned, I thought it'd be funny to stick my ass out the window of my Jeep as I drove by her. She didn't think it was funny. So at the end of the year I was asked not to return to Tampa Prep, and my father was surprised when they turned down his bribe to build the school a new baseball stadium.

PAUL BILZERIAN

Father, Corporate Raider

Dan returned to Tampa for tenth grade and attended Tampa Prep. He made the varsity baseball team as a sophomore. Dan was not only a great pitcher, but he was also the greatest clutch hitter I ever saw. I coached him on fourteen teams, so I saw him play close to three hundred games. Getting a clutch hit one out of three at bats is exceptional. In three hundred games, I cannot recall one time when Dan failed to get a clutch hit. He reminded me of The Natural. Thirteen of those teams came in first place, and a good deal of that success was due to Dan. So we were rather excited about Dan's baseball prospects for his junior and senior years. Unfortunately, Dan mooned his math teacher on the last day of school his sophomore year, and he was permanently expelled, so we never got to see him play his junior year. Of course, as everyone knows now, he was arrested on the first day of school in his senior year and was ordered to leave the state of Utah, so he never played baseball his senior year either. Four years in the Navy later, and his baseball days were over.

Some birds just have to fly free; some men must blaze their own paths. I have no doubt when Robert Frost was writing his great poem, "The Road Not Taken," he had someone like Dan in mind.

Two roads diverged in a wood, and I—
I took the one less traveled by,
And that has made all the difference.

CHAPTER 8

First Fight

I spent the summer back in Minnesota. Tanya, the Puerto Rican girl I had a crush on, had gotten knocked up, had a kid, and dropped out of school. So she was just desperate enough to agree to sleep with me, and I finally lost my non-condom virginity. I got some confidence and continued sleeping with her to accumulate experience with someone who wasn't a Mexican hooker.

For my junior year, my parents enrolled me in public school, which had always seemed cooler than the private schools I was used to. However, I wasn't allowed to play baseball that year due to the same district school change. Since I couldn't play ball, I hung out with more of a juvenile delinquent crowd, one of them being a Hispanic kid named Fabian. This friendship lasted until a girl told him I was talking shit. I was not; the girl just wanted attention, but he believed her and called me out to fight him.

Fabian was a big dude with about five inches and sixty pounds on me. I didn't want to fight him, but I hadn't done anything wrong, so I refused to back down. I'd never been in a fight before, so I was scared, but I also wouldn't be able to live with myself if I pussed out. So it was either get beat up by him or internally beat myself up. Nothing was worse than the latter.

An audience gathered at the parking lot where kids met for fights, cheering like bloodthirsty Romans watching gladiators in the Coliseum. I threw a jab at Fabian just to get this thing going. He lunged and cracked me in the head with a right hand. I felt his metal rings hit my face, and it hurt, but the pain somehow didn't register.

I got a few shots in before he put me in a headlock and repeatedly pounded the back of my skull. Every time he hit me, I wondered if it was lights out. I saw stars, and each blow was like a concussive blast where everything went quiet and then slowly came back to normal with all these kids yelling.

I eventually slithered out of his grasp, and we traded punches on the asphalt until I thought my heart would explode. I'd never been so tired and out of breath in my life. He was heaving and throwing looping lazy punches that shouldn't have landed, but I was too exhausted to move out of the way. This continued until he couldn't punch anymore and stopped the fight.

As soon as it was over, I remember thinking, *I can't believe I was so scared of fighting my whole life,* and *I really need to start doing cardio.* Taking a punch to the face didn't hurt nearly as bad as I imagined. When you're in a fight and you know it's coming, your adrenaline is going, so you barely feel any pain.

He beat my ass, but technically didn't win the fight since he's the one who stopped. It was simultaneously my first defeat *and* my first victory. The crowd was happy, I had blood on my face, and I was smiling, relieved that it was over. That could have been much worse, I thought. I didn't quit and learned I could take a beating. It was a lesson that I would relearn many times.

CHAPTER 9

Approach Anxiety

Halfway through my junior year, my family up and moved back to Utah so my father could be closer to his work. We rented a house in a nice neighborhood outside of Salt Lake City called Sandy, where I finally started to find my place.

This was my seventh new school in five years. Though some kids feel like moving a lot fucks them up, the upside is you get a fresh start and that allows you to learn how to reinvent yourself, a skill that has served me well in life.

In Salt Lake City, I ran around with a diverse group that ranged from jocks to Samoan thugs. I kept lifting weights, joined a Mexican car club, and tried mushrooms for the first time. It was all coming together, and I was actually happy for the first time in my life.

My friends and I would typically meet up at the mall to get high and pick up girls. I was pretty shy, and like most seventeen-year-olds, I was scared of talking to hot girls. The fear wasn't of actually speaking to them but of being rejected by them. My buddy Wayne was the opposite, he didn't give a fuck. He would talk to every girl he saw, but he had a different approach than we did; he wouldn't hit on them. Sometimes he would even start conversations by making fun of them, something I never thought would work, but it did. Usually, he just asked a question, something innocuous to get them talking, and if they tried to dismiss him or act like they were too good, he would just crack jokes and turn it around on the girls, making them feel insecure.

His approach was genius if you understand the psychology, but this wasn't something he had figured out from textbooks on the human brain. It was natural, and it worked because he genuinely didn't care, and that telegraphed confidence. But most importantly, by never hitting on them or displaying direct interest, he *set it up* so the girls never really had the ability to reject him.

It was inspiring to see a guy who wasn't afraid. I hated being scared of anything, and this was the perfect way for me to conquer that fear. After watching how Wayne worked, I began building up the confidence to approach women. I wasn't as witty or as comfortable talking to girls as Wayne, but the more I failed, the less I cared. And I quickly learned that not caring was the most important attribute you could have when picking up women.

Also, once I made it about talking to girls instead of hitting on them, I approached with more confidence. Before, I used to get anxiety because being rejected seemed like a big deal, but with my new strategy, I had less to be afraid of. I didn't get laid that much; in fact, I don't think I got laid at all from doing this, but I was making progress, and Rome wasn't built in a day.

APPROACH, APPROACH, APPROACH. Volume is the key. The more you fail, the less you will care, and the less you care, the more you will succeed.

I had a buddy who would only talk to girls he was positive were into him. He pursued two girls and slept with both of them. I tried with a hundred girls, and I fucked three. Sure, he may be "batting a thousand," but I still fucked more girls.

Do this at the mall or the beach. Get some practice with girls you aren't gonna see every day and just start a casual conversation or ask a question. If they seem interested, invite them to tag along to something you're gonna do anyway; that way their involvement doesn't seem important. For example: "My friends and I are about to go to a pool party/winery/lake house/concert/Chipotle/whatever if you wanna come."

Don't hit on them.

Around the time he broke ground on the Tampa house, Dad bought a peninsula of land in Minnesota with five homes on it. I'd been spending summers up there ever since, so when school got out in Utah, I loaded up my Jeep and drove north. My parents agreed to let me stay in one of the guest houses, so the only thing I needed was a wingman. I called my buddy John, a neighbor from Tampa and invited him up. He was a state champion wrestler but as much of a fuck up as me. After winning state, he went to nationals but was kicked out of the tournament for buying beer with a fake ID. The good news was he still had the ID.

It was summertime in a lake town, and girls in bikinis were everywhere. My cute five-year-old cousin Nick was a better accessory than a puppy dog for picking up chicks, so we'd send him in to ask girls if they wanted to come on the boat with us. My ski boat and the cooler full of beer helped continue the conversation. We wake-boarded and drank while blasting music from my carefully crafted mixed tapes. I was good, but my wakeboarding skills always seemed to improve when there were hot girls on board.

After an hour or so, buzzed, we'd head to my house to keep drinking. I finally started hooking up with girls and, surprisingly, without much effort. This was the moment when I first started to understand the importance of *The Setup*. My "game" with girls hadn't really improved, but my environment was now conducive to getting laid, and that made all the difference.

In the past, I tried too hard, and it was counterproductive. I noticed the less "I tried," and the lower my perceived effort, the more the girl would try and make me interested in her. I also realized the more fun and exciting my life was, the more girls wanted to be a part of it.

When my five-year-old cousin wasn't around, John and I took turns approaching girls. During the day, it was, "Hey, wanna go boating? We're wakeboarding and need a spotter." At night, it was, "Hey, wanna go to the keg party on Cross Lake" or "Wanna smoke?"

Inviting a girl to join us for something we were doing anyway made it a lot easier to talk to them, increased our success rate, and showed less interest than randomly approaching them. Then by doing something fun together, we could avoid the forced conversation and pressure that makes a regular date awkward.

John looked like an athletic Matt Damon, so he was usually pretty good at getting girls. One day, he was cruising around the lake on my WaveRunner when he saw a hot blonde laying out on her dock. He picked her up, took her for a ride, and somehow convinced her to suck his dick. Unfortunately, the girl's dad had binoculars, so he was waiting when they pulled up to the dock. After some hostile words, John panic-shoved the girl off the back into the water and sped off. The problem was that we lived directly across the lake from the girl's family.

We knew that her dad would be coming to talk to my dad about what happened, so I figured it was best to lean into this thing and not hide. John took a shotgun, I grabbed my AR-15, and we both started shooting cans and shit in the front yard. Moments later, we saw her dad's red pickup truck peel out of their driveway headed towards us. As he got closer, he must have heard the semi-automatic gunfire because he never made it to the house.

When summer was over, I packed up my shit and drove back to Utah in my Jeep. The drive took a couple days, but I was, for the first time in my life, actually looking forward to school.

CHAPTER 10

Utah Code §76-10-505.5

I had an AR-15 that I kept in the back of my Jeep, which kids thought was cool.

I laid out my best outfit the night before and couldn't eat much at breakfast because I had butterflies in my stomach. It was the first day of class, and I was excited to be a senior. I was eligible to play baseball again, I had a lot of friends, and people thought I was cool. Everything was set for this to be my best year yet.

On the way to school, I picked up a couple buddies, and as they tossed their backpacks in the trunk, they saw my AR-15. It wasn't an accident; I was proud of that thing and was always trying to show it off. They thought it was badass too, and as soon as we got to school, they told all their friends. Halfway through my first class, I was asked to step into the hall.

A cop stood there with some of the school faculty.

"Do you have any weapons in your car?" he asked.

"Yes."

"What are they?"

"I have a hunting rifle, a shotgun, and a pistol." (Ok the hunting rifle was a bit of a stretch, but technically you are allowed to hunt with an AR-15).

The cop glanced over at the administrator, who seemed to be trying to get her breath under control.

"Can I search your car?" he asked.

"Yeah, sure."

My whole life Dad had taught me to always tell the truth. But he didn't give me any lessons on dealing with the police, where the truth was not always on your side. Considering he was a convicted felon and I was in constant trouble, that was the kind of mentoring I could really have benefitted from.

Had I refused to speak to them, gotten in my car, and driven home, there would have been zero trouble. But I naively gave them permission, so they searched my car and slapped handcuffs on me.

Dad rushed down to the juvenile detention center. I was sure he'd be pissed, but he was very calm and said he was going to get me out. I was shocked because he would get so upset about petty shit, yet he was calm about me being in jail. Mom offered some encouraging words. I told them, honestly, that I didn't know why I was in trouble since the guns were legal. I was parked about a quarter mile away from the school, and I had told the truth.

I asked optimistically if he thought I'd be able to get back into class that week. My dad said no matter what happened, I would never be allowed back at that school again, and my lawyer said I might never be allowed at any school again. Then my father gave me the bad news.

They were charging me with "possessing a firearm on or about school grounds." This was shortly after the Columbine shooting in Colorado, and that's when I understood why Dad wasn't mad. He knew this was serious, and I was looking at years in prison. I sat there stunned while he told me not to worry. The last time he told me not to worry, he ended up in federal prison, so I didn't feel very confident in his assertion.

I laid in my cell that night contemplating how one mistake had completely derailed my life. I'd busted my ass to make a bunch of friends, I was finally popular, and for once in my life I actually wanted to go to school. My mind was still holding out some hope that my life would go back to normal, but one glance at the iron bars made it register. I was locked in a cage. I looked around the room at the metal mirror with gang symbols cut into it and the dented steel toilet with no seat and wondered, *Am I gonna have to get used to this?*

Two weeks later I'd accepted my fate, I was actually much happier in jail than I was when I got caught jerking off a few years prior, so I guess it's all relative. I was just upset they weren't feeding me for shit, and there was no weight room. I'd worked so hard over the past two years to put on what little muscle I had, that losing it actually bothered me more than losing my freedom.

When I finally stopped caring I got the news...My lawyer negotiated a good deal since it was my first offense. I pled guilty and was sentenced to time served, which by then was twenty-one days, but there was a caveat. I had to leave Utah and not come back. I had never heard of someone getting kicked out of a state before, but it wasn't the first time I'd been booted out of something, and it certainly wouldn't be the last.

The drive with my mother back to Tampa while my brother and Dad stayed in Utah, was forty-eight hours of uncomfortable awkwardness. It was my fault. I'd singlehandedly split up the family. On top of that

My dad, mom, brother, and me.

I couldn't get into any high schools in Florida because of the conviction, so I had two options: go to a shitty community college in hopes of transferring to a better university after two years of good grades or I could join the military.

Slinking into a community college was essentially admitting I was a failure so that was out. My father went into the military a high school dropout and came out a decorated war hero. He used that distinction to get into Stanford University, which at the time was my dream school. The path was clear. My whole life I'd wanted to get my father's respect and I knew he, along with everyone else would respect me if I became a Navy SEAL. It would also mean that I wasn't a loser or a pussy. But that wasn't the only reason I made that choice.

PART 2

Military

CHAPTER 11

Welcome to the Navy

I wanted to be a part of something serious and impressive, I wanted people to respect me, but, most importantly, I figured it would get me laid.

I went down to the Navy recruiter's office and asked what I had to do to become a Navy SEAL. The recruiter looked at me like a sucker who'd wandered onto a used car lot; he smiled and told me to take a seat. After asking a series of questions to make me qualify myself, he went on to tell me how great military life was.

I asked what the training was like and what I should do to prepare. He didn't know anything other than "It's really hard, you have to run and swim a lot." And "90 percent of the guys don't make it." When I pressed him for more information, he handed me a pamphlet that said "BUD/S (Basic Underwater Demolition/SEAL) Warning Order," which contained a basic description and the minimum requirements to be eligible. I went to the bookstore and looked up books on how to be a Navy SEAL. Nothing. I started asking around, and I couldn't find anyone who even knew anyone who was a Navy SEAL.

I hired a swim coach and started training my ass off. Every day I would do some form of cardio, calisthenics, and eat every three hours. Things were not progressing as fast as I'd hoped, and I wanted to delay shipping off because I kept getting shin splints any time I'd run more than a mile. But Dad wanted me out of the house, and he told me to build up my running base in boot camp.

I enlisted in the Navy and shipped out on April 29, 1999, four months after my eighteenth birthday. I was 165 pounds, and I'd never run further than two miles in my life.

Upon arrival to Naval Station Great Lakes, we were ordered to strip off our civilian clothes and put all of our personal items in a Ziplock bag before they shaved our heads. The reality of it all hit me hard. I was truly on my own for the first time in my life, on equal footing with everyone else, and there was no turning back. I was also much uglier bald than I'd anticipated.

Boot camp sucked, but for different reasons than I expected. The food was unhealthy, and we barely slept. I expected to get into better shape, but the workouts were designed for obese couch potatoes. The farthest we ran was a couple miles and it was at a snail's pace. We stood watches, cleaned bathrooms, shined boots/belt buckles, and learned how to make beds and fold clothes. I thought this was going to be like the movie *Full Metal Jacket*, but it felt more like learning how to become a sleep deprived maid than a soldier.

After nine weeks of boot camp, it was on to six weeks of Quartermaster A School, where I would learn how to navigate a ship. Going through boot camp changed my perspective. All of a sudden I was appreciative of everything I used to take for granted. Getting eight hours of sleep felt amazing and food from normal restaurants now tasted better than Michelin Star dinners I'd had in the past. Even little shit like having the freedom to workout in comfortable clothes and shower whenever I wanted brought me a disproportionate amount of joy.

In QM A school, I met a squared away quiet guy named Matt who was going to BUD/S* as well. He was a good runner who followed the

---

* Basic Underwater Demolition/SEAL.

rules and rarely got in trouble. We were completely different but shared a willingness to endure pain and an abhorrence to quitting.

Matt and I would do calisthenics, lift weights, and go for runs around the base. I preferred run-swim-run circuits because it allowed me to get good cardio exercise without putting too many consecutive miles on my legs. Lake Michigan was cold, but my shins loved it. After a few weeks of keeping up with him on runs, my shins began to really hurt. I went to medical, and after an X-ray, I was diagnosed with bilateral tibial stress fractures. The doc put me on crutches and ordered nine months of limited duty.

I was really happy to get this news because I knew I wasn't physically ready to go to BUD/S, and this would give me time to get in shape while my tibias healed. The Navy detailer who handled assignments had other ideas. "If you can't go to BUD/S now, then I'll put you on a ship for two years after your limited duty is finished."

"But then it will be three years before I can start! I can't wait that long."

"I don't care. Either you get declared fit for full duty now and go to BUD/S or you take your limited duty time and go to the ship."

I went back to the doctor and told him that I no longer had any pain in my legs.

"Sir, I'd like to be taken off limited duty please."

"Keep weight off of your legs as much as possible and take it easy," the doctor said as he signed the papers.

I called my detailer and informed him that I was now fit for full duty. He cut me orders to BUD/S and shipped me off to California. San Diego is beautiful, and the weather is 72°F and sunny during the summer. But when I arrived for training in October, it was cold and overcast.

The first thing you have to do at BUD/S is report to the infirmary with your medical records and complete a "Dive physical." Trainees must get cleared by the DMO (Dive Medical Officer), who, at the time, was Lieutenant Mosier. Doc Mosier was a no bullshit Vietnam SEAL, and he was intimidating. He glanced at me, scanned my paperwork, and then looked back at me.

"What are you doing here?" he asked. "Why aren't you on crutches? You were documented with stress fractures four weeks ago."

"The doc at A School cleared me for fit for full duty, sir," I replied.

He didn't buy it and ordered a fresh set of X-rays, which told the same story as they had a month earlier: bilateral tibial stress fractures.

"You're not fit to train. I'm dropping you from the program."

"Sir, can you roll me back to the next class?" I pleaded.

"There are no *white shirt* roll backs," Doc Mosier said referring to the color of T-shirts aspiring SEALs wore before completing Hell Week. After, trainees are given *brown shirts*. "And there is absolutely no way you can complete training with broken legs. Go to a ship, let your body heal, and then come back."

With my back against the wall, I played the only card I could, one that was guaranteed to piss off every single person in my chain of command.

I requested Captain's Mast.

Enlisted men essentially lose all personal freedom and rights. But you have one undeniable right: to request Mast. It's the ultimate fuck you, the military version of Karen demanding to speak to a store manager. It goes all the way up the ladder to the base commanding officer. Once submitted, it can't be stopped unless you withdraw your request.

Doc Mosier was pissed.

I ended up in the office of the captain, the highest-ranking officer on the base who was also a SEAL. In the military, you're broken down and taught to fear and respect rank, particularly the officers, so it was extremely intimidating.

"I only joined the Navy for one reason, sir," I said, standing stiff as a board, trying to keep my voice from quivering. "I want to become a Navy SEAL, and I will do anything in my power to accomplish that. Please clear me to train, sir."

"I don't think you're going to make it very far," he said. "But I'll let you train."

I was thrilled but also dreaded the trip back to Doc Mosier's office. He was visibly irritated by the captain's orders but seemed to offer a grudging respect.

"I'll bet you twenty bucks you don't make it through Hell Week," he said.

"Yes, sir, you're on." I was bluffing. I didn't really think I would make it. I was a massive underdog medically and statistically but felt like I'd look like a real fucking asshole if I didn't accept.

He wanted to bet, he was confident, and he had a big ego. The *setup* was right to get a good bet; I should have asked for long odds, but I was young, and I had a lot to learn about gambling.

CHAPTER 12

Basic Underwater Demolition/SEAL Training

Before starting BUD/S, trainees have to complete PTRR (physical training rehabilitation and remediation) and Indoc (indoctrination). These courses are supposed to build trainees up and get them ready for first phase, but I think more guys quit in PTRR and Indoc than in the actual training. We were running twelve to fourteen miles a day, swimming, doing calisthenics, and completing obstacle courses, all while being wet, cold, and sandy.

My first roommate at BUD/S looked like a ripped-up *GQ* model hired to play a Navy SEAL in a movie. He told me that he lived off base during his prior stint at BUD/S. I was interested, but he said they'd only approve requests to live in private housing if the applicant is either married or an officer.

"Fuck it, I'll submit the paperwork anyway," I told him.

People who work in military administration roles often make mistakes. They shuffle endless amounts of paper each day, and sometimes they don't read forms properly. And since they generally would never see this kind of request from an E-2 (my rank), I figured maybe I'd get lucky. And I did.

Through some mix-up in the bureaucracy, my application was approved. I didn't talk to Dad much, but I called to share this good news. He was impressed and offered to send out my mother's Jeep so I could commute to and from my apartment. The first thing I did was spend all of my saved boot camp money installing a lift kit and huge mud tires to transform it from Soccer Mom to Swamp Buggy. Then I outfitted a one-bedroom apartment in Coronado.

Moving off base was the first mistake I made in BUD/S. It took my pay from just under a thousand dollars a month to almost three thousand, but it separated me from my classmates and made me stand out. Growing up, I craved attention, so I liked to stand out, but in BUD/S, the last thing you wanted to do was stand out. It also meant I couldn't ask questions or share tips at night like the guys in the barracks. Plus, I lost almost an hour of sleep a day when my round-trip commute was tallied up. That recovery time was important, given that part of BUD/S is intended to deprive you of sleep to test how you perform.

Each day started the same. My three alarm clocks would sound, and I'd wake up at 0300. I stood in the mirror and shaved, knowing the sun wouldn't rise for another four hours. I thought Southern California was supposed to be warm, but it wasn't unusual for the base temperature gauge to display temperatures in the forties during those early winter mornings.

It was pitch-black as we ran from the barracks to the CTT (combat training tank). The air was crisp, and I could see my breath with every exhale. It had been unusually cold that week, and the sign as we entered the base flashed between the time, 0350, and the temperature, 39 degrees.

The first step before entering the CTT was Decon, which was short for decontamination, where we were subjected to hundreds of gallons of freezing water from industrial pinpoint high-pressure hoses designed to wash dirt off military vehicles. As I felt the cold water seep through my uniform, I fully abandoned all hope of being dry and warm for breakfast, the one thing I usually looked forward to.

We stripped down to our UDT shorts, which were like Daisy Dukes made of a thick, heavy-duty canvas. They seemed designed by a sadist with special effort paid to pinching your nuts and chaffing the skin off your inner thighs. We sat down in our boat crews "nut to butt" on the cold concrete pool deck to wait for the instructors to arrive. The highlight of my morning would come if the guy behind me couldn't hold it any longer and pissed on my back and ass. It's funny how a stranger pissing on your back, something that at any other point in your life would lead to a lay down drag out fight, would, in this strange situation, be welcomed.

Headlights shined into the CTT, indicating the instructor's arrival. We did twenty push-ups, followed by acknowledging them in order of rank with "Hooyah, Instructor Patstone! Hooyah, Instructor McCleland!"

"Backs!" one of the instructors yelled. We flipped over, backs on the cold concrete while they turned on hurricane fans and sprayed us with water. After what felt like an eternity, the instructors ordered my half the class into the pool. Excited to warm up, I eagerly got to my feet and jumped into the water. Shit! The pool heater was either broken or turned off, because the water was freezing. If I had to guess, I'd say low sixties.

I swam as fast as I could, trying to warm up. After twenty minutes, I was exhausted. The water still felt cold, and I knew I had hours more to go. The negative thoughts quickly began piling up, and I started to question everything. *What the actual fuck did I sign up for? Why on Earth did my dad think I could do this? There's no way I'm gonna make it!* I thought as I swam.

I tried to imagine picking up a hot girl in a bar by telling her I was a SEAL or sitting on a warm tropical beach to distract myself, but my mind kept settling on *this sucks*. It was actually better when the instructors were yelling at you because at least there were distractions, other things going on. In the water, it was just you and your thoughts.

After hours of swimming and other drills, we raced to put on our cold, wet uniforms. Over half the people in my class ended up quitting because they were sick of the cold. Being cold for ten or twenty minutes sucks, but being cold sixteen hours a day for seven months straight is downright soul crushing.

Breakfast provided a few brief moments of rest and nourishment before we ran the mile back to the other base to a concrete training area called "The Grinder." There we would complete a rotating circuit of exercises that totaled around five hundred push-ups, almost a hundred pull-ups, and a seemly never-ending amount of sit-ups, flutter kicks and leg levers.

Rubber boats full of ice cubes and water were positioned near the pull up bars. If you couldn't finish your set, you had to dive into the boat and crawl under the rows of inflated cushions and climb out the other side. If you reached failure during push-ups or sit-ups, the instructors would order you to "Get wet and sandy!" That meant run two hundred yards to the ocean, jump in, roll around in the sand until you looked like a sugar cookie, and then sprint back.

After an hour and half of calisthenics, we mustered on the beach for a run. The thick wool socks we were issued held water like sponges, so it felt like I had anchors attached to my ankles. I looked around, and the other guys didn't seem to be struggling too much, which was a big mind fuck. The hardest thing for me to do was run next to a guy who didn't get winded or show pain. If I saw a guy suffering, it gave me confidence and sometimes a second wind. But no such boost happened for me in the early days of BUD/S.

I was out of breath just a few minutes into the run. I tried to relax, but when the instructor led the class into the soft sand, I thought my heart was gonna explode. The soft sand was less painful on my shins, but each step took much more effort.

After about thirty minutes, I started to fall off the group's pace and ended up in my first "goon squad." This was a general term for people who couldn't keep up or failed a test. The instructors had us get wet and sandy and then told us to "drop" and "push 'em out." If you heard "drop," it meant a minimum of twenty push-ups, and you would stay in the push-up position until you heard "recover." They "beat us," which was a term for having us do repeated sets of various calisthenics with no breaks.

After about fifteen minutes of this, the goon squad was ordered to go into the surf, interlock arms, and lay down. The fifty-seven-degree ocean crashed over our heads, sand washed into our eyes, noses, and ears as we lay there, wondering how long this would last. This was called "surf torture," and it usually lasted about twenty minutes but felt like an eternity.

The remainder of the day was spent doing some combination of surf passage, an obstacle course, drown proofing (swimming with hands and feet tied behind your back), underwater knot tying, log PT (workout with a half telephone pole), a two-mile timed ocean swim, etc. When we were finally dismissed around 1900, everyone was exhausted but we still had to clean and prepare our gear. Trainees were expected to appear with polished boots, a sharp knife, clean UDT life jacket, and a perfectly painted helmet every day. All metal would rust when it hit saltwater, and my helmet regularly required a new paintjob after getting punted by instructors who didn't like me, which was pretty much all of them.

Painting a helmet doesn't sound hard, but it took hours to sand, prime, paint, dry, and then apply all the stickers. Hours that were destroyed in a split second with a swift kick. I can't count the number of times I watched in horror as my helmet spun through the air and crashed on concrete. I felt like the instructors were kicking me in the stomach, not to knock the wind out of me but worse—to make sure I lost three or four hours of sleep.

I was in the bottom 10 percent of the class physically, probably lower in terms of maturity. Aside from the stress fractures, I was suffering from iliotibial band syndrome, which manifested itself in golf ball-size lumps in my knees and caused sharp pain by pulling my kneecap to the side. I also had bilateral extensor tendonitis, and the Navy's answer to all of this was Motrin, which had given me acid reflux and almost burned a hole in my stomach.

I was immature, inexperienced, scared, broken, and unconfident. This was not what my class or the instructors were looking for, and I knew that in this pitiless environment, things would only get worse. And they definitely did.

CHAPTER 13

Hell Week

It had been over two months since I'd checked into BUD/S and I was extremely over trained. My body was breaking down, and on Thursday when I started hacking up green flehm and it hurt to swallow, I knew I was in trouble. Medical encouraged us to inform them of any issues, warning that students had died in Hell Week from untreated respiratory infections that lead to pulmonary edema. I knew if I went into medical, they'd most likely pull me from training, and for the first time I considered taking the easy way out.

I sat in my car shaking with the heater on full blast thinking, *What choice do you have? Your cardio is shit without the bronchitis or pneumonia, why put yourself through all this? You're not gonna make it anyway. What's the point?* After five minutes of acting like a bitch and feeling sorry for myself I came up with an idea.

I called my dad's best friend Lane, who lived a couple hours north, and asked him if there was any way he could bring me antibiotics. A month after graduating bootcamp I'd gotten pneumonia from swimming in Lake Michigan. The bad news was, I'd be much more susceptible to getting pneumonia in the future now that I'd had it once. But the good news was a heavy dose of antibiotics had gotten me healthy in a week. Lane came through on Friday night, forty-eight hours before

Hell Week was going to start, with a Zpac and a recommendation from his doctor "No strenuous activity for a week." *That's funny,* I thought as I swallowed two of the pills.

Hell Week is five and a half days of training with no sleep or breaks other than to eat and one two-hour nap on Wednesday. They said during the week we'd run a total of 144 miles, all while carrying 200-pound boats on our heads. The rubber boats would bounce up and down as we ran like perpetual jackhammers pounding us onto the pavement and sand. It was the test of all tests, and we knew it would be unrelenting.

Sunday night the class voted, and we selected the movie *Predator.* Everyone yelled at the screen and recited Arnold Schwarzenegger and Jessie Ventura's lines, but I couldn't concentrate. I knew Hell Week could start at any moment. I just didn't know when. About forty-five minutes into the film, right after Jesse the Body died in the jungle, one of the instructors kicked in the door and fired an M60 machine gun into the classroom ceiling.

"Hit the surf!"

We poured out of the classroom and into the dusk, crossing the Grinder as explosions and smoke grenades detonated everywhere. What seemed like twenty instructors were yelling on bullhorns and firing belt-fed machine guns.

I ran over the beach and into the dark ocean. Right before the water hit my waist, I turned around and fell back. The cold took my breath away—the first time getting wet is always the worst.

The instructors use the term "evolution" to describe a different task or exercise in training. One of the first evolutions we had to do in Hell Week was called rock portage. This was equal parts dangerous and scary. We paddled our rubber boat toward an outcropping of huge rocks when the surf was at its most fierce.

It was a moonless night. All I could see was the green chem lights on our lifejackets and the distant headlights of the support trucks on the beach. It was difficult to see the waves, but we could hear them thunderously breaking around us. I knew they were big because as they formed, the lights on the beach disappeared. We waited outside the surf zone until the instructors gave the signal to come in.

The red chem light waved; it was game time.

We paddled our asses off toward the rocks. Once we'd gone thirty meters, I knew we were in the impact zone (dangerous section where the waves are breaking). I looked back at a growing ten-foot wall of water, and I thought, *Oh fuck, we're gonna get smashed.* We picked up speed quickly as we rode the face of the wave. I paddled as hard as I could, but the nose dug in, and before we knew it, our boat turned sideways, and we were ejected. I held onto my oar, covered my face, and went into the fetal position. The wave came down like an engine piston and held me underwater as I tumbled like a rag doll in a laundry machine.

When I finally surfaced, I took a big relieving breath of air. It took a second to get my bearings, but when I saw the chem lights on the boat, I made a beeline. Everyone scrambled to right our craft, and guys pulled each other in by the tops of their lifejackets as a wave crashed down behind us. The whitewater pushed us forward as we paddled, trying to stay straight. We rode it in and braced for impact as we approached the rocks.

Upon arrival the coxswain leapt out with the bowline. We quickly exited. Fast but careful because if you fell between the boat and the boulders as a wave hit, bones could get broken.

After carrying the boat over the rocks, our boat crew mustered on the beach, backs straight, eyes front, boat resting on our heads. Boat crews were assembled based on height because everywhere we went, we had to run carrying the boat on our heads. Everything was a race, and "It pays to be a winner!" the instructors taunted. The winning boat crew got fifteen minutes of rest while the rest of the class got beat. That's what I heard anyway; my boat crew never won a race.

The one thing we had to look forward to every six hours was a break to eat a hot meal. A couple times they yanked that rug out from under us and instead of hot mess hall chow in the warm mess hall, we got cold MREs while sitting waist deep in the ocean. Saltwater got into my food, and I couldn't look down to see what my fork was hitting because I had a boat on my head.

On the second day, an instructor took me to the surf alone, which was very unusual for Hell Week. He told me to lay down in two feet of water. After about twenty minutes, my whole body was shaking uncontrollably, fighting to generate heat. Eventually, it stopped. When you shake frantically, that means you're really cold. When you stop shaking, that means you're hypothermic. Your body isn't shaking because it's shutting down. Delirium often follows.

Instructors watch the trainees pretty closely and usually bring them in while they're still shaking. When he didn't let me up, I began to get worried because I certainly wasn't going to get up on my own. I just hoped I wouldn't "hyp out" (pass out from hypothermia).

"Get in here, Beelzebub!" the instructor finally yelled. Nobody could pronounce my last name, so they substituted all sorts of nicknames.

I came into the beach and stood in front of him at attention, waiting for him to ask me questions to determine my level of hypothermia. He didn't; he just looked at me.

"It's time to go away."

"Negative, I'm not going to quit, instructor!" I said, feigning confidence.

His face seemed to soften, and he took on a different tone, not angry, more like a father offering advice.

"Listen I'm not saying this to be an asshole. I'm not trying to make you quit; I'm being completely honest with you. You are not going to graduate, the instructors don't like you, the class doesn't like you, and no matter what you do, they will not let you graduate. I'm being serious, I'm telling you this man to man, not as an instructor at BUD/S. I think you're a tough kid, but you need to go away, prepare, and come back in two years if you really want to be a SEAL because you will not graduate with this class."

Instructors had beaten my ass before, and they'd tried to get me to quit many times. But this was different. He was serious, and I could tell he wasn't lying. It meant I would be enduring all this pain and misery for no reason. There was no light at the end of the tunnel. No good outcome. This hit me like a ton of bricks.

I took it in and processed it.

I could quit and come back when I was healed up, or I could go through all this pain for nothing. Seemed like an obvious choice, but I never wanted to do what I was supposed to do. After hearing this,

I really didn't believe I was going to graduate, but I also wasn't going to quit. I looked at him and calmly said, "You're gonna have to kick me out because I'm not quitting."

This wasn't because I was some badass, in fact quite the contrary. I was a 160-pound insecure weakling who'd been bullied, shamed, and humiliated for the better part of my life. I just didn't want to add self-loathing to the list.

When times were tough in Hell Week, the instructors would try to seduce you into quitting. They offered hot chocolate, warm blankets, and donuts to anyone who rang out. To quit in training, you are required to ring the bell three times, signifying that you have reached your limit and don't wish to continue. I watched guys in far better shape than me, who'd suffered way less, ring that bell.

Sometimes I'd see a guy with a thousand-yard stare and just know he was gonna quit. Guys would get glossy-eyed and emotionless; lights were on, but nobody was home. When they finally left, it was as if their soul had been plucked from their body and just a shell of a man was trudging off the beach. Other times a guy would be doing fine, smiling, and then out of nowhere, he'd just quit. But every time I heard that bell ring, it sent a chill down my spine. They call it the BUD/S curse because that decision will haunt them for the rest of their lives.

The Steel Pier was an evolution notorious for making guys quit. The instructors waited until the middle of the night when the temperature was at its lowest, and then they hauled out the hurricane fans. They had us strip down to our Speedos and instructed us to lay on the cold steel pier. The instructors sprayed us with hoses and turned on the fans. The steel felt colder on my skin than the ocean, but it was a slower, more controlled drop in core body temperature, so they were able to drag it out longer.

When I saw the first guy get up off the pier and slink towards the SUVs carrying a Styrofoam cup of hot chocolate, I squeezed my eyes shut and just concentrated on making it to Wednesday. If you could hang on until Wednesday night in Hell Week, then you could make it, nobody quits after that.

WHEN YOU ARE GOING THROUGH something difficult, set achievable goals. Don't look at it like this is seven months of hell; take it a day at a time. Don't think *I have to stay up for five and a half days*. Look at it like *I just have to make it to the next meal or get through this evolution.* If it's really shitty, take it a minute at a time. You can do anything for a minute.

We were finally granted an hour of sleep on Wednesday afternoon. I wasn't planning on sleeping; my uniform was soaked, and I was freezing. I laid down on the uncomfortable metal cot, pulled the sleeping bag over me, and curled into a ball trying to warm up.

I unexpectedly woke up to whistles and machine gun fire.

"HIT THE SURF!" the instructors screamed through bullhorns.

I tried to stand but my hip flexors were so knotted up, I couldn't even extend my legs. I rolled out of the cot onto the sand, temporarily paralyzed in the fetal position. I pushed myself up and hobbled my way to the surf wondering, if any second, my hip flexors would tear.

Every twelve hours there was a medical check. The medics examined everyone's injuries, but it was frowned upon to verbally express anything that wasn't life-threatening. If you said, "My back hurts," then the doctors would be obligated to do something. Some guys used that as a way out of the program to avoid the humiliation of ringing the bell. If they could articulate a spinal injury or something serious, then the doctor would have to diagnose and treat, which almost always meant being pulled out of Hell Week.

I was in bad shape, but the antibiotics had worked, I was still spitting up flehm, but my sore throat was gone. As I got through every medical check, Dr. Mosier appeared more and more surprised. On Wednesday, he personally examined me.

"How do you feel?" he asked, hoping I might take the easy way out.

"I feel great, it's so weird. I'm not in any pain at all. That Motrin really works, Doc."

This was the only time that lying to an officer's face would not result in court martial. The dishonesty was actually encouraged. Dr. Mosier smiled, knowing that I was completely full of shit, and looked at my file. He reached down and pinched my shin. An indescribable pain shot through my entire leg. I started sweating, and tears welled up in my eyes and ran down my cheek.

"Are you sure?" he asked. "Your leg feels extremely inflamed." He put his thumb directly on my fracture and pressed like he was being fingerprinted.

"Hooyah! It's just a little tender from banging against a log on the O Course."

He kept his thumb on the fracture and looked at me. I swung my gaze to stare him eye to eye. This was a major no-no. In the military, you're expected to look straight ahead and always avoid eye contact with someone of higher rank. But I looked into his eyes and without saying a word, I communicated everything I needed to say: I might be broken, but none of you motherfuckers are going to break me.

I probably looked like a big fucking pussy with tears coming down my cheeks, but I took my tiny victories when I could get them. Doc Mosier smiled and released his thumb. He paused like he was going to say something but just stared at me curiously with what I interpreted as a look of respect. It was the only time in the military I had felt respect from anyone higher ranking than me. He and I both knew that I was going to finish Hell Week, and he was gonna lose that bet.

By Thursday, I was a zombie. We'd just set our boat down in front of the obstacle course after a long run. The next thing I knew, the instructors were yelling at me. I'd actually fallen asleep standing up, and they were screaming at me to "hit the surf!" Normally instructors yelling at me would incite fear, but for the first time, I wasn't afraid.

The instructors operated a lot like bullies, preying predominantly on the guys who were weak or scared. Now that I knew I was going to pass their ultimate test, my perspective changed. The mystique was gone, and now all of a sudden SEALs didn't seem superhuman. Once

I viewed them as normal people and removed them from the pedestal in my mind, I noticed they gave me more respect. This is no different than women, when you put people on pedestals, they know they don't belong on, they respect you less for putting them there.

Things were getting worse but my outlook was improving. My knees hurt, my body was breaking down, and the searing pain in my tibias was there like a constant beacon in the darkness reminding me that this wasn't a dream. The good news was, I'd been in pain for so long that I'd learned to accept its presence. Once you reach a certain point of discomfort, a confidence develops because you know things cannot possibly get any worse.

Twenty-four hours later, I found myself doing backward summersaults in the thick mud. My eyes were burning, my ears were plugged, and I was choking on saltwater that'd made its way up my nose. I laughed because somehow, they'd figured out a way to make it even worse—impressive really.

I low crawled through the demolition pits under the barbed wire. Every cut, rash, bruise, and open sore on my body burned from the gunpowder and nasty shit in that sludge we had to wade through. Nothing mattered, though, because I knew it would end soon.

We ran back to base, and the commanding officer came out to inform us that Hell Week was secured. I remember proudly standing there on the beach, hoping he would notice and recognize me. He had to remember. We started with 119 guys, and there were only 17 of us left. I was sure I was going to get at least a smile or a nod, maybe a "congratulations" or "I can't believe you made it!" He pivoted and walked off.

Of all the pain I endured and all the hell the instructors gave me, the CO simply not acknowledging me hurt the most. There was pizza and brown T-shirts laid out for us. I put my shirt on, staggered to my Jeep, and drove to my hotel.

I'd accomplished the unimaginable, but it felt like nobody cared. Like winning the lottery only to find you're the last person on earth.

CHAPTER 14

Tijuana Steroids

I turned nineteen the day after Hell Week was secured and for my birthday my father got me a room at the Hotel del Coronado to recover. I was beyond exhausted, but I couldn't for the life of me sleep for more than an hour or two at a time. Every time I woke up, I felt worse than before. The pain seemed to be increasing, and everything was becoming more swollen by the hour. My ankles didn't want to bend, and my feet looked like rubber gloves that had been blown up like balloons. The bulk of my toenails had fallen off from the swelling, and my shins hurt so bad that even the thought of touching them made me wince. The ITBS in my knees had gone from golf balls to Easter eggs, and my extensor tendonitis had gotten so bad I couldn't lift my foot upward an inch. On top of that, I couldn't take any more Motrin for the pain or swelling because it was burning a hole in my stomach lining.

When I woke from the second nap, my body had locked up so bad that I needed to literally crawl to the toilet to avoid pissing myself because walking was no longer an option. As I was crawling, I remembered laughing cockily at one of the medical staff who offered me crutches after we secured Hell Week. *If only he could see me now*, I thought.

Training started that Monday morning like always, except the class was allowed to walk for the week instead of run. Some of the guys bounced back quickly, but not me. I was in bad shape physically, but honestly, I was in worse shape mentally.

I've noticed when I work really hard on something, I feel melancholy upon completion. I put everything I had into finishing Hell Week, and it remains the hardest thing I've done in my life. Maybe it's because I expected to feel happier, or maybe because of the suppressed hormone levels, but I really felt like shit. Instead of feeling like I'd climbed a mountain, I felt more like I'd fallen down one.

I made it an additional three weeks in training before imploding. Doc Mosier was the only person who knew about my stress fractures. The instructors just thought I was a shithead who sucked at running, which was true, but having fractured legs certainly didn't help. I was limping, skipping, and galloping to try and reduce the pressure on my tibias, but the pain was completely debilitating. No matter how hard I tried, I couldn't complete the four-mile timed run in under thirty-two minutes.

The instructors sent me to medical, and I was given a rollback. I was slated to continue training with the next class in two months after they finished Hell Week and was tasked with quarterdeck watch during the days. When you get this assignment, you're not supposed to leave base for the full twenty-four-hour "duty day." However, I had watch every day, and I lived off base. To the letter of the law, I was not allowed to go home at all, even though my stuff, my clothes, my bed, and everything was in the apartment.

One of the instructors who didn't like me spotted my unmistakable Jeep rolling out the gate, and he reported me. The next day I was called into a review board. I stood there stiff as a board as the instructors took turns telling the commanding officer what a poor performer I was. This kangaroo court was just a formality. They wanted me gone, and there was nothing I could say or do to change it. I was subsequently dropped from training and put in X-Division where they house quitters awaiting orders to their next duty stations.

I checked into X-Division with a chip on my shoulder. I had gone through all of that for nothing, all the pain, all the cold, and I was right there with the guys who rang the bell the first day. My brown shirt, the thing I was most proud of in the world, had been taken from me. I'd only worn it for a few weeks, but it felt good to be given respect for something I earned. Now I was back at the bottom. Back to being a loser.

My body hadn't recovered from Hell Week, and I was in a bad place mentally because my cortisol levels were sky high, and my testosterone was low. My buddy Matt from Quartermaster school was in a similar situation. He'd been medically dropped from training after injuring his back, and his mind worked like mine.

"You wanna go to Tijuana and shoot some 'roids?" I asked.

"Fuck it, let's go."

I had toyed with the idea of steroids ever since I saw my cousin gain twenty pounds of muscle one summer on a heavy cycle of Dianabol. Going to Mexico for a trip like that could get you sent to military prison, but Matt and I felt like we didn't have a lot to lose. Information about juicing (taking steroids) was limited before Google and YouTube, but I'd read a couple books, so I wasn't flying completely blind.

The bus let us off right before the border, and we marched into the nearest pharmacy. "Do you have any steroids?" I asked. The only anabolic steroid they had was fifty milligram *rediject* Deca-Durabolin. I'd read that Deca was pretty safe, so I dropped my drawers in the back of the pharmacy for some guy who barely spoke English and didn't care much for proper sterilization practices. He swabbed the site with alcohol, then open hand slapped my ass before jabbing me with an eighteen-gauge needle and hammering in two ccs of oil totaling 100 milligrams. I later found out that the massive needle was about twice the size it needed to be, and the Deca dosage was absurdly low. Small dose or not, the shit worked. My body finally started recovering and after a few days felt better than it had in months. I upped my caloric intake and began lifting weights.

The following week, I went back to Tijuana and had the guy shoot me with 150 milligrams. I gained about ten pounds. It was mostly water, but my muscles looked full, and I was getting a lot stronger. My attitude improved immensely, and for the first time in my life, I actually *looked* like I was in good shape.

Third week, I did two shots of 100 milligrams, one in each butt cheek. People say your first steroid cycle is where you make the best gains, and that was certainly true for me. I'd transitioned from all calisthenics to weightlifting, my daily calories went from a deficit to an excess, and I was able to get decent rest. It was the perfect scenario, and I went from 160 to 173 pounds in three weeks. I was looking and feeling great when the brass gave me the news.

I was required to report to San Clemente Island to work as a janitor while class 227 finished Third Phase. Anger built up inside me; I wanted to break everything in my apartment. I was more pissed about that than I was when they dropped me from training. Hormones play a big role in your thought process and mentality. Overtraining lowers your testosterone levels, making you more passive and more willing to tolerate bullshit; the opposite is true when you're juicing.

There was no way to bring the Deca with me, so my hormone levels would inevitably crash, and my first steroid cycle would be ruined. I'd been railroaded out of the program, and now these dickheads were sending me to a barren island that didn't even have a weight room. I was pissed, but I had no choice. I went out there, lost most of my newly acquired muscle, and swept floors for a few weeks while I came up with a plan.

STEROIDS

Do not take steroids before you have stopped growing! Steroids will fuse your epiphysial plates and stunt your growth. It isn't worth it.

If you want to take steroids after you turn twenty, then do it correctly. Get your blood work done and establish a baseline testosterone level. If you have naturally low testosterone levels, then have your doctor prescribe you testosterone replacement therapy (TRT) along with Armidex to prevent aromatization (when excess testosterone turns converts to estrogen). If your testosterone levels are normal or high, I would not recommend doing steroids because you can possibly irreparably damage your ability to produce testosterone.

Steroids can cause side effects, especially if you use high doses. Most will cause your estrogen levels to increase dramatically, and you'll need to know what to look for in order to determine how much antiestrogens to take. Night sweats, water retention, mood swings, and nipple sensitivity are all indicators that your estrogen levels are too high. Having your hormones elevated or out of balance can cause acne, hair loss, prostate enlargement, and it can even cause a man to grow breasts or a woman to grow a beard. The crash after you stop taking steroids can also be shitty; many people lose most of the muscle they put on, and moving backwards always sucks.

If you don't give a fuck and you want a performance advantage or you have shit genetics, then I would recommend doing a lot of research before you start a cycle. Always error on the side of doing less. The risk versus reward of doing really high doses is rarely worth it.

The heaviest cycle I ever did was:

- 100 mg of testosterone and 200 mg of Equipoise every three days.
- 1 mg of Armidex every three days.
- 3 IUs of HGH every day.
- 10 mg of Dianabol twice a day.

Testosterone is your base; it is essential for sexual function and mental state. You can add anabolics, but you should never do a cycle of just an anabolic like Deca or Winstrol unless you don't want your dick to work. The converse is true as well;

you should never just do large doses of testosterone by itself. Combining an anabolic will give better results with a lower incidence of side effects. Low doses of HCG are typically administered during or at the end of the cycle to get your nuts producing testosterone again and to prevent testicular atrophy.

There is a plethora of information out there, so don't be lazy. Do your research and make an informed decision. Talk to a hormone replacement doctor. But keep in mind most doctors don't know jack shit about juicing, so do your homework and find one who does. Be responsible, get your bloodwork done frequently, use proper sterilization techniques, and only take what your doctor prescribes—black market drugs can be mislabeled, unsterile, and inaccurately dosed.

CHAPTER 15

The Nuclear Half Marathon

While in X-Division I received orders to the USS Mount Vernon. I was supposed to be on crutches working a desk until my legs healed. Instead, I was motoring towards Okinawa, standing watch because my CO (commanding officer) was an asshole. He refused to honor the medical recommendations for me to be on crutches. Instead, he wanted me to rely on an improvised cane they made like I was Jiminy fucking Cricket.

After three weeks at sea, our ship arrived in Okinawa, Japan. As soon as we pulled into port, I requested to see the dentist on base because my wisdom teeth were getting impacted. I didn't really give a shit about my teeth, but it was an undeniable medical condition that would put me in front of a doctor who wasn't on my ship and that was all I needed.

"My legs have been fractured for six months, and they just won't heal," I told the base medical staff. The doctor ordered a nuclear bone scan, where radioactive tracers are sent through the blood stream. After a couple of hours, the tracers gravitate toward tissues that are injured and working to repair themselves. It also helps reveal how much damage has been done to bone material. The staff told me to come back in two hours for the next step of the examination when they would look at the tracers in action.

This was my chance. I shut the door to the medical building and took off running. I wasn't gonna let the CO of that boat fuck me over for one more day. I was supposed to be on crutches, and I was gonna make sure that happened even if it took breaking my legs completely in half. I ran around the base for almost the entire two hours, and the pain was just as bad as it was in BUD/S, so I knew they were still fucked up.

Back at the hospital after my little jaunt, the staff asked a series of questions.

"How much pain are you in?"

"It's pretty bad, sir."

"On the scans, your tibias are lit up like Christmas trees. What did you do on the passage over?"

"My commanding officer had me on the bridge standing watch for eight-hour shifts."

"Your medical records say you're supposed to be on limited duty with crutches."

"Yes, sir, but I always follow orders, sir. They did provide me with a cane."

I told him everything. Everything except for the half marathon I just ran. He rang up the ship CO and chewed his ass, threw in some references to gross negligence, and then recommended a medical retirement for me from the United States Navy. I was ecstatic; I didn't even know that was a possibility.

Medical retirements don't happen overnight, but me leaving that ship certainly did. I packed, said some proper goodbyes along with a few fuck-yous, and got the hell off that boat.

I stayed in Okinawa for four months letting my legs heal and waiting for the retirement paperwork. I spent my free time working out and I was really happy to finally have some normality in my life. I hadn't had sex in over a year but didn't really stress over that. I'd been so physically beat down that I didn't even have the vigor to jerk off.

CHAPTER 16

If at First You Don't Succeed

I was ready to make a second run at BUD/S.

Over eight months had passed since I started the process of retiring from the Navy. I'd gotten up to 180 pounds swimming, lifting weights, and doing steroids. After five months of staying off my legs, I was finally running with zero pain. I trained like an animal, fanatically monitored my diet of five or six lean meals a day, didn't chase pussy, or drink booze. I lived like a monk. A monk with a monkey on his back.

At first, the idea of getting out of the military sounded like a gift from God, but my failed attempt at BUD/S was eating at me. I had literally nothing going on in my life and it was all I could think about. During my workouts, I imagined the respect people would give me if they saw a SEAL trident on my uniform. I imagined a girl asking me what I did for a living and how cool it would be if I didn't tell her and she later found out. I thought being a SEAL would solve all of my problems. When I enlisted, I didn't really think I could do it. I looked at it like a Hail Mary pass—if I caught it, I would be a hero. Now things were different.

I knew I could do it, and I knew if I didn't finish what I started, it would haunt me forever. I had to go back.

When my OIC said he wasn't going to approve my request to go back to BUD/S, once again, I had nothing to lose, so I requested Captain's Mast.

"You are at a limited duty command because a panel of highly-respected naval doctors determined that you're permanently disabled to the point you can't perform regular duty. You're currently scheduled to be medically discharged from the Navy, and you want me to approve your request to go to SEAL training? Is this a joke?" the captain asked.

I assumed these were rhetorical questions, so in a rare show of good judgment, I kept my mouth shut.

"Request denied. Get out of my office!"

My father wasn't surprised at the CO's reaction.

"Son, you're going to be medically retired. That's better than honorably discharged. You're going to receive money and benefits for the rest of your life. If you go to BUD/S and don't make it, you'll be on another ship for two years...You should take the retirement."

I appreciated his perspective, but, of course, his advice just made me want to do the opposite. Nothing inspired me like proving people wrong, and the best way to motivate me was to tell me I couldn't or shouldn't do something. That said, I was out of options, and I was desperate. I hated asking my dad to use his connections, but I saw no other way out.

"Dad, you're probably right, but I have to do this. Can you call in a favor, please?"

Pops came through.

"I don't know what kind of shit you pulled, Petty Officer Bilzerian," my CO growled. "But if you end up back here because you quit, I'm going to make your life hell."

I couldn't help myself. I held in the laugh as much as I could, but the thought of going through all this shit and then quitting was a pretty funny punch line to me. I sputtered and smiled.

"You think that's funny? You think BUD/S is easy? Less than 10 percent of the guys that show up make it through, and I've seen guys a lot tougher than you quit."

I'd like to tell you I said something witty like, "Are you taking bets?" but I didn't. The truth is I just smiled and said, "Hooyah, sir." Hooyah was a great word because of its ambiguity; it could mean many different things. Here, it meant "Fuck you." Guys like him were the exact reason I wanted to go to BUD/S. I loved that he doubted me.

When I left BUD/S, I was a broken, near cripple of 160 pounds. But when I checked in this time for BUD/S Class 238, I was a rock hard 178, and the instructors barely recognized me.

About a month into PTRR, I was eating breakfast in the chow hall when all of a sudden, the place got real quiet. Forks were lowered, and everyone's eyes were glued to the TVs that were on with no audio.

It was September 11, 2001, and two planes had just crashed into the World Trade Center.

As we ran back to the NSWC (Naval Special Warfare Center) base, things escalated quickly. Snipers appeared on the rooftops, soldiers patrolled with full combat loadouts, and armored vehicles with manned .50 caliber machine guns were rolling down the street. The base went into Threatcon Delta, the highest level of threat assessment possible, indicating threat level *critical* and terrorist attack imminent.

For hours, we waited with no clue what was going on, until we finally received word. Shit was about to get serious. The country was going to war, and that meant *we* were going to war. At this point, there were SEALs who'd been in for ten years without seeing any combat. But that was all about to change.

CHAPTER 17

Looking for an Edge

BUD/S is one of the few military training programs where officers and enlisted guys go through training side by side. This created an interesting dynamic because the instructors were mostly enlisted guys, and they were ordering around and "beating" the officers. Officers who, one day, could potentially be in charge of their platoon, team, or their entire base for that matter. The officers in the class were usually the boat crew leaders, enlisted guys had to call them sir, and fraternization was not allowed.

Chris Regan was my "swim buddy," the Navy's version of the Army's "battle buddy." It meant anytime I had to hit the surf or do anything, Chris was right there with me. Students were never allowed to go anywhere without a swim buddy, so Chris and I got to know each other pretty quickly. We shared a similar sense of humor, and I respected that he wasn't a pussy.

Being pushed to your limits mentally and physically usually brings out the worst in people, but when things got bad, Chris didn't falter. He was regularly there by my side to get beat because I had a tendency to get creative with the rules. I took my medicine with a smile, and Chris did too; he never bitched; he took the beatings like a man.

CHRIS REGAN

Former US Navy SEAL

I met Dan during our early twenties—that formative time of life for young men when they're testing themselves. Meeting in BUD/S meant taking that test to a whole other level. All of us showed up wanting to be Navy SEALs, to do crazy shit and be violent, so it attracted a certain type of person. But even the toughest guys quit at the beginning.

Those who passed the test and were eligible, met at the Grinder where the physical education selection is done. That's where Dan stood out to me immediately, as the guy who commented out loud on the ironies that were apparent during this intense process, things that other guys didn't have the balls to say. So I liked him right away—and, with a similar height, we were partnered together in a boat crew and got to be friends. With Dan in my crew, we received a lot of extra attention. By that, I mean the physical beatdowns you get when you're not quite in line. But I was unconcerned about it, and so was he. So when I watched him do this shit, it made me laugh, and I didn't mind the extra push-ups or whatever punishment we were given that day. We knew we'd get through it, and we did.

He was a team player but also on his own program, getting creative with the rules. Like, at the beginning of training, you're given all the gear you need. There's no option to bring your own shit. But Dan, he brought his own—these split fins that I would never keep up with. I looked at him and said, "You realize we're not going to swim; we're going to get our ass kicked." And they looked at us, and looked at his fins (they were like Ferraris compared to the issued Fords), and we proceeded to get our ass kicked. I had to give him credit for trying.

I value our friendship because you get the real, unvarnished truth—and that's rare these days.

Tiko Crofoot was an officer and one of the top performers of our class. He graduated from the Naval Academy, but he didn't have the same sense of smug entitlement that most of the Academy guys did. A lot of officers acted like they were better than you, but not Tiko. Which was funny because he was one of the few who was actually better than me at almost every single thing. He was an elite athlete, and I don't say that lightly; the guy did a 163 consecutive pullups, ran sub six-minute miles, and all while looking like a bodybuilder.

We were the only guys that I know of who'd go lift weights at night during first phase. I remember one time I was driving us to the gym, and he asked me why I wanted to be a Navy SEAL. I told him the only reason I wanted to be a SEAL was to tell people that I was a SEAL. That answer surprised him, and it's probably not what he wanted to hear considering he's spent his life in the teams, but that was the truth.

TIKO CROFOOT

US Navy SEAL, Commander

No matter how prepared you were on the first day, BUD/S had something that would humble and devour you. For some, it was the endless running or always being wet and sandy. For others, it was the swims; choking on saltwater while trying to fight the waves and the currents. For all, it was the cold water, sapping willpower and desire twenty times faster than the air.

It was incontrovertibly hard, and it left most exhausted at the end of each day.

Most went home, showered, and fell into bed dreading the next morning. However, a few of us traded precious hours of sleep each day for the "fix" of the gym. Dan was one of those few. I would see him there each night, often still with dried salt on his skin and grains of sand in his hair. He loved the gym as much as I did, and he wasn't doing maintenance workouts either. Every one of his workouts was as intense as the day we'd just finished, and I respected him immensely for the sacrifice I knew he was making to be there each day.

I got to know Dan well over the months we spent together in BUD/S and at the gym. Often, he and I were the only two from our class in the gym at the end of a long day. He had a ready sense of humor, flecked with sarcasm and a sharp knack for pointing out the irony of much of the military dogma that was constantly being purveyed. He was a kindred spirit in that respect as he and I shared much of the irreverence and disdain for the more rote and perfunctory tasks we would regularly perform. He was intelligent and looked for ways to accomplish things smarter and faster, even when it ran counter to the rules.

Dan showing up to a swim with the latest technology in fins only made sense to the two of us. Actually, it made sense to everyone, but not everyone was brave enough to buck the system so overtly. Chris and Dan paid dearly for his slight to decorum, but he never stopped looking for ways to do things better. Ironically, a short time after Dan showed up for his swim with split fins and got punished severely for doing so, BUD/S recanted and began issuing them to all new SEAL candidates. Being Icarian is not always painless or without its setbacks.

However, Dan turned out to be right, and I've never forgotten that lesson.

Throughout training I was always looking for an edge. If there was a better, more effective way to do things, I wanted to figure it out. After my stress fractures healed, I figured out the reason I was getting shin splints and fractures was because I was an overpronator. So I had custom orthotics made for my boots to fix my gait. When we were doing land navigation and pack space was limited, I went to REI and bought freeze-dried food to replace the bulky and unhealthy MREs (meal ready to eat) we were issued. My vision was 20/70, so I had a hard time seeing the targets at three hundred meters with iron sights. In BUD/S, students weren't allowed to wear glasses or contacts, except at the range, you *had* to wear shooting glasses, so I had custom ones made with prescription lenses. Able to see the targets, I went from being a good shooter to the best shooter in the class.

Steroids seemed to be the ultimate edge. Winstrol was the water-based steroid that got Ben Johnson, the world record Canadian sprinter, busted in the 1988 Olympics. My books said it would offer strength without water retention, leading to very lean muscles. I mixed it with Equipoise, the oil-based horse steroid that I was doing, and injected it into my quad. It was painful, so I just assumed that I'd hit a vein or a nerve. But as the day went on, the pain got worse and worse.

I later learned I shouldn't have mixed the oil and water in the same syringe because it can cause an abscess, which is exactly what happened. This sucks under normal situations, but when you're running fourteen miles a day in BUD/S, it's crippling. My leg muscles kept giving out, and I had tears in my eyes from the pain, but it wasn't like I could stroll into medical and say, "Hey, I shot some bad gear, can I take a couple of days off?"

I was shooting 100 milligrams of test and Equipoise every four days while popping twenty milligrams of Novadex every day to prevent estrogen buildup. These were Mexican veterinary steroids, so I'd get abscesses from time to time due to a lack of sterility. It was horrible. Sometimes I'd get flu-like symptoms and feel like I was going to die; but there was nothing I could do other than laugh at the absurdity of my predicament.

Guys in my class probably thought I was nuts, crying and smiling, but I didn't give a shit what anyone thought. I just wanted to graduate. I thought about giving up steroids a few times, but I looked good with my shirt off. And no one likes a quitter.

CHAPTER 18

Adventures in Keistering

Billy, Dale, and I were cruisin'. The sun was out, so I rolled down the windows and shut off the air conditioning. We were on a cliffside stretch of coastal highway, about an hour south of the Mexican border on a quick trip to restock our steroid inventory.

I was starting to figure out that many of the guys going through BUD/S and at the teams were juicing. Dale had done a couple of mule runs for our group, but we knew training was going to get super intense, and we wouldn't be able to go down every week. So I decided we should all keister (put up your ass) a couple bottles and save ourselves the constant trips. This was a big risk because if we got caught, we'd all be thrown in military prison and kicked out of the program. But the juice was worth the squeeze.

Dale was a former truck driver and part-time model. A tall, loud, outspoken Norwegian with blond hair and blue eyes who looked like Ivan Drago from *Rocky 4* but with a full sleeve of tattoos that continued up his neck. Billy was an older, squared away ex-Marine. He was a big

Native American Cro-Magnon-looking motherfucker with a strong chin and a constant dip in. Our various looks and personalities could not have been more different, but we had one thing in common: We fucking loved steroids.

At this point, I was hanging out with a cute Navy girl-next-door type who cleaned my apartment, bought me groceries, and would cook while me and the guys watched movies. It was a strange relationship because, despite some occasional flirting, we never hooked up. Even though I was getting almost no pussy, I still didn't want to sleep with her because she was about ten pounds overweight. I'm not sure why she did all of this; maybe she liked me, or maybe she just liked doing stuff and hanging out. Either way, none of us wanted to use our vehicles for the Mexico run, so we borrowed her truck but didn't say what for.

A couple hours later, we arrived at a veterinary shop in Ensenada that sold local ranchers the steroids for their livestock and racehorses. After some intense haggling and pretending to leave, I got a bottle of Testosterone, some Winstrol, and Equipoise. Dale and Billy bought their gear, and we headed to the truck like kids toting Christmas presents. Then I stopped at a pharmacy where we purchased some condoms and lube. On the way home, our last stop was a bathroom in a sit-down Mexican restaurant close to the border. We each piled into a stall, shut the door, and got to work.

"Fuck, this hurts."

"Use more lube," Dale advised.

"There's no way this is going to fit in my ass," Billy replied.

"Stop being such a pussy," Dale instructed.

Brain surgeons operating on Ebola patients don't scrub their hands as much as we did before leaving that bathroom. All three of us shuffled out sweaty, guilty, and bow-legged. I'm not sure if there was someone in the bathroom who heard us or if the walls were just thin because the restaurant went silent and everyone stared at us as we exited the bathroom, which made our walk of shame that much more awkward. To this day, I still don't know if they thought we had chosen that bathroom to buttfuck each other or if they figured we were smuggling drugs, but considering the looks we got, I'd say buttfucking.

As we waited in the never-ending line to cross the border, I cranked the A/C as high as it would go to alleviate my sweating. I'd never been so uncomfortable in my life. It felt like I had a flashlight in my ass and my body was doing everything in its power to get rid of it. *Oh, shit it's escaping*, I thought as I gritted my teeth and clenched my ass in an attempt to retract the turtlehead that was now sticking out.

As I got closer, my mind began racing with possibilities. I couldn't help but imagine what would happen if they pulled us into secondary and I couldn't hold it any longer. *What if I actually shit myself?* I was on the verge of panic as we approached the booth, I handed the customs officer my military ID and nervously answered a few questions. "Pull forward," he said.

Fuck, I'm screwed, I thought as I approached the secondary inspection.

"Stop." He looked in the bed of the truck and then back at the military decal on the window before waving us through.

Thank God.

We'd barely spoken a word the entire drive, but as soon as we passed the checkpoint, Dale screamed at me to pull over. I took the first exit and turned into a Goodyear parking lot as Dale yelled, "Stop! Stop! Stop!" He leapt out of the truck before it had fully stopped and exploded a pile of shit onto the concrete in broad daylight. We were only ten minutes away from my apartment, and we didn't want to follow his example, so we yelled at him to get back in the vehicle. He scooped the condom of drugs out of the pile of shit and gingerly climbed back into the truck, trying not to touch anything. The smell was grotesque, and it required all the windows rolled down not to vomit. We had accomplished our mission and were on the home stretch, even if we looked like the fucking three stooges doing it.

I double parked sideways at my apartment, slammed the shifter in park, and bolted out of the cab. I did some version of an epileptic sideways crabwalk to the door and burst into the apartment. I darted right into the only bathroom and immediately shit in the toilet without bothering to even close the door. I had been clenching so hard for so long, that when I finally let go, it sounded like a shotgun blast.

Billy made a frenzied beeline to the kitchen, where he, without hesitation, lifted one leg like a dog pissing and fired a shit right into the kitchen sink. Dale calmly strolled in, hands covered in shit, holding a stretched-out condom like those sticky rollout sheets of flypaper, and patiently waited for Billy to finish so he could wash his hands. Billy, meanwhile, grabbed a dish towel to wipe his ass. All of us exhaled like we'd been holding our breath for a record-setting free dive in the Pacific.

My girl, clearly horrified at what she'd just witnessed, screamed "Oh my God!" and ran right out of the apartment. I mean, the poor girl was preparing lunch for us, and Billy literally fired a shit right into the sink she was using to wash the chicken. I'd left the truck running, so she must have gotten in and just drove off because we never got a chance to explain, not that we really wanted to anyway, so maybe that was for the best.

The fucked-up part of the whole thing was that I did all of this to save a hundred and fifty bucks because Dale would have happily smuggled mine back if I paid him a premium.

CHAPTER 19

Soft-Ass OIC

I'd gotten up to 193 pounds by the time first phase rolled around. The extra muscle didn't help me with almost anything in BUD/S; it was more of a hindrance, but I didn't care. It felt good to be big.

My experience was a complete 180 from the first time I showed up at BUD/S. Going through training unprepared, scared, and broken was absolute torture. But it made going through strong, confident, and healthy seem like a walk in the park. The Seven P's—Proper Planning and Preparation Prevents Piss-Poor Performance—was a long-winded military way of saying my mantra: *Life is all in the setup.*

The time off had healed my injuries, the training and the steroids had gotten me stronger, and the strict diet made me ripped. The previous suffering and persecution had turned my mind into an impenetrable fortress of fuck-you confidence that declared, *Your mouth will get tired of telling me what to do before my body gets tired doing it.*

Instructor McCleland remembered me from before, and he'd beat me every chance he got. While we were in the classroom, he had me doing air chairs while holding my canteens straight out and vertical push-ups against the wall. I laughed and smiled as I pushed them out and said, "Hooyah, Instructor McCleland." The instructors liked to instill fear in the students; they liked when we played the game. So the more

I showed I didn't care, the less enjoyment he got out of hazing me. When he told me to hit the surf, I smiled and said "Hooyah" as I ran out of the classroom. I made it very clear I would happily do this shit all day, every day. After an hour, he gave up.

I'd won that battle, but they would win the war.

The OIC* of our class had a different attitude. He was a big pussy, scared of making mistakes, scared of getting beat, and scared of the instructors in general. I told him flat out, "They're gonna beat us anyway, no matter how good we do, we're gonna get beat." Their goal in first phase is to make guys quit.

ARIK BURKS

Retired US Navy SEAL, Master Chief, Former BUD/S Instructor

By the time Dan's class rolled around, I was the lead instructor for Hell Week, specifically Alpha shift, which was four to midnight. I remember Dan and his fucked up last name, but he didn't stand out, and that rare distinction is only because he didn't suck. You ask any First Phase Instructor, and they will tell you that you remember the students that are really bad or the ones that get rolled back. Dan was not one of the shitbags who refused to perform or hid among the guys that did. That being said, I did remember his OIC, who was one of those prior fleet lieutenants. From being an instructor in First Phase, I ran into just a handful of prior fleet officers, and I would give them a 50 percent score. Some guys were great and used their experience and maturity to lead their men well while also dealing with their own performance struggles. Others were not so good. Some were complete spaz monsters that thought every student sent to get

* Officer in charge.

wet and sandy was a direct reflection of their leadership. His OIC fit into this group.

He was very entitled and hated that an E-6 like me could tell him that he was a horrible leader. In the regular Navy, that type of interaction was intolerable, and you could tell it rubbed him the wrong way. Despite being a SEAL with multiple deployments and ten years in the SEAL teams, I could tell he disliked that I had authority over him and an opinion on his poor decision-making. These officers who end up making it to the SEAL Teams struggle. They ignore advice from senior enlisted men who have much more experience, and in an effort to prove themselves, often step on their own dicks.

The instructors would tell the OIC this was the worst class they'd ever seen; I would roll my eyes because they used to say the same shit to my last class, but his asshole would pucker; he would panic and yell at us. Fear breeds fear, and pretty soon all the officers were buying into his bullshit. I just put my head down and focused on passing my runs, swims, and O courses, and I kept not giving a fuck about our whiney-ass OIC, figuring a dude that soft would surely quit anyway.

CHAPTER 20

Trust Fund Seizure

I was pulled out of class during the second week of First Phase and led into an office with a judge advocate general.

"Petty Officer Bilzerian," the stiff JAG started. "The United States Securities and Exchange Commission and the Justice Department are seeking to settle your father's dispute and release him from custody."

Earlier that year, my father ran afoul of the feds again and was found to be in contempt of court by a judge in Washington. In classic Bilzerian fashion, rather than lay low after his first indictment and prison sentence, he had sparred with the government ever since. The judge decided to teach Dad a lesson and send him to jail until he "purged" the contempt by handing over documents and paying his fine. Between the intensely long hours of SEAL training combined with my usual family oddities, I didn't communicate much with Mom and Dad during that time. I didn't even know he was in jail for the first six months because my parents "didn't want to worry me."

While he was away, the FBI raided our home and even went through our trash bins. They took every file and computer he had. The feds wanted him to prove that he didn't have money hidden in offshore accounts, but it's hard to prove you *don't* have something, especially when all your documents are locked up in an FBI evidence storage facility.

Meanwhile, Dad was experiencing what longtime inmates referred to as "diesel therapy." The judge had ordered him to be bussed all over the state from one maximum-security prison to another in an attempt to get him to break. It was a terrible punishment, but if the judge knew anything about my father, he'd have known that the more you kicked him when he was down, the more it would motivate him to fight.

They'd been negotiating with my mother, which primarily consisted of threatening, "We're going to send you to jail along with your husband!" Mom agreed to give up the Tampa house, sell some stock, and hand over some cash. But before opening the cell door for Dad, they had one additional request. They threw it in like it was nothing. An "oh yeah, by the way..." kind of thing.

They wanted one third of the trust fund established for my brother Adam and me.

At one time, that fund was worth about $96 million. But the government seized more than half during Dad's first fight. The stock had fallen dramatically in the interim when they dumped all the seized shares on the open market. As I sat in the JAG's office that day, the fund was worth slightly less than $10 million.

"You sign off on this," the JAG said, "and your dad will be released in short order. Your family has struggled with this hanging over your heads for more than a decade. Do this, and your mom can finally sleep easy."

I scribbled my name on the line on the piece of paper. Adam got 33 percent, I got 33 percent, and Uncle Sam walked away with 33 percent. After being locked up for over a year, my father walked into the bright Florida sunlight a free man.

Dad was so pissed that I'd gone along with the settlement that he refused to speak to me for months. He was genuinely convinced that he'd done nothing wrong and that his conviction was for political reasons.

My father would've gladly stayed in jail the rest of his life if it meant not giving the government another dollar.

The $3 million in stock left in my trust fund dipped as low as a quarter million and was finally sold in 2019 and 2020 for a grand total of $1,339,160 and one cent.

SCOTT ROHLEDER

Accountant, CPA

I have served in the capacity of accountant and financial advisor to Dan Bilzerian for the past seven years. I have intimate knowledge of his financial affairs, and I would like to provide the facts regarding Dan's trust fund.

Dan was the beneficiary of "The Paul A Bilzerian and Terri L. Steffen 1994 Irrevocable Trust." The trust initially had two assets, which were 2,313,500 shares of Cimetrix ("Cimetrix Shares") stock and 8,847 shares of Retail Holdings, N.V., formerly Singer, N.V. ("Singer Shares").

However, on January 16, 2002, a court order in the case Securities Exchange Commission vs. Paul A. Bilzerian removed 665,000 shares of the Cimetrix Shares from the trust, leaving 1,648,500 shares in the trust. This is public record and can be easily researched by referencing Securities Exchange Commission vs. Paul A. Bilzerian, Case 89-1854, Docket No. 603, pp. 4–6.

On April 1, 2013, Dan was provided ownership of the Cimetrix Shares, and on April 30, 2013, Dan was provided ownership of the Singer Shares, which are the only assets of the trust.

Dan held the Singer Shares until May 2019 when they were sold in the amount of $269,052.35. He held the Cimetrix Shares until they were sold in December 2020 in the amount of $1,070,107.74.

4602.0643

COMMON SHARES

PAR VALUE $.01

COMMON SHARES

8847

INCORPORATED UNDER THE LAWS OF THE NETHERLANDS ANTILLES

SINGER N.V.

SEE REVERSE FOR CERTAIN DEFINITIONS

CUSIP N74108 10 6

THIS CERTIFIES THAT

DAN [illegible] BILZERIAN
1500 BLUE JAY WAY
LOS ANGELES CA 90069-[illegible]

8847
8847
8847
8847
8847

EIGHT THOUSAND EIGHT HUNDRED FORTY-SEVEN

IS THE OWNER OF

FULLY PAID AND NON-ASSESSABLE COMMON SHARES OF THE PAR VALUE OF $.01 PER SHARE (EACH) OF

Singer N.V. [illegible] transferable by the holder [illegible] of Incorporation of the Company [illegible] This Certificate is not valid unless countersigned by the Transfer [illegible]

In Witness Whereof the Company has caused this certificate to be executed by its duly authorized Managing Director

CERTIFICATE OF STOCK

NAME CHANGED TO RETAIL HOLDINGS N.V.

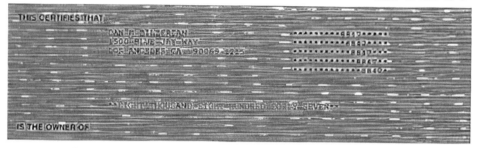

Dated 11-NOV-2013

COUNTERSIGNED AND REGISTERED
MELLON INVESTOR SERVICES LLC
TRANSFER AGENT AND REGISTRAR

BY

AUTHORIZED SIGNATURE

SINGER N.V. CORPORATE SEAL 1999 NETHERLANDS ANTILLES

MANAGING DIRECTOR

THE BACK OF CHECK HAS AN ARTIFICIAL WATERMARK. HOLD AT ANGLE TO VIEW.

WELLS FARGO ADVISORS
One North Jefferson
St. Louis, MO 63103

May 8, 2019
Check No. 16655937

WELLS FARGO BANK, NA
CHAPEL HILL, NC 27514

68-7270
2560

Pay Exactly Two Hundred Sixty-Nine Thousand Fifty-Two and 35/100

$269,052.35

Carlos Bilbao
Authorized Signature

000205 DKP2T128 000001
DAN B BILZERIAN
6005 LAS VEGAS BLVD S STE 7
LAS VEGAS NV 89119

THIS CHECK MUST BE CASHED WITHIN 180 DAYS.

PRINTED WITH BLUE BACKGROUND ON WHITE PAPER

⑈0016655937⑈ ⑆053101561⑆ 2079900058945⑈

12/30/2020 WIRE TYPE:BOOK IN DATE:201230 TIME:1533 ET TRN:2020123000474956 SNDR... C 1,070,107.74 [redacted]

Edit Description

Type: Credit

Description: WIRE TYPE:BOOK IN DATE:201230 TIME:1533 ET TRN:2020123000474956 SNDR REF:20CUE1405K790N69 ORIG:COMPUTERSHARE INC AAF CLI ID:XXXXX99265 PMT DET:PDF SOLUTIONS INC C106232

Merchant name: COMPUTERSHARE Edit

Merchant information:

Transaction category: Income: Other Income Edit

Print transaction details

COMMON STOCK

9073

COMMON STOCK

1,648,500

Cimetrix INCORPORATED

INCORPORATED UNDER THE LAWS OF THE STATE OF NEVADA

SEE REVERSE FOR STATEMENTS RELATING TO BUSINESS PREFERENCES, PRIVILEGES AND RESTRICTIONS, IF ANY

CUSIP 17185E 10 0

THIS CERTIFIES THAT ***DAN BILZERIAN***

IS THE RECORD HOLDER OF ***ONE MILLION SIX HUNDRED FORTY EIGHT THOUSAND FIVE HUNDRED***

100,000,000 SHARES AUTHORIZED, FULLY PAID AND NONASSESSABLE SHARES OF COMMON STOCK, $.001 PAR VALUE, OF

CIMETRIX INCORPORATED

transferable on the books of the Corporation by the holder hereof, in person or by duly authorized attorney upon surrender of this Certificate properly endorsed. This Certificate is not valid until countersigned by the Transfer Agent and registered by the Registrar.
Witness the facsimile seal of the said Corporation and the facsimile signatures of its duly authorized officers.

Dated: July 8, 2014

CHIEF FINANCIAL OFFICER

CORPORATE SEAL CIMETRIX INCORPORATED STATE OF NEVADA

PRESIDENT AND CHIEF EXECUTIVE OFFICER

COUNTERSIGNED AND REGISTERED COLONIAL STOCK TRANSFER SALT LAKE CITY, UTAH TRANSFER AGENT AND REGISTRAR

AUTHORIZED SIGNATURE

CHAPTER 21

Graduation Is at Hand

Just like I learned how to adapt from switching schools and getting to start over again, this second chance at BUD/S was going much better. The ability to learn is far more valuable in the long run than natural talent.

First Phase finally ended, and we swapped out our canteens and guard belts for big Gatorade bottles and dive tables. Second Phase, referred to as Dive Phase, was a big step; it was also uncharted territory for me. Pool competency is where the instructors really test how comfortable you are in the water, and it's one of the scariest things a trainee can face. If someone ran out of air and bolted for the surface, the instructors would grab his ass and drag him down to the bottom. This wasn't to be dicks: If a trainee inhaled from his tank at the bottom, freaked out, and didn't exhale on the way up, his lungs could burst.

I was good in the water but terrible at holding my breath. The instructors are supposed to let trainees get a full breath of air before they simulate a surf hit (getting smashed by a huge wave). I figured they were going to fuck with me because I'd been cocky with them, so I never fully exhaled. Sure enough, right as I exhaled, the instructor yanked out my air source and started tumbling me around. Another instructor ripped my mask off and tied my scuba hoses in knots. I already felt like I was out of air, but I tried to remain calm and follow the protocol. Just as I was certain that darkness was coming, I untangled the last knot and gratefully sucked in air from the tank. Air was like so many things in life; you don't appreciate it until you lose it.

Passing pool comp was a big milestone. It was pretty much the only thing a student could get kicked out of BUD/S for after finishing Hell Week.

Third Phase was Land Warfare; it consisted of land navigation and weapons/explosives training. The instructors loaded us up on busses, and we went to the mountains for a week at a time to learn to navigate various terrain using a topographical map and a compass. We'd patrol at night and take turns standing watch while we slept in the woods. There were no showers, so after five or six days, we came home smelling pretty ripe.

Before graduating BUD/S, students had to go to The Rock. Three solid weeks on San Clemente Island, no days off. Just explosives, live fire drills, underwater demolition, and lots of physical training. Inspection of our gear upon arrival at the island was routine, so I didn't dare bring my steroid supply. I had enough juice in my body for the first week, but I knew I'd crash in the second week, quickly dwindling down to prepubescent testosterone levels.

After the inspection, we had to knock out twelve dead-hang pull ups with thirty-five pounds of gear on to avoid getting wet and sandy before dinner. We ate, put our gear away in the barracks, and went to the classroom for a brief.

The instructors screened a National Geographic documentary about the waters around San Clemente Island serving as a breeding ground for great white sharks. The thick kelp beds around the island attracted hundreds of seals and sea lions, which in turn attracted dozens of monstrous great whites. This was a legitimate documentary with respected marine biologists lecturing on how sharks liked to feed at dusk.

It was followed by actual footage of great white shark attacks. I remember thinking, *The sun is about to set. That means dusk, right?*

"Jock up for a three-mile ocean swim!" the instructors yelled.

You gotta be fucking kidding me, I thought.

Every stroke through those kelp beds, I'd feel the slimy weeds brush against my legs and shit started playing with my mind. I could see dark shapes in the water dart in front of me. They were probably seals, I told myself. The instructors on the surface periodically fired shotguns to add to the ambiance.

After the swim, my OIC informed me that I had the "midwatch" that night. The dickhead really didn't like me, so he regularly scheduled me for the midnight to two in the morning watch, which pretty much guaranteed that I wouldn't get more than a couple of hours of sleep. There was nothing I could do, and by the end of the second week, I was delirious.

The class regularly went to the range to do IADs (Immediate Action Drills), which involved moving and shooting as a group. The instructor ordered us to drop and aim down range, so we did. He ordered us to rise and walk towards the targets, so we did.

"About face!" he yelled. "And drop!" This meant to turn 180 degrees, drop down, and prepare to shoot.

So we did.

Essentially, our entire group did as commanded, which meant we pointed our weapons the wrong way on the range, right at the instructors. This wasn't a trick. The military didn't exactly train for free thinking; they wanted you so intensively drilled that your body responded to orders with muscle memory. That's exactly what we did. The instructor had made a mistake. Regardless, they gave half the class safety violations for pointing our weapons the wrong way. We didn't argue; it wasn't even a conversation. We just signed the paperwork and continued training.

After almost three weeks, we had one night left on the island, and everyone was exhausted. I was in rough shape with the testosterone of a little girl and all those midwatches ruining my sleep. We practiced shooting and then peeling out, one by one, until every guy in the platoon was running. We did this for thirty minutes and then switched while the other half of the class took their turn.

It was about eleven at night, pitch-black, and we all wore earplugs. Some guys took catnaps while others talked about their family coming in for graduation, which was only thirty-six hours away. My own family was beginning their travels to San Diego to see me, at long last, graduate from something. I laid back and smiled. It had been almost eight months since I checked into BUD/S, and I couldn't help but think about how good it was going to feel to be finished. I closed my eyes and envisioned my father's face at the graduation ceremony. I knew he would be proud of me.

Suddenly there were instructors standing over me, screaming. They ordered me to climb into a tub of ice water. As the cold shock rolled over my body, I tried to figure out *what the fuck was happening.*

"Why didn't you show up to muster?" one yelled.

"Why were you sleeping during live fire drills?" another one shouted.

I assumed that I'd fallen asleep, and my boat crew leader hadn't woken me. The instructors gave me a safety violation and said I was being submitted for a review board. They told me to pack up and be outside the barracks ready at 0600. My mind was racing as I grabbed my things and threw them into the big green duffle bag. I laid in bed for five hours watching the seconds tick by on the white wall clock.

The instructor didn't say a word as he drove me to the island airport. I was sick to my stomach. It felt like I'd just come home to find my safe with everything I cared about *empty*. Usually when you get robbed, you never get your stuff back, but there's always a chance. On the plane back to San Diego, I couldn't help but wonder if by some act of God maybe they would still let me graduate.

In front of the master chief and captain, I was at a loss for words. The instructor read my list of violations, and it sounded really bad on paper. Bilzerian pointed his weapon at the instructors. Bilzerian was sleeping during live fire drills.

The CO asked me if these violations were accurate. I really wanted to explain what happened, but we were told to never make excuses, and my father taught me not to be a snitch.

"Yes, sir, they are, sir," I said calmly.

He presented two options. I could go to another duty station and come back to BUD/S in a year, or I could join the next class at the very beginning of Second Phase. Instead of four hours until graduation, I was now looking at four more months.

"I'll do it again, sir."

I had been royally fucked, but I didn't rat on the instructors. I hung my head and walked off.

That was the longest drive home ever. I was too tired and beat up to even get angry. I was just sad. My parents, brother, and friends had their bags packed. They expected to see me graduate, and I was going to have to tell them I was going back almost to the beginning. Making that phone call was the last thing in the world I wanted to do; I was depressed, humiliated, and I felt like a failure.

I sat on the floor of my apartment and began to sand the red paint off my helmet. Trainees in First Phase wear green helmets. Second Phase means blue helmets. Third Phase proudly sport red. It took a while to get the paint off, but finally I polished it, sprayed a coat of primer, and waited for it to dry. I didn't have any blue paint left. I took off my uniform and put-on jeans and a T-shirt so I could go into town to purchase a new supply of blue spray paint.

CHAPTER 22

Class 239

I went into base the next morning to muster up with my new class. It was embarrassing to drop down a phase, but my new classmates found me useful because I could tell them what to expect.

The OIC of BUD/S class 239 was a big boy; he weighed around 240 pounds and was built like a linebacker. He had a hard time passing his timed runs as big as he was, so he was used to getting beat, and so was the class. This was music to my ears. It was a complete change from 238. This class didn't whine, and they would laugh when the instructors sent us to the surf. They had a completely different attitude, and the difference was our leader.

I got along well with everyone in the class, and it felt good, like I was finally part of a team. So when one of the guys got hypothermia during our 5.5 nautical mile ocean swim and needed a swim buddy to accompany him, I volunteered to swim it again. And during land navigation, when I finished early, I went back out to help some of the weaker guys.

Things were going well with the class but not with the instructors. I knew they were trying to figure out a way to drop me when I received a safety violation for taking a shit in the woods six feet from my gear instead of three feet. The instructors were clearly trying to fuck me for anything they could, but it was hard because after doing so much training, I was good at most everything.

The day before we were scheduled to go to The Island, one of the instructors pulled me into the office and said they were going to drop me from training. They didn't have any real safety violations—I'd passed everything—so they just decided to "admin drop" me. My OIC and my LPO went to bat for me, but the instructors didn't care; they'd heard enough from my previous OIC and decided I wasn't a good fit.

I'd rubbed my previous OIC the wrong way, and he quickly turned the rest of the officers against me. The instructors followed. The officer in charge has a lot of power, and he dictates how the group thinks. SEALs aren't the John Rambo cowboys the movies portray. The guys they want aren't the free-thinking risk takers; they want guys who follow orders. It's pack mentality. If there is a guy who doesn't kiss ass or mesh well with the leader, they'll all gang up on that person. They don't like outliers, and I've seen it happen to some solid guys like David Goggins and Jesse Ventura.

I was pissed; I'd just done an entire year straight of BUD/S with no break. But these motherfuckers had yanked the rug out from under me so many times, I wasn't even surprised at this point. I fucked up. I honestly thought if I passed all my evolutions and didn't quit that they had to let me graduate. I didn't think the instructors had as much power as they did, and I was wrong. I was cocky this time, but I believed they would look at this like my father and respect the lack of fear.

I figured, I'd go to college, have fun, and finally fuck some girls. I could endure endless amounts of pain, but I wasn't built to take orders, and I wasn't the best at following rules. I was a leader, not a follower. I didn't do well kissing ass, and I was ready to get the fuck out of the military and begin a new adventure.

PART 3

Gambling

CHAPTER 23

Frat Orgy

After four years, I was honorably discharged from the United States Navy on the anniversary of the day I joined, April 29, 2003.

I was accepted to the University of Florida, while my brother Adam attended the University of South Florida which was located in Tampa. He lived at home and worked part-time at Ernie's car dealership. He spent his spare time playing golf at the country club and hustling Dad's friends in poker games. He was working hard studying, striving to transfer to a good school in two years. Adam didn't date much, and his only real social activity was his membership in Pi Kappa Alpha fraternity.

I had a BMW, money saved from my time in the military, and monthly disability checks from the Veteran's Administration. You get a percentage score at discharge for injuries sustained while on active duty, and after 510 days of BUD/S, my medical record was pretty thick. The VA rated me 60 percent disabled, which meant I would receive 60 percent of my military pay and free medical care for life. I was also expecting my GI Bill cash any day, which meant I would be getting almost five thousand dollars a month tax free.

Adam heard about all my extra money and decided I should learn how to play poker, primarily so he could separate me from the loose cash. The whole summer, we battled Texas Hold 'Em at the kitchen table. My losses had a silver lining because Adam rushed me as a PIKE at USF so I could essentially go onto campus at UF in the fall as a brother and not deal with rush and hazing. I felt I'd paid enough dues in SEAL training that if some nineteen-year-old kid was hazing me, I might have just killed him, so I was doing the right thing.

All the PIKEs were jocks and meatheads, so I fit right in. My first semester, I had a 4.0 GPA and fucked thirteen hot girls, which was more than my whole life combined prior to college. I was in amazing shape, I had money, I was popular, and I was banging superhot girls. Finally, this was my time.

In San Diego, the local women hated military dudes and poor guys. I was both. They had heard every line in the book and expected men to take them to dinner and pay for overpriced bottles in the club. But in college, the freshmen girls were accustomed to nervous high school guys with no money and no game. They were away from home for the first time and just wanted to get drunk and have sex with strangers. After four years of getting my teeth kicked in, I was in fucking heaven.

PIKE had a big party at least once or twice a semester. There was Hawaiian, where the pledges had to import thousands of pounds of sand and palm fronds. Platoon, which was an army theme, and Day Glow, which was the best one by far. The themes gave girls the excuse they needed to wear next to nothing and not feel slutty about it. There were around fifteen good sororities on campus, and we invited all of them. This ensured an absolutely ludicrous ratio of girls to guys as no fraternity ever threw a party on the same night as another house.

Day Glow was a body painting party where the women started out in bikini bottoms or thongs with white T-shirts or wife beaters. The guys wore board shorts or boxers. Girls gravitated towards the guys they were interested in and asked to be painted with glow in the dark paint. When the guy finished painting the girls, those girls would then paint him. It was basically an excuse to grope each other. Some girls took full advantage, going right for the dick. This got absurd; multiple girls would rub each guy down, and it got competitive because there was a massive shortage of guys. The setup was pure genius.

After everyone was painted, they'd shut off the regular lights and turn on the black lights so everyone glowed in the dark. The DJ started getting everyone hyped up, and pledges went around pouring shots down people's throats like it was spring break in Cabo. People would dance/grope each other until they couldn't take it anymore. The party gradually moved upstairs to the showers, which, as everyone got drunker and more sex crazed, turned into a full-blown orgy.

It was fascinating to see dudes who wouldn't get laid in San Diego in a million years banging two girls at a time. Some guys went for the easiest girl they could find while others searched for a girl they wanted to date. I had a more pragmatic approach, fucking the hottest girl who was into me as quickly as possible and then going back out for seconds or thirds. It was like shooting fish in a barrel.

Day Glow showed me how important the setup is. Everyone had a room within fifty feet that they could go have sex in, so the logistics were solved. The ratio was absurd, so girls had to compete for the attention of guys. There was no need for awkward conversation because everyone was drinking, the music was loud, and the girls had already made the first move by painting the guys they were into. The environment was good because everyone was hooking up openly and the girls felt comfortable because there was no judgement.

I had been taught about the laws of supply and demand in economics class, but now it clicked. This was by far the most valuable thing I learned in college, and I would be implementing that knowledge soon.

IF ANY OF YOU GUYS READING THIS are about to graduate high school, I would highly recommend going in the military for four years and then going to college. This allows you to fuck around for a few years with no consequences and no worries about your GPA. You'll get some real-world experience to help figure out what you want to do with your life. Plus, you'll get into a much better school as a veteran because universities value diversity.

When you are eighteen and male, no girls want to fuck you, and no guys want to hang out with you. However, when you go to college at twenty-two, you get to have four years of basically being a senior. You will be older, more confident, more attractive, and more experienced—plus you'll have more money and value the degree.

Then there are the financial benefits: You get your school paid for, you're eligible for more grants and student loans with zero interest, and you get free medical. Trust me, it's the move.

CHAPTER 24

Going Broke

Toward the end of my first year of college, I began playing more and more online poker. A couple of my fraternity brothers would often play for ten to sixteen hours straight at the frat house. I'd watch them, and they'd let me play on their accounts until my addictive personality gave way to a full-blown gambling addiction. Poker was a rush like nothing I had experienced before, and even when I wasn't playing, I was thinking about it.

I downloaded Party Poker, and soon I was skipping meals, the gym, and class. Instead, I was joining the brothers in their marathon poker sessions and playing the local $200 buy-in game with *Rounders* looped on the DVD player in the background.

I had a roommate who was as addicted as I was but with a different style. I had a super-aggressive style that, if played with discipline, could make a lot of money but with a couple missteps could also lead to big losses. He, on the other hand, was a very tight, disciplined player who always maintained a balance in his online poker accounts.

Living with him made it pretty much impossible for me to stop playing poker. I would come home after a night of drinking, and gambling always sounded like a good idea, but it never was. Poker requires patience, so it may come as no surprise that a drunk guy on steroids with ADD is not a winning formula. I knew this would happen, so I'd cash out before the weekend. The problem was he always had money in his account, and I knew all I had to do was kick his door in and force him to transfer me money. No matter how many times I told him I wouldn't pay him if he ever transferred me money again, I would still cut him the check in the morning, knowing that he really had no choice.

It all came crashing down halfway through my sophomore year; I was broke and in debt. Unpaid loan on my BMW, maxed student loans, savings drained to nothing, and I owed money. Even my own family, from Dad to Adam, was smart enough not to help me. I was a total degenerate and had gone from having more money than I could spend in college to having nothing.

I scraped together $750 for one last shot at a win by selling two pistols and a shotgun on Craigslist, then took that money to a gambling boat in St. Petersburg. If I lost on that boat, I wouldn't even have gas money to get back to school.

I played the $200 buy-in until I had $1,500. Then I played the $500 buy-in for six days straight, only stopping to sleep until I reached ten grand. I was easily outplaying the guys on the boat and figured I was ready, so I bought a one-way ticket to Las Vegas to take a shot, just like Matt Damon in *Rounders*.

At the Bellagio, I played every day for sixteen hours a day. My soundtrack was 50 Cent's "Get Rich or Die Tryin'" and I daydreamed of having enough money to tell everyone to fuck off. I wanted financial freedom. I wanted "fuck-you money."

There was Internet now, so after a quick Google search, other players in Vegas assumed I had financial backing from my father, which wasn't true, but I leaned into the perception. I played super aggressive, and players called me with barely anything just because they were frustrated. I bet, bet, bet until I met resistance. I would rarely make huge bluffs, but I was capable of it, so as a result I'd get paid off in spots that nobody else would. This unpredictability made me much harder to play against, and it threw players off their game.

Starting with that boat in St. Petersburg, I had played every day for a month, sixteen hours a day, and made $187,000. I went to the main cage and exchanged my remaining chips for cash. At that moment the win became real; it was the most money I'd ever seen, and it felt amazing knowing it was all mine. It gave me confidence and the ability to do what I wanted. I no longer had to answer to anyone. All the stress about paying my bills and debt was gone. It felt like freedom in a briefcase. Winning was like a drug, but the high lasted longer, and it was more addicting. I wanted more.

CHAPTER 25

Fuck-You Money

I took my briefcase full of cash straight to the Range Rover dealer. I had daydreamed about paying all cash for a car ever since I saw 50 Cent do it in *Get Rich or Die Tryin.'* In the movie, he goes to the dealership and the guy doesn't take him seriously, so he later returns with a backpack full of cash and throws it at the car salesman before driving his new car off the lot. Maybe it was the snobs at my country club when I was younger, or maybe it was all the people in my life who told me *no*, but nothing seemed more appealing than flexing on them and seeing the shocked expressions on their faces. None of that happened at the dealership, but it was fun to play out those scenarios in my head. I traded in my BMW plus forty thousand in cash for the best used Range Rover I could afford.

I had noticed that players were more willing to gamble with me when I had a bunch of money on the table. I saw the value of being perceived as rich. So buying the Range Rover wasn't totally reckless spending, but even if it was, I didn't care. I wanted to present an image of being as rich as possible to the gambling community, and the Range Rover was the perfect car because, at the time, it was the most expensive SUV out there.

I was a new man who no longer had to break down doors to drunkenly demand a loan. I had a newly discovered discipline, developed in my intensive month of grinding at the poker tables. I figured out when to put on the brakes and be patient, which screwed up all my old online opponents. They had notes on me saying "always bluffs, never fold to him," and so forth. I got paid off on all my big hands and ended up winning $87,000 in a week just playing a $1,000 max buy-in game. Around this time, Chris Moneymaker won the World Series of Poker on ESPN and turned twenty-five bucks into millions of dollars. That was the best thing to happen to poker as it attracted tons of newbies, and just like that, poker became the new gold rush.

I spent weekends in Vegas, the Bahamas, Monaco—wherever there was a poker tour event. Everyone else tried to get famous for being the best poker player; they wanted to win tournaments and collect shiny bracelets. I did the exact opposite. I never played in the actual tournaments. I looked for cash games. My goal was to be perceived as being a rich, shitty player so that I could get into private games with other rich, shitty players and beat them for the big money.

At a Bellagio 25/50 game, where I was splashing around and playing loose, I met Nick Cassavetes, the guy who directed *The Notebook*. And probably because he thought I was a sloppy player, he invited me to play his private home game in the Hollywood Hills. Porsches, Ferraris, and Range Rovers lined the street, and there wasn't one pro player in the place.

It was a 50/100 ten thousand-dollar minimum buy-in cash game. I played a lot of hands and showed my cards if I made a bad call and mucked like I was bluffing if I got cold-decked. A cold deck is when two players have extremely good hands, and the loser has no choice but to put his money in. A lot of poker players would bitch when they got unlucky, but I didn't say a word. I wanted them to think I was playing bad, not *running bad* (getting unlucky). It wasn't hard to figure out how everyone played; I made my adjustments, gave good action, and cashed out for six figures the first night.

I enjoyed college, but I really only got one good year in before going over to the dark side (gambling). I was much happier my first year, but

I loved the action and excitement of poker, not to mention the freedom and power the winnings provided. For a college kid in Gainesville, Florida, where a pitcher of beer was a buck fifty, I had stupid money. And that money went a long way. I paid one kid fifty bucks to drink a shot of warm piss. I gave another guy forty to eat a live roach and then later a hundred and fifty dollars to fuck the fattest, ugliest girl I could find at a street festival.

My priorities had begun to shift; I used to lift weights almost every day and run thirty to forty miles a week. Now I was only lifting four days a week and barely doing cardio. Even when I was having fun, going to parties, banging girls, and hanging at the frat house, poker was constantly in the back of my mind. I couldn't escape it; it was always there, twenty-four hours a day, seven days a week; I could get on my computer and be in action.

By my fourth year at Florida, I was superficially a senior, but I didn't have that many credits because I'd dropped so many classes. It was impossible to pay attention to school given how much gambling I was doing.

The poker books and self-help courses will never tell you this, but the first step toward succeeding at anything—from poker to attracting women to life in general—depends on finding a way to cram the most experience into the shortest period of time. That might seem obvious, but I looked at the average live poker player and did some simple math. Playing in a home or casino game, live players see, on average, around twenty hands an hour and usually sit for a ten-hour stretch. That works out to seeing around two hundred hands per day.

I would play ten online tables at once, seeing around one hundred hands per hour at each table. So, by playing fourteen hours a day, I looked at roughly fourteen thousand hands each day. It wasn't long before I'd seen more hands online than what even the most obsessive live players saw in a lifetime.

And this was when online poker was still relatively new. The poker fad was coming but wasn't huge yet, so you couldn't find tutorials online, and solvers hadn't been invented. The best you could hope for was a poker book providing a very rudimentary explanation.

My volume of play gave me a monster edge, especially because certain aspects of the game—like learning people's bluff/call tendencies—were only learned through experience. Lots of experience.

An even bigger advantage was understanding my table image. How I was perceived by other players usually dictated the way they reacted to my hyper-aggressive style of play. Recreational players usually did one of two things:

The first approach—They would play really tight, refuse to bluff, and wait for me to bet. This strategy was easy to defeat. I ran them over, stole pots, and bet huge on my big hands.

The second approach was to play back at me, which meant they bluffed more frequently. This was harder to counter, but it yielded the most profit. And the most fun. When a bad player tries this, it leads to all sorts of mistakes: bluffing at the wrong times, taking betting lines that make no sense, and giving off tells. I mopped up with those guys.

Earlier that year, I'd found a poker site with an online sports book attached called Bodog. This was a big deal because sports bettors would wander into the poker room and blow their newfound winnings. I recorded the biggest monthly win in Bodog's poker history, clearing around $400,000 only playing three tables with a max buy-in of only $2,000 per table.

That week, I was sitting in class, tired from the long hours in front of the computer, when the professor said something to me in a condescending way. In no mood to take shit, I replied, "Who the fuck do you think you are?"

"I'm your professor!" he screamed. "And you will not use profanity in my class."

I never liked academia, I didn't respect him, and his sense of entitlement bothered me, so I doubled down.

"You think you can talk down to me because you've read some books?"

He looked bewildered and declared, "I have a master's degree!" as if that somehow settled the argument. He said it like he'd landed on the moon.

I rolled my eyes.

"And what have you done?" he hissed, clearly getting himself worked up. "Graduate high school?"

"Nah, I got a GED. But I'm a veteran, and I made more money in the last week than you will in the next three years."

The professor stood there dumbfounded for a second and then fired back, "If you're so rich, why are you in college?"

As stupid as it sounds, I hadn't really considered dropping out, but the asshole did have a point. I sat there in silence for about six seconds and thought about it.

"That's the first intelligent thing you've said all semester. You're right, I'm out. Enjoy earning thirty thousand a year, you fucking dipshit."

The kids went crazy as I walked out of the classroom and shut the door on my college career.

CHAPTER 26

Russian Hitman

It felt good to tell my professor to fuck off. I'd always wanted to do that since I was a little kid. As I drove back to my apartment, I couldn't help but smile. For the first time in my life, I had no obligations and nobody to answer to. I was free.

Bouncing between private games in New York City, Las Vegas, and LA was more lucrative than I thought. My parents couldn't say shit about me dropping out because I was making so much money. Dad kept telling me to take the money and run, but that was his style as a corporate raider, not mine.

Eddie Ting ran a private game in New York with super rich businessmen and the occasional pro he took a piece of. Some nights, he raked (taking a percentage of the pot for the house each hand) over a hundred thousand dollars from the game. But it didn't matter; the players were so bad, I could beat the rake easy. I almost always won. Eddie saw all the angles and knew I had skill, but I was liked by amateurs, and I was good action, so he let it slide. The New York guys had big money and liked to push it around, so I had to play tighter there.

Vegas games were usually smaller and tough to get into because the moment a whale (rich bad player) would come in, a game immediately built around them. I tipped the floor people $100 for seating me, I gave out $500 for a heads-up that a bad player had come in, and I would tip up to five grand for doing me a favor. Casino employees became like family, and I always took care of family.

Showing poker legend Johnny Chan my hand while playing at Bellagio.

I met Tom Goldstein at the Bellagio poker room. People were all watching the game and talking about what a fucking maniac he was. When I walked up, he had been playing without looking at his cards for two hours straight. Occasionally on the turn or the river, he would look and then fire huge bluffs.

To this day, I have never met anyone with less respect for money proportionate to their net worth than Tom. And I've met some true degenerates. He wasn't very good at fundamental poker, but he was super intelligent and savvy enough to read people and situations. Those skills enabled him to play blind (without looking at his cards) and actually win.

He loved the action, but it was almost like he subconsciously wanted to lose. I think he liked that everyone at the table loved him so much, and as a ruthless lawyer, he probably didn't get that kind of a warm welcome elsewhere. The more he lost, the happier everyone around him got, and I think he was partially addicted to that feeling, but he was fully addicted to the rush of gambling.

I also met John Dolmayan, the drummer for System of a Down, at the tables in Vegas. John and his entire band were proud Armenians, so when he discovered I was Armenian, a bond quickly formed. Needless to say, with his shaved head and goatee, he looked more like a Mexican gangbanger than an Armenian rock star.

One time, a casino regular, who was a crotchety old bastard, mouthed off to John after getting beaten in a hand. The drummer bit his tongue, staying quiet and respectful before he finally had enough of the old buzzard and stepped away for a break.

"Do you not know who that fucking guy is?" I asked the geezer.

"No, who is he?"

"He's a trigger man for the Russian mob," I told the old man to fuck with his head.

"Are you serious?"

"Yes, you fucking idiot, what's wrong with you?" I warned him. "He's got a shaved head, wears the same clothes every single day, and loses tens of thousands of dollars in cash here every week. What did you think he does for a living? Did you think he was an orthodontist?"

The old buzzard sputtered and stammered, asking if John was going to hurt him.

"Have you ever seen anyone react so calmly after getting yelled at?" I asked. "You know you were being a dick. Has anyone ever taken that kind of shit and just quietly walked away from you?" I paused for effect. "If he snapped back, or even punched you, I'd say you're fine. But that was cold, the way he just left. That's not normal to be so emotionless. I've got chills. You better beg for forgiveness."

The buzzard spilled his drink while scooping up his chips. I didn't see him for another week, and he was usually an everyday regular.

A few weeks later, I was playing with the buzzard, and John walked up to the table. I had totally forgotten about my story or I would have clued John in. The old guy leapt up from the table.

"I'm really sorry about the last time," he stuttered. "I have a bad heart, and they switched my prescription. I wasn't myself. Let me buy you a drink or dinner. I'm sorry about the misunderstanding."

"No problem, I appreciate the apology," John said, looking around confused.

"Are you sure? Is everything okay? Is there anything you'd like me to do?"

I now remembered the whole thing and was grinning from ear to ear, doing my best to contain my laughter. John looked at me and knew something was up. He took me aside, and I explained the story to him. I saw the look in his eye when he realized this was perfect retribution. He returned to the table and fucked with the buzzard, scaring him for twenty minutes before saying that he would let the old guy live.

CHAPTER 27

Molly's Game

I rented a house in the Hollywood Hills and a Ferrari F430 for $45,000 a month to give the LA scene a shot and was paying for it all from Nick Cassavetes's home game. People saw the house and the car, and it bolstered the trust fund kid image I was building. I also played in the now famous "Molly's Game," which was stocked with celebrities or super rich businessmen and absolutely no pros. I made my living playing these games, but I wasn't winning tournaments or playing tight, so no one considered me a pro. They thought I was just a spoiled kid living off the money my father was presumably hiding offshore. While I acknowledged that I had a trust fund, I never discussed how much it was actually worth or that I would not have any access to it until my thirty-fifth birthday.

They recently made a movie about Molly's Game, and I'm not sure they did it justice. I walked into a $6,000 a night suite at the Four Seasons in Beverly Hills that had every type of booze, cigar, and food you could want. Top agency models slinked around in revealing cocktail dresses, and the minimum buy-in was $50,000 with no maximum.

Molly was a straight hustler. Cold and calculated, she saw all the angles. She had a genius level IQ and could read a room well. Within two games, she'd figured out that I was a good player. Incredible, considering she wasn't even playing poker. I'd watch her smile and flirt with the guys, convincing them they had a chance, but it was all business. She used girls like pawns and quickly accumulated dirt on most of the guys, a useful tool if they decided they didn't want to cover their losses. Her goal was the same as mine: to make as much money as possible by any means necessary.

MOLLY BLOOM

Author of Molly's Game

Dan showed up to the game and played the part of the trust fund kid fish perfectly. Almost—maybe because I didn't belong in that room, I recognized he didn't either. Bilzerian was an excellent card player; he was hustling them, no doubt. I saw through it in an instant—he would have bankrupted that table if I let him play regularly.

The other thing about him was that, under the surface of his gun-toting, womanizing, arrogant demeanor, was a man who had been through a lot. His childhood was pretty fucked up, his dad had gone to prison, and the instability and chaos that ensued with all of that surely left a mark. I saw the human being underneath. I recognized the damage and the mask.

CHAPTER 28

Heart Attack

I was gambling in Vegas when I got a call from my frat brothers who wanted to meet up in Lake Tahoe to snowboard. I booked a flight, and four hours later, we were having beers in a Tahoe casino.

I met a surprisingly hot girl on a chair lift, and I went out that night with her and a bunch of her friends. I'd just won $40,000 gambling and was in a good mood, buying drinks for everyone in the dive bar. Later in her bedroom, it was my typical hookup. We made out for about twenty seconds while peeling off our clothes, she sucked my dick for a minute or two, and then we started fucking. After a few minutes, I remembered why I hate drinking. My dick was becoming more worthless by the second.

"Give me like ten minutes," I said. "I just need to get some water and something to eat, and I'll fuck you properly."

I ate some bread and a banana and pounded a jug of water. I knew if I didn't fuck this girl right, my ego wouldn't let me sleep. I smoked some weed and hopped in the shower. By the time I got back into the room, she was half-asleep, so I swatted her in her face with my dick a couple of times. She laughed, and the sex was great. I showered again, drank more water, ate another banana, smoked more, and fucked her again until the sun came up.

Moral of the story? Alcohol is a dick killer. Carbs, potassium, and hydration are important and weed is vital.

I didn't sleep; I went back and spent that last day in Tahoe riding the mountain hard. When I got to my hotel room, I was exhausted and didn't feel well, so I laid down. I couldn't sleep, and once I started throwing up, I figured I had altitude sickness. There wasn't any water in the room, so I slurped out of the sink because I knew if I got dehydrated, things would only get worse. Then I started shitting, which was more like pissing out my ass. I spent the whole night puking and didn't sleep.

The following day, I took a bus ride into the airport in Reno and puked in the bathroom repeatedly. I couldn't keep fluids down. I felt weak and knew I needed an IV, so I asked the baggage check attendant to get a medic.

"If I give you an IV," the EMT said, "I cannot let you fly."

We went back and forth until I promised that I would cancel my flight, return to the hotel, and rest up. As soon as he slipped the IV into the disposal bag and left, I dashed off for the departure gate to catch a flight to Vegas.

At the Bellagio, I still felt like shit, but the poker tables were located between the valet and the elevator, so I never made it up to my room. I played all night and was up about twenty grand when some poker buddies said they had had a bunch of drugs and were going to meet some strippers. I snorted some coke in the Maserati on the way to the club.

I never really liked blow; it just always sounded like a good idea, even though it never was. I like to eat, workout, fuck, and sleep—and blow messes all of those things up. I lose my appetite, and coke is a vasoconstrictor, which messes up blood flow, thereby reducing oxygen to the muscles. It keeps you up all night and also makes it tough to get your dick hard, which for a sex addict like me is a deal breaker. It's honestly the worst drug in my opinion, and it sucks for girls too. They don't shut the fuck up.

I'm not into strippers or hookers, but I have, on occasion, had a moment of weakness. This night was one of those times.

I saw a stripper in a schoolgirl outfit, and I'm a sucker for short skirts, so I called her over.

"Would you like a dance?"

"I'm not into awkward lap dances," I said. "But I'll give you $500 to suck my dick."

"I'm not a hooker."

"I didn't say you were. I just don't want a lap dance."

"Then why are you in a strip club?"

"I was gambling and got dragged here by my friends."

She smiled and stared into my eyes, which, given my current drug regiment, probably looked like saucers. The girl was sexy, but more importantly, I thought her tits were real.

"Well, when in Rome..." she implied.

"I just don't see the point of lap dances."

"So what are you going to do with yourself?"

"More drugs and hopefully get a blowjob."

The girl asked if I had any Molly. I smiled and covertly gave her one before heading to the bathroom to do more blow. I was pleasantly surprised to find her still sitting there when I returned.

I was all jammed up from the coke and wanted to talk, so I ran a pickup artist routine I read in the book *The Game*, and it was well received. Then I took her hand and put it on my dick. She didn't remove it, which was a good sign. She rubbed a bit and—surprisingly, given the amount of drugs I had taken—my dick came to life. She started grinding on me, and I stopped her. "Look, I'm not trying to get blue balls. What do you want to do?"

"Give me thirty minutes. I gotta cash out and change."

"Please don't change."

My buddy offered me a Viagra while I waited for her to finish up. I had never taken one before, but I hadn't slept in days, I was sick, dehydrated, and on Molly and blow. I needed the help. A few minutes later, nothing was happening, so I asked the guy for another.

"No way, you've had plenty."

"This shit isn't working, just give me the fucking pill!"

"Bro, these are hundreds."

"I want it for tomorrow," I lied. "Give me the pill."

On the ride back to the Bellagio, I still didn't feel anything, so I tossed down the second pill. In the room, we kissed, and the clothes came off. By that point, I felt like my dick had grown an extra inch, so I guess the Viagra was finally working. After what seemed like an hour of hardcore fucking, I could barely feel anything, my heart was pounding though my chest, and I was covered in sweat. Cumming did not seem to be an option for me.

I went to take a shower and was shocked at my reflection in the mirror. My face was beet red, and my eyes were bloodshot. I looked like I'd just gotten out of an over-chlorinated pool. After an ice-cold shower, my dick was still rock hard and wasn't going down. I ordered room service and had to place my dick against my stomach and tie the towel around my waist when the food arrived forty-five minutes later. The stripper noticed, and we went at it again. It was late morning when we finished, and I couldn't sleep, so I went downstairs to retrieve the suitcase I'd left in the poker room.

I bet ten grand on the Florida game at the sportsbook and got a cab to meet John Dolmayan for lunch. We grabbed some greasy Mexican food at this hole-in-the-wall spot near his comic book warehouse. I was trying to be good company, but I felt like shit. I hadn't slept in days and couldn't even pay attention to the football game.

Back at the Bellagio, my shoulder started hurting as I walked to my room. I tried to stretch it out and massage it, but the pain felt deep in the muscle. I tried doing push-ups to get the blood flowing, hoping the pain would subside, but that seemed to make it worse. I called my mom and asked her to phone our family doc. While I was on hold with his office, I started having a hard time breathing. I didn't know what was wrong, but I knew it wasn't good.

I should have just called 911 and gotten an ambulance, but I thought it would be quicker to take a cab to the emergency room since it was only ten minutes away. That was a mistake because I ended up trapped in the waiting room for an hour before seeing a doctor. The girl at the desk wasn't moved by my symptoms or by my bribe of $10,000 to get a doc immediately.

After what seemed like an eternity, I was admitted. A nurse took my vitals and quickly returned with a doctor.

"He's having a myocardial infarction," the doctor said in a surprisingly calm voice.

"What the fuck is an infarction?" I asked.

"You're having a heart attack," the doctor said as he applied nitroglycerin patches to my arm and chest.

I thought I was dying, so I called my parents. It wasn't easy to talk because I felt like I was breathing through a narrow straw, but I did my best to explain what was happening. I told them I loved them.

That's when I started to feel warm and happy, like I was floating in a field of flowers. I wondered if this is how it felt as you were about to die, but it was just the morphine kicking in. When I opened my eyes, my parents and my on-again, off-again girlfriend Nadine were at my bedside.

Nadine and I.

Dr. Conrad Murray had been my grandfather's doctor, and he later achieved some notoriety (and jail time) as Michael Jackson's infamous propofol administrator. My grandfather had died of a heart attack the year before under his watch, and we all know how the King of Pop turned out. So maybe I wasn't in the best of care, but I didn't know at the time. He held a clipboard and took notes.

"I am going to ask you a series of questions, and I need you to be completely honest," he said.

"What drugs did you take in the twenty-four hours leading up to your heart attack?"

"I smoked some weed."

"I need you be thorough and exact."

"And I did some cocaine."

Mom perked up when I said that.

"And some Ecstasy."

Dad looked surprised.

"And I took some Viagra."

Nadine yelled, "What?"

"How much Viagra?" Dr. Murray asked.

"I think it was 200 milligrams."

"You took 200 milligrams? What were you doing?" He didn't look up but kept writing frantically.

"Yes, what *were* you doing?" Nadine squawked.

"Is that a lot? I've never taken it before."

"That's an insane amount," the doctor answered. "A normal dose is twenty-five to fifty milligrams."

This was a lot to wake up to. I sat there in my hospital bed with everyone concerned and upset, and I kind of zoned out a little bit. I had put my body through so much hell in SEAL training that I legitimately thought I was unbreakable. I'd stayed up for five days with no sleep, so I thought this wouldn't be a big deal, but I didn't account for the drugs. At the time, I thought it was the coke and Viagra, but only years later did I realize it was the horse steroid, Equipoise, that I was taking. That coupled with my sleep apnea had raised my hematocrit levels dangerously high, essentially thickening my blood into mud.

The next night after my parents went back to their hotel, I had a second heart attack. I asked to see my doctor, but it was late and most of the staff had gone home for the night, so they said I would have to wait till morning. I was short of breath, but I was able to call my father, and I begged him to come down and raise hell. Dad came through and got the on-call doctor's lazy ass out of bed, and sure enough, I was having a full-blown heart attack...again. They administered more nitroglycerin and morphine.

The following day, doctors made an incision in my inner thigh and performed an angiogram to look at my heart. The results indicated I didn't have any lasting damage or blockage. They chalked it up to a combination of stress, travel, illness, dehydration, and lack of sleep. And a lot of drugs.

I'd like to tell you that two heart attacks at twenty-seven, hospitalization, and my near-death experience changed me. But the truth is that I stopped taking my prescriptions after a couple of weeks and got right back on the horse. Gambling and fucking.

"It's better to have a short life that is full of what you like doing than a long life spent in a miserable way."

ALAN WATTS

CHAPTER 29

No Remorse

When I was a kid, the first concert I went to was Paula Abdul. My second concert was twenty years later standing on stage watching Metallica after I fucked a girl in the bass player's trailer.

System of a Down had broken up due to "creative differences," whatever the fuck that means. The lead singer left and started his own band. The guitarist and my drummer buddy John Dolmayan followed suit and started their own band called Scars on Broadway. John invited me to watch their first big show when they opened for Metallica in Tucson.

At the Phoenix airport baggage claim, I saw a tall, blue-eyed, superhot model-looking girl. We had both flown in on the same flight from Cabo.

"Wanna see Metallica tomorrow?" I asked her. "My buddy is opening for them."

A couple of hours later, she texted me about meeting up that night.

Where would I stay? she asked.

You can stay with me if you want.

I'm not going to have sex with you.

Who said anything about sex? I texted.

I just don't want you to be upset.

You could be a total weirdo. I'm not promising sex to some girl I just met in an airport.

John and I went to a seedy strip club where the owner made a big deal about having a famous musician in the house. He tried to welcome us, but the pizza was subpar, and the dancers were all pretty beat. After a couple hours of drinking, John wrangled some hyena that looked rabid, but she had big tits, and after eight whiskey sours, I guess that's all that mattered.

The airport girl and I went to my room, where she changed into a semi see-through nightgown. Because of the texts, I considered not even trying to kiss her, but I'm not a big fan of the long game, so I said fuck it. She got in bed, and I pulled her on top of me. We kissed, but when I went to slide down the straps on her nightgown, she stopped me. So I got out of bed, went to the bathroom, and popped a sleeping pill.

"Are you mad?" she asked.

"Nope. All good, let's get some sleep."

I didn't say it in a bitchy way since I wasn't angry or dejected. I was only irritated at myself since my gut told me to wait until "it was her idea." I certainly wasn't going to whine, keep trying, and keep getting shot down like most guys. The more a girl rejects you, the lower your perceived value becomes in her eyes. It's like when you get stuck off-roading—the more you spin your tires, the harder it will be to eventually get out.

The following day, we met up with John and headed to the venue where they assigned us a golf cart to get around the massive festival grounds. We had all access passes, so we could go anywhere we wanted. My girl and I both started drinking the minute we arrived.

We were hanging in John's trailer after he finished his sound check when Metallica's manager came in. He asked John to come to his trailer next to the stage so they could talk business. We went to their trailer until it was time for John to perform.

Watching him and his band from the side of the stage was intense. I looked out at the sea of people, banging their heads in unison. After a few songs, my girl and I went in search of more booze. We walked down from the stage to the trailer we'd all just vacated. I knocked but no one answered, so we walked in. I poured some drinks, and she was right next to me, staring at me, so we started kissing. She was all over me. I put her hand on my dick, and without hesitation, she dropped to her knees and started giving me a blowjob.

A small amount of rational thought remained in my head. I knew this was not John's trailer, and we were definitely going to fuck; so I waddled over to the door with my pants around my ankles and locked it shut. She bent over the kitchen table, and I started fucking her. After some riding on the couch, I picked her up and put her back on the table when there was a loud banging on the door.

"Gimme a minute," I yelled. The knocking continued. I didn't even consider stopping. I'd waited a long time to fuck this girl. Yes, I know it was technically only twenty-four hours, but I'd shared a bed with her, and we'd had the equivalent of six dates within that time period. Whatever. Fuck those guys. There's no doubt they knew what was happening. Eventually, they gave up. Airport Girl dropped down and asked me to cum on her face.

I find these glimpses into the female mind fascinating. She wouldn't let me take her top off, but after breakfast, two beers, and three songs, she let me do whatever I wanted. By me being willing to accept a no and then still hang out with her afterward, it allowed her to feel safe and think that I liked her for more than just sex. And this allowed her to then have dirty, cheap sex with me. Go figure.

Most guys are persistent and keep trying. That's a bad tactic. I quickly came to realize that if a girl says no to me, music stops and I'm out. I don't play that beggar bullshit. No games. If she isn't super into me, then I'll find a girl who is.

Don't get in the habit of begging or allowing the possibility of sex to control the situation. If you shut it down, it communicates that you aren't going to let her pussy run the show. Whether it's a business negotiation or a hookup, the person willing to walk has all the power.

During the turnover of festival bands, I saw the bass player from Metallica giving John shit for me fucking in their trailer. John apologized out of respect for the headliners, but he thought the whole thing was hilarious. We watched Metallica play a few songs and took off. I love their music, but they're some grouchy old bastards.

A couple years later, System of a Down got back together, and John invited me out for their European reunion tour. It was the craziest shit but not in a good way because, despite being massive rock stars over there and playing huge festivals, they didn't do anything fun. They didn't hang out, do after-parties, or go to nightclubs. The lead singer Serj was married, so he just hung with his wife. Daron the guitarist had a girlfriend, so they did their own thing. Shavo, the bass player, was doing a decent amount of drugs at the time, and John only drank, so they didn't hang out either. The tour was a big letdown with respect to partying, but their shows were actually amazing.

I'll never forget the energy of the crowd. When the curtain dropped, the people went insane. There were times when the fans were singing so loud it overpowered the seemingly endless amount of speakers on the stage. I'd heard a few songs of theirs on the radio, but I'd never listened to an album, and I was shocked that I liked almost every song. To this day, those were the best concerts I've ever been to.

During the show in Nuremberg, the lead singer spread his arms, and the crowd parted like Moses with the Red Sea. He put his arms together, and the crowd charged at each other like a battle scene from *Braveheart;* they hit so hard I actually saw one guy fly up in the air a couple feet.

After the show, a couple hot girls somehow ended up in John's tour bus. He took one of the girls in the back as I sat somewhat awkwardly in the living room with the other. There was no music playing, we were all sober, and nobody hooked up. The whole thing seemed off to me, but I did learn some valuable lessons.

John was a perfect example of a guy who wanted to get laid and should've been getting a lot of pussy but massively underachieved. He had the trifecta of what makes it easy: fame, money, and social status. He is also known for having a big dick, which should also make it easier. The reason he wasn't getting laid as much as he should have was because of one thing and one thing only: His setup was wrong.

John is kind of an introvert who didn't have a lot of girls around, so there wasn't a sense of competition and a scarcity of dick. The two girls on the bus were probably surprised to see no other girls there. The scarcity of women lowered his perceived value while at the same time raising their relative value in the process because this made *them* the commodity in short supply. The laws of supply and demand apply the same to women as they do in business. In case you slept through economics class, I'll give you the formula: an abundance of women plus a shortage of dick equals getting laid with minimal effort.

John should've had an assistant prior to the show cherry-picking from the female fan mail and then combing the crowd for hot girls. At the end of each show, John shoulda been putting down his drumsticks and stepping onto a tour bus full of hot women competing for his attention. Then if he brought those same two girls in, the one he wanted would perceive him as desirable, instead of desperate. Her inclination to hook up with him would be validated, and she would also feel pressure to do so, knowing if she didn't fuck him, then he would most likely fuck someone else.

Giving her undivided attention, which in the previous scenario was a negative, would now be a positive. Because any attention he shows one girl means less attention for the rest of the girls, creating scarcity, which breeds competition. This isn't exactly rocket science; in fact, it's obvious when you *actually* consider it. But most guys never do. When it comes to attracting women, most guys neglect—*or flat out ignore*—an intelligent setup and rely on dumb luck.

And luck, as the saying goes, is for the unprepared.

JOHN DOLMAYAN

Drummer from System of a Down

Dan and I met playing poker at the Bellagio; at this time my band (System of a Down) was on "hiatus," which is a nice way of saying we had disbanded. I was in a toxic relationship, my future was unclear, and my life was an economic mess, so what better choice could I make then to play poker, risking tens of thousands of dollars a day?

I remember thinking, Who is this fucking loudmouth who never shuts up across from me? He's giving me a headache and plays almost as poorly as I do. I hated him straightaway until I saw his last name was Armenian. Being a proud Armenian and adhering to the adage that when any two Armenians meet, they will form a new Armenia, I announced to Dan that I was also Armenian before slow playing a full house and relieving him of about $8,000.

It didn't take long for us to become friends; I think we went to eat after the game and fairly soon after were hanging out nearly every day. You see, Dan can come off as an uncouth ass, but he is actually an incredibly kindhearted, intelligent, and charismatic person who attracts and helps people in need. I've seen him bend over backwards to help people with no benefit to him, myself included, with never a thought of payback. We shared years of friendship, and I would say we could have counted on each other for almost anything.

Here Are a Few Fun Times with Dan

- *Dan once had a heart attack and blamed me for taking him to a Mexican restaurant I frequented, not the three days of drugs, pussy, drinking, poker, and strip clubs he imbibed in.*
- *Dan fucked a random in Metallica's bass player's private dressing room when we opened for them. The guy had to wait for Dan to finish so he could get dressed for the show. Our dressing room was right next door, by the way.*
- *Dan fucked a random (this one was a ten) in my bass player Shavo's dressing room while we played on stage. Unfortunately, Shavo's entire family decided to go in while he was doing so. I heard shit about it for days and could never understand why Dan didn't simply use my room instead.*

- *I invited a few girls to my house. Dan came over and after a quick hello got a blowjob from one of them and came all over my guest bedroom sheets. Then he accused the girl (who had an ankle bracelet because of a DUI and could only leave the house to go to work) of stealing $2,000 from his wallet. He then left, saying he didn't care about the money, it was the principle. The girl (ankle bracelet) looked confused, sitting naked on my couch as Dan left. I slept with both girls but never found the $2K.*

CHAPTER 30

Don't Be a Sucker

In 2009, I moved to a penthouse in Panorama Towers so I could live in Las Vegas full-time. It was close to the Bellagio and Aria, so I had around-the-clock access to games and I played a lot of poker as a result. I trained at world-famous MMA gyms and got into Muay Thai, boxing, and jujitsu. I loved the city, but I can't say the same for the women.

Women in Vegas are polished like a marble countertop. Their bodies, yes, are porcelain smooth. But their mentality is cold and hard as well. In college, socializing was a whole different ball game. The girls were young and innocent and just interested in fun. In Sin City, they were surgically enhanced, attitude-drenched financial predators.

In Vegas, you're either hustling or you're *being* hustled.

Women always had some sob story or unpaid bill while secretly taking cash from four different dudes. If a girl told you she wanted to hang out but had to work because she *needed to make money*, then she was dangling the sucker carrot over your head. She wanted you to take the bait and say, "Don't go to work tonight, I'll give you some money."

The money wasn't an issue; I just refused to establish a framework where someone shook me down to hang out.

One night in a strip club, a stripper came up with the usual hustle wanting me to buy lap dances. I get it. That's their job, and we had entered her place of business. So I tried to think of a way that we could both come out happy. She tried to get me drunk and bragged about her own prowess indulging.

"I'll pay you $1,000 if you can do a shot a minute for ten minutes and not puke for an hour," I taunted.

She accepted the bet, and I'll be fucking damned if that bitch didn't do it. She didn't even get up to piss. I was impressed, and I paid her the thousand bucks.

She asked to come back to my place, but she was so sloppy that I wanted nothing to do with her. I put her in a cab, gave the driver a hundred bucks, and told him to make sure she got home safe.

The whole thing had been entertaining, and that was the goal, but it got me thinking. Could I offer this to Vegas girls trying to hustle me with the "pay me to take the night off work" routine? Ten shots was way too much, but what if I cut it in half? I bet a couple of cocktail waitresses, and they did it with ease, but it was still better than a typical date.

I'd been paying people to do dumb shit since college, but what was interesting about this challenge was the simplicity and the subtle complexity of what it accomplished. The hustler gets paid to entertain you, and it shows you don't care about the money. It also challenges her to prove herself. Had you just given her money for nothing, then you'd be a sucker. If that happens, you can't escape that designation. A hustler's number one goal is to tax the sucker.

Most important of all, however, is this: When it comes to *setup*, you always want to conserve your most valuable asset—time.

One of my few regrets in life is how much time I've wasted talking and hanging out with girls. But that's the price I pay for being a sex addict who doesn't like hookers. I always envied the guys who loved hookers and were cool with fucking girls who weren't into them. It makes life SO MUCH easier: The girl gets money, you get sex, and there's no jealousy, no mindless conversations, and no wasted time. It is the purest interaction; both parties are completely honest and upfront about their expectations and everyone gets what they want.

Before all this social media shit where my life was on display and women knew exactly what they were getting into, I had someone I was dating freak out on me.

"Are you sleeping with anyone else?" she asked.

"Yes."

"Recently?"

"Yeah."

"Who was it?"

"You wouldn't know them."

"It was more than one girl?"

"Yes."

"How many?"

"What time frame are we using here?"

"This week."

"Three," I calmly replied.

"You fucked three other girls this week? It's only Thursday!"

"I used a condom."

I never apologized because I hadn't done anything wrong. I'd never promised her monogamy, and I didn't pretend she was the only woman in my life. In about a week, she came around. And our relationship was infinitely better because of the honesty; she opened up about things she hadn't told anyone because she knew she could trust me. Plus, she was accepting of everything I did after because I set the bar of acceptance pretty high to start.

The quickest way to build trust is to answer truthfully even when you know the person won't like your answer. It also shows that you aren't going to go out of your way to make up a lie to try and make her like you, which indirectly communicates confidence and shows you aren't desperate. If I ask a girl how many guys she's fucked in her life and she says seven or nine—which they almost always say—then I don't *know* she's lying, but I assume she is. However, if she looks me in the eye and says she's fucked seventy-eight dudes, then I'd bet she's telling the truth. That isn't a number a liar would spit out.

I can't trust someone unless I have a little dirt on them. Give your partner honesty, give them unapologetic dirt, you'll be very surprised at how far it goes in building trust quickly and making you two closer. One thing I've learned on my crazy journey is that everyone has dirt. Some people are just better at hiding it.

CHAPTER 31

Antonio

After a few months living in Vegas, I was approached to join an online site called Victory Poker. A guy named Dan Fleyshman was the founder, and he offered me equity without investment. He hired superhot models to host fun events that involved racing cars, tropical vacations, or blowing up vehicles in the desert.

All the Victory Poker pros lived at Panorama, which had become like a fraternity house. We'd see each other in the gym downstairs during the day, and there was usually some kind of after party going on at night. You could always get stoned, jump in the elevator, walk in your buddy's door, and play *Call of Duty*. There was also a bunch of strippers and bottle girls who lived there as well. So many, in fact, that when you arrived late at night, there was a reasonable chance you'd take home a hot girl from the valet or lobby.

Antonio Esfandiari, a famous poker pro, and I butted heads as the alphas of the group. He liked to punish his friends by hustling them into prop bets where he'd propose something and wager on it. For example, "I bet you can't get below 10% bodyfat in 6 months" or "I bet you can't eat $1,000 worth of McDonald's food in 48 hours." He even had a TV show called *I Bet You* based on this exact kind of thing.

He had a big ego because of his money and fame, so I had to check him once in a while with my typical honesty. I openly acknowledged that I didn't like him, and strangely enough, I think he appreciated that.

Antonio had a fitness trainer called All-American Dave. He was a clean-cut, good-looking guy with morals, so no steroids. We worked out together at Panorama, and he accompanied us when we traveled. I always gave him shit about his client Antonio, and we would go back and forth on why he should/shouldn't start juicing.

"Look at his physique. It's absolutely pathetic," I said.

"He hasn't been very dedicated lately, and I'm working on upping his caloric intake."

"He still has a belly and skinny arms. What are you feeding him, doughnuts and soymilk?"

"He doesn't need steroids," Dave replied.

"His genetics are awful; he looks like a fat Ethiopian."

Despite having a body that resembled the Grinch, Antonio got a lot of girls, and I respected that. He hosted parties in his apartment with a professional chef, and he performed legitimately impressive magic tricks and illusions. He was the focal point. Antonio understood the setup and capitalized on it, managing his fame and persona well. He had a lot of standing in the poker world and got into good games because bad players wanted to say they'd sat with Antonio Esfandiari.

My neighbor Ernie opened my eyes early on to the power of money and having the confidence to live unconditionally. He didn't hide his women and that worked in his favor. They competed for his attention. College experiences demonstrated the power of having a good ratio of women, the impact of jealousy, and the value of a good setup. Las Vegas taught me how to leverage money and status without overtly bragging. And Antonio gave me a glimpse into the power of fame and how people reacted to it.

ANTONIO "THE MAGICIAN" ESFANDIARI

Three-Time World Series of Poker Winner, Two-Time WPT Champion

Dan Bilzerian is a living, breathing, red-blooded stream of consciousness, strangely doing it without the assistance of drugs. I don't think I could do it; you know, merge my inner and outer monologue, unleashing his unfiltered train of thought locomotive across the world, saying whatever I wanted, to whoever I wanted, twenty-four seven. The words that escape his mouth are often refreshingly pure, slicing through boring small talk of everyday existence. Other times, his diarrhea mouth can be straight up offensive, shitting brutal truth all over unsuspecting egos. Either case, Dan's interlocutors always share the same nonplussed, surprised reactions that spew from this apathetic chatterbox of a man; a man with no fear of being judged, a man with cojones you can't help but respect.

One time we caused serious damage on KandyKruise, a three-day, twenty-four-hour debaucherous cruise ship party. At the end of the marathon party, Dan, was GONE, walking off the ship and into US Customs Control wearing nothing more than a speedo, stumbling, high as a kite. The stunned look on the custom agents' faces made me howl so hard that I nearly bust my gut. Needless to say, they skipped the search, Dan's airtight miniature speedo clearly not hiding anything.

I first met Dan at the Bellagio poker room in a 50/100 No Limit game. I noticed that Dan was actually a decent card player, a knucklehead in smaller games but consistently rising to the occasion when the stakes were high. Admittedly, we have always had a love-hate relationship over the years, not always seeing eye to eye. But the one thing I have to admit is that he is a man of integrity. In my book, it means a lot.

CHAPTER 32

Jessa

Jessa Hinton was a gorgeous 5'9", 115-pound, blue-eyed Jessica Rabbit-looking blonde with DD tits.

I met Jessa towards the end of 2009 when she worked as a commentator for Victory's first poker tournament. Her intelligence and wit were obvious as she effortlessly hosted the show. The Victory crew was headed to a racetrack we'd rented for the day, and I asked Fleyshman to put her in my SUV. She showed me a meme in the car; I laughed and told her to text it to me. I didn't really want the meme, but I did want her phone number. We were two feet away from each other texting instead of talking like Gen Z kids. After she sent a couple modeling pics, I replied with a naked pic of myself.

Sadly my modeling career hasn't taken off like I'd hoped, I texted wanting to cut to the chase. It was an aggressive move, not one I would recommend, but it worked. I fucked her in the bathroom of my apartment later that night while her best friend made drinks in the kitchen.

After working my way through half of the Victory models, I ended up dating Jessa exclusively. I didn't want to like her. Deep down I knew it would eventually turn into a nightmare. But we got along super well, and the sex was phenomenal. We quoted *Step Brothers*, *Bridesmaids*, and *Dumb and Dumber* back and forth without missing a beat. Everything was great in the beginning.

Jessa was a showstopper. She would walk into a room, and everyone would stare. She got tons of attention, and she loved it. Going out with her was fun, until she started drinking, then she'd turn into a mess. All the warning signs were there, glaring in my face. But I really liked hanging out with her, and we'd have sex three or four times a day. I couldn't get enough. This is probably when I started jokingly referring to myself as a sex addict. And there's a half-truth in every joke.

Jessa.

Jessa was loyal, though. One night in Vegas, I packed up my Range Rover with a couple guns and a bulletproof vest. I'd been cheated out of $50,000 in Bellagio chips by a card mechanic (card cheat who specializes in sleight-of-hand and manipulation of the cards) in LA, and I intended on getting my money back. I decided to drive so there wouldn't be any flight records if things went sideways. I told Jessa that she should stay home because I had no idea how this was going to turn out, but she insisted on coming.

The mechanic was a seemingly harmless out of shape old white guy, but his partner was a six-foot-four black dude built like a linebacker. I offered to buy the chips back for cash at a slight discount, and they agreed. My plan was to hand over a brick of one-dollar bills wrapped on both sides with hundred-dollar bills in exchange for the chips. I got a couple of knuckle draggers to come in a separate vehicle in case the cheats had back up.

I met up with the black guy in Beverly Hills. Before we could make the exchange, he spotted my goons and immediately took off running. I sprinted after him down Rodeo Drive, and my goons followed in their car. It was almost midnight so the streets were empty, but he came across some construction workers doing an overnight job, and he yelled at them to call the police. I probably should have just left, but pride is a powerful thing, and I couldn't stomach this guy getting away with robbing me.

I dialed 911 myself and told the dispatch that this motherfucker had stolen $50,000 from me and I was actively chasing him down Rodeo Drive. The cops arrived, but nothing made sense. His version was that I, along with my backup, were trying to rob him. My version was that he had stolen my chips, and I was just trying to get them back.

"The casino can verify that I have play history with those chips," I offered.

Jessa pulled up in the Range Rover and corroborated my story. It made the most sense. I mean, what is more likely, me randomly chasing a huge 250-pound black guy through Beverly Hills trying to rob him or that he stole my two $25K chips and was running away? I was in the homestretch until one of the cops asked to look at my phone. The officer saw a slew of missed calls and checked my messages. There were multiple voice mails from my thugs saying they were bailing out because there were cops everywhere. That didn't look good.

The cops asked Jessa for the keys and then proceeded to search my Range Rover. When they found my pistol and bulletproof vest in the trunk, it was all over. I was cuffed and put in the back of the squad car. The female officer was going through my phone while her partner interrogated Jessa on the sidewalk. He told Jessa that I was going to prison, and said that she would be, too, if she didn't tell them the truth. He said she'd lose custody of her son, and the female officer even showed her naked pictures of other women on my phone, but she never cracked.

I spent the night in jail while Jessa called around trying to get me out. She managed to find a lawyer and got me out on bail the next day. I was sure I was going to prison, but my lawyer said the case would never see the light of day. He was right; the cheats had a criminal history and didn't want to testify against me, so the authorities were forced to drop the case.

Jessa had demonstrated that she was a ride-or-die type of girl, and loyalty goes a long way with me. After this, I had no choice but to take her seriously and give the relationship a real shot. I played poker while she worked at the Playboy Club in the Palms Hotel & Casino and did modeling jobs.

I fell in love with her. She was the hottest girl I'd ever seriously dated and the smartest as well. It was more than that though: We could hang out for weeks at a time and never get sick of each other. It was hard because, despite everything, I still didn't fully trust her. I'd seen girls do so much fucked up shit in the past, usually at my instigation, that it warped my view. Jessa didn't have the best relationship with her father, plus she was sloppy when she drank, so I had reason to be careful. I wasn't used to being this into a girl, and I didn't like having that feeling of being out of control.

I think I got that from my father because he was a huge control freak. That was the primary reason my dad wanted so much money. It was never about buying things; it was because he liked the power and control it gave him. Well, there is nothing that will make you feel more power*less* than being in love with someone you don't fully trust, especially a girl who gets and enjoys so much attention.

She was very independent and didn't want to have to rely on me to support her because she had similar issues and didn't fully trust me.

However, to prove her devotion, she got my name tattooed on her. Twice. One *Dan* above her vagina with a heart and another *Dan* on her ear.

We went to the Bahamas for the PCA poker tournament in early January 2011. As usual, I wasn't playing the tourney but getting in on the juicy cash games that happened on the periphery. One of those games was being hosted by Eddie Ting on a big yacht he chartered and docked by the casino. There was only one open seat, so Andrew Robl, a Victory Poker pro and I agreed to share it, taking turns playing and splitting the profits or losses.

ANDREW ROBL

High-Stakes Poker Player

The high-stakes gambling world is full of larger-than-life characters. But there is none bigger than Dan Bilzerian. Back in the day during the big game, Bobby Baldwin sarcastically told Dan after a big bluff, "You're gonna be a big star." Sarcastic or not, Bobby was right, and Dan turned himself into one of the biggest celebrities in the world.

During the process of becoming a "star," Dan was able to monetize his outrageous personality into unheard of profit at the poker table. Dan taught me that turning a profit at poker wasn't all about being good at poker. Honestly, I never thought Dan was better than a mediocre poker player. But everyone always wanted to play with him. He entertained the players with his outrageous personality, and he could always make people laugh with his stories.

But his best trait at the poker table is that people always underestimated him. I was amazed at how often Dan could get people to do exactly what he wanted at the poker table and make horrible plays against him. He would act like an idiot and show outrageous bluffs then for the rest of the night show the player he bluffed the "nuts" (the best possible hand).

I witnessed Dan win all the money at the poker table time after time despite being what I considered to be not very good! And the wealthy people he beat always wanted to come back and play him again, often for bigger and bigger stakes. He ended up capitalizing on this and played some of them for outrageous sums and came out on top. These abilities made him one of the winningest poker players of all time.

I was up a few hundred thousand when Jessa texted me a picture of her in the hotel room wearing only my boonie hat and socks. I figured this was as good a time as any to hand over the seat to Robl. When I came back to the table, I learned that Robl had lost the $300,000 that I was up and was now in the hole $100,000.

"Get the fuck out of the seat," I said. I was not in a good frame of mind, but I wanted to win the money back. It's the last thing I should have done, going on tilt and playing poorly because I was angry. I made a bad call, and suddenly we were down $200,000. I was really pissed at Robl, so when he offered to split and let me play on my own, I leapt at the chance to be rid of him. Shortly thereafter, a seat opened up, and Robl sat down. He and I got into a pot where he beat me for another $100,000, and it really put me over the edge. I was furious, and I went on to lose another $400,000 before I finally quit.

When it was over, I had lost over half a million dollars. It was the most I'd ever lost in a poker game, and it was about 20 percent of my entire bankroll. I went from winning in the game and feeling good to losing my ass and feeling like I'd been kicked in the stomach.

The following day, I woke up hoping it was just a bad dream, but I knew it wasn't. I didn't even want to get out of bed. Jessa didn't understand gambling, and she didn't know what losing felt like. I also didn't have the heart to tell her how much that sum of money meant to me at the time.

When it went poorly, I hated gambling, I absolutely loathed it.

Jessa got a phone call from her agent with an offer for a one-day TV commercial shoot in Las Vegas. The pay was $800, and she had to get back to Vegas in less than twenty-four hours. She accepted the gig and informed me that the flight cost $850 and she needed me to pay for it.

"I'm paying more for the flight than you're going to make on the job!" I yelled. I felt like she was abandoning me right after I'd lost my ass. "After this, you're on your own. Work wherever you want and pay for your own shit."

When I got back to Vegas, I mentally checked out of the relationship and wasn't feeling great about life in general. I felt shitty about my meltdown in the Bahamas, but the silver lining was that Eddie saw it and invited me to his game in New York City. The first night, I won $325,000.

It's hard for a normal person to understand the emotional swings losing and winning that kind of money creates. Playing on the edge of your bankroll can drive you insane. It's why most pros will never get rich; they can't handle the mental stress, and they're scared to take a shot. But like Wayne Gretzky said, "You miss 100 percent of the shots you don't take," or as I less eloquently stated, "You won't get rich betting like a bitch."

Jessa started working at Encore Beach Club doing bottle service and drinking. I didn't like her working in nightlife and wasn't any more enthusiastic about the kind of modeling she was doing. There was no longevity in it, and the work consisted mostly of guys trying to fuck her. She resented my view and said I trivialized her career.

Modeling, to her, was an opportunity to become famous and get bigger opportunities. She liked bottle service because it was the quickest way for her to make good money, and that cash would allow some independence and security if we broke up—which, in her defense, could happen at any minute because our relationship was becoming pretty volatile.

She became a Playmate, and her *Playboy* issue came out in July 2011, back when that was a good career move for a model. She started getting a ton of attention, and things changed. Celebs began hitting her up, and rich guys offered to pay her $5,000 to have coffee with them. Her social media was blowing up, and I remember her bragging about having one hundred thousand Instagram followers.

After trying to suck it up for a while, I came to the conclusion that I didn't want to date a bottle service girl. I said I would support her if she wanted to start a business, but I wasn't going to continue down this path. She agreed to start a company making bikinis, and I got her a Lexus in the business name to drive, plus a few thousand a month for expenses.

We would have weeks of normality and then get into crazy fights. She was pretty intent on moving to Los Angeles to model. I hated the idea. I didn't like the people, I didn't like the scene, and I didn't want to do a long-distance relationship. We had come to a crossroads. I was making hundreds of thousands in a night, and for her to expect me to uproot my life to support her modeling career was a slap in the face to me. The more money I made, the less bullshit I would tolerate. Winning made me cocky, and losing made me angry. This combination did not lend itself to peacefully settling disagreements.

Jessa and I would fight and break up frequently, mostly because of her drinking problem. She would drink after promising not to, so I'd break up with her and fuck other girls to get even. Then she'd come over to "get her stuff," which always ended in her seducing me. We'd have amazing sex all night and wake up happy as honeymooners, thankful to be free of the pain of the breakup.

Just like that, we'd be back together without any discussion of what I'd done during our break or addressing the reason for the breakup. This lasted until Jessa's curiosity would get the better of her. Eventually she'd ask if I'd slept with anyone, and I'd tell the truth. She'd go crazy, and I'd run down a laundry list of things she'd done wrong, thus carrying even more animosity into the relationship. This cycle continued longer than was healthy for both of us.

CHAPTER 33

Ford vs. Ferrari

Tom Goldstein, my maniac bluff-happy attorney, texted me that he bought a new Ferrari 458. The sticker was around a quarter million dollars, but due to availability, you couldn't get one for under $350,000. According to the online articles, it was faster than even the million-dollar Ferrari Enzo. I was jealous, so I did what most jealous people do. I talked shit.

"I'll blow your doors off in my '65 A/C Cobra," I told him.

In college, I wanted a fun car to accompany the Range Rover. I couldn't responsibly afford a brand-new Ferrari, so I settled for a classic vehicle. I figured something like Eleanor, the Ford GT500 from *Gone in Sixty Seconds*, or a Chevy SS would be cool and bolster my rich guy image. I started searching, and I came across a Shelby Cobra; it looked like something James Bond would drive.

Original 1965 Shelby Cobras were designed by the legendary Carroll Shelby, and they were monsters. They were also worth millions of dollars. Or there were cheap fiberglass replicas you could buy for $30,000. But in the late nineties, Shelby American remade the classic in a limited production run they called CSX. They bought the rolling chassis from a company based out of Utah called Kirkham, and they were mint.

I found one with 700 horsepower and under a thousand miles. The car only weighed 2,150 pounds, so it was an absolute rocket ship. There wasn't any cage, crumple zones, or airbags, so it was super dangerous, but I didn't care; it looked amazing. The polished aluminum body was flawless. It shined like chrome and had two matte brushed racing stripes down the middle. It was listed for $150,000 by a seller in Laguna California. There was no question. This was the car. I put some cash in a backpack and flew out there the next day.

The Cobra was immaculate, and it was hands down the fastest car I'd ever driven. I handed the guy a few bricks of cash, and he signed over the title. After arranging for the car to be shipped to Tampa, I headed to the airport. I was giddy; this was by far the coolest thing I'd ever bought.

I started racing the Cobra at Sebring International Raceway, a Le Mans-style road course in Florida, and easily passed Lambos and Ferraris on the backstretch. Nothing street legal could touch it on the straightaways.

"My car has a wooden steering wheel, and it'll still smoke your Ferrari," I bragged to Tom.

"Wanna bet?" he said.

Our initial wager was for $100,000 on a road course, but he changed his mind when I told him I'd raced at Sebring. He said he wanted to do quarter-mile drag races instead. I felt like this adjustment favored him since my car was a stick and I had no experience drag racing, so he agreed to spot me two-tenths of a second. The salesman had assured Tom that the 458 was the fastest production car on the planet, so he offered to up the bet to $300,000.

For all my talk, I wasn't totally confident. However, the math was in my favor. My car was 2,200 pounds and had 700 horsepower while his Ferrari weighed 3,600 pounds and had 560 horsepower. But if I couldn't put the power to the ground and get my tires to hook up, it wouldn't matter. His tires were wider, and I wasn't allowed to run drag slicks, so he had the traction advantage. The Ferrari had cutting-edge engineering, nine gears, automatic dual-clutch shifting, and launch control to ensure a perfect start every time. But being a math guy, I took the bet.

In practice, I recorded thirteen something to hit the quarter-mile mark. *Car and Driver* reported that the Ferrari 458 could do it in less than eleven seconds. We both took preparations seriously. I hired a drag race instructor, and Tom haunted online Ferrari and Shelby forums for advice and opinions on the outcome. 1965 was the year Ford famously beat Ferrari in Le Mans, so there were passionate enthusiasts eager to weigh in on both sides.

I was able to get down to twelve seconds or so, but not any lower. Nailing the takeoff and shifting the gears at precisely the right time was more difficult than I expected.

Tom talked shit the entire time.

"I'm going to buy a billboard outside your apartment and put my face on it to celebrate my victory," he taunted. He tried to piss me off by saying he wanted Jessa to ride in his car. *I want her to see what a winner looks like*, he texted.

You got it! I replied. They say every hundred pounds adds a tenth of a second, and I needed all the help I could get.

As the race neared, his shit-talking got worse. The night before the race, he posted his $300,000 in Bellagio chips and begged me to up the stakes of the bet. I said it was enough, but when he offered me an additional $85,000 to my $40,000, I had to accept it. He wanted to add that if I lost, I could not have sex or masturbate for a month. As a sex addict, this scared the hell out of me, but I figured I'd be too depressed anyway, so I agreed under the condition that if he lost, he had to get high with me.

Tom had taught law at Harvard and in his practice, he'd developed a special expertise for skillfully arguing before the United States Supreme Court. Despite his craziness at the table, he was a square in many ways and had never done a drug in his life. Gambling was one of his few vices, but he was a sicko, so he agreed to smoke weed if he lost.

Poker players and car enthusiasts from the forums showed up at the track early, eager to see the outcome. There'd been a lot of money bet on the side, and it seemed like everyone had a strong opinion.

I wore a helmet, gloves, and arm restraints that strapped my hands to the steering wheel, per track regulation. I also wore a fireproof suit in case my gas tank blew up and the car caught on fire, which Cobras were known to do from time to time.

I revved the engine to 5,000 rpm and dropped the clutch; the back tires broke loose, and smoke filled the wheel wells. This heated up the rubber, helping to maximize traction. I pulled up at the starting line and refused to look to the sides or acknowledge that anyone was within twenty miles of me. I was laser focused.

The drag tree lit up yellow, and I revved to 3,800 rpms like I had practiced. When the light hit green, I dropped the clutch and rolled into the gas. The tires didn't spin or slip at all; they just hooked up. My head flew back, and the car took off like a runaway freight train. Shift point, banged second gear home. Shift point, smoothly went up and over for third. Pedal buried to the floor. Shift point, slammed straight down into fourth. Crossed the finish line, hit the brakes.

It was the fastest ten seconds of my life. I hadn't accounted for how sticky a prepped drag strip was; my tires stuck to the track like glue.

Everyone was yelling and screaming as I pulled into the pits. The board read 10.75 seconds, 133 miles per hour. I'd won the race. No way he could beat that time, not without putting a jet engine in his car anyway.

Tom pulled an 11.51 at 121 miles per hour. It wasn't even close. Everyone was celebrating or upset, but Tom refused to acknowledge that it was over. He was like one of those people at a funeral who, despite seeing the body, refuses to accept that the person is dead. For the next thirty minutes, he checked his tire pressures and tried different start techniques, but it was hopeless.

I liked Tom, but he'd talked a huge amount of shit, so I didn't feel too bad for him. We met at my apartment to get high. I had made brownies the day prior with slow-roasted weed oil. It usually took forty-five minutes to an hour for the high to kick in, so we hit a few bong rips to get started.

"I don't feel anything," Tom insisted. He started saying that he couldn't get high on pot, that he was immune. It sounded like bullshit, but he was definitely inhaling, so he'd upheld his end of the bet. I couldn't hold it against him if he couldn't feel the high, so I cut him loose and let him go.

The phone rang ten minutes later.

"Blitz, the weed worked," he yelled.

"Where are you?"

"I'm in the poker room at the Bellagio. I couldn't drive anymore, so I left my car."

"Where's your car?

"On Las Vegas Boulevard."

I raced down there, and, sure enough, that asshole had left his brand-new Ferrari sitting on the boulevard with the keys still in it. He didn't even turn the lights off. I parked the car in valet and went to the poker room.

"Blitz, I need to borrow some money to gamble."

"No, you don't," I said. "You shouldn't play poker under any circumstances right now. You play bad enough when you're sober."

"If you don't loan it to me, I'm going to borrow it from someone here. I promise to only play with the money you give me, and you can keep the Ferrari until I pay you back."

"Dude, you should not gamble right now. You're gonna lose."

"Either you give it to me, or I'll get it from someone else."

"Fine."

He obviously lost the money I gave him. It took him six months to pay me. But for once in my life, I had collateral on a loan, and with that car I didn't care if he never paid me.

CHAPTER 34

Ponzi Scheme

Black Friday. April 15, 2011.

The day the United States Department of Justice shut down online poker in America. They effectively banned the game, seized everyone's assets, and generally fucked up players lives. I had millionaire friends begging to sell their online money for pennies on the dollar just twenty-four hours later. Private games suffered as players became credit risks.

Molly's Game fell apart when Tobey Maguire got sick of her making so much money in tips and ran her out of town. Also complicating matters was that Bradley Ruderman got busted for operating a Ponzi scheme. He'd stolen from his investors and lost over five million of their dollars in Molly's Game. In 2011, the feds and the victims tried to claw back the money by suing everyone who had won money from Bradley. They sued Tobey Maguire, Nick Cassavetes, Rick Salomon, and me.

I'd just turned thirty, and the last year had been some of the worst times for me in poker. I'd been cheated, stiffed, sued, and shut out of games.

Nick said that if I paid off the Ruderman lawsuits we both faced, then he'd let me back into his game. They were going after Nick for $73,000 and me for a $100,000. Nick had stopped letting me play because I'd said in an interview with *Star* magazine that Tobey Maguire played like a tight bitch. It was a big *no-no* to talk to gossip magazines and mention anything about celebrities, but I was new to this, and didn't know.

Nick and I would have been cleared if we aggressively fought back. But fighting required attorneys, and attorneys cost money. There was no upside in going to trial, so I settled both lawsuits for around $75,000 total, which was a gamble; I was betting I could make more at Nick's house.

Nick's game had a dream lineup—the guy who owned 7 for All Mankind jeans, *The Hangover* director Todd Phillips, Tobey Maguire, Owen Wilson, and more. I won $85,000 in my first game back, so paying off the lawsuit turned out to be the right choice.

CHAPTER 35

San Diego Vindication

Shortly after moving to Vegas, I realized promoters were the biggest cockblocks in the city.

Promoters would bring girls to their clients' tables and introduce them while secretly talking shit. The promoters didn't want their clients to get laid, they just brought the girls to drink the champagne. Clubs would pay promoters 10 percent of what their client spent, so the goal was to run up their tab. Waitresses would get 18 percent via auto gratuity, so their goal was the same, but their hustle was different. Waitresses were trained to flirt with the client, upsell bottles, and ask for drinks. They'd then take full glasses of champagne to the bathroom, dump them out, and repeat. The whole thing was a hustle designed to milk the sucker for all they could.

This was 2011, before the rise of social media, sugar daddies, and Only Fans. Back when hot girls went to nightclubs. I wanted to get laid, but I refused to take part in this scam, so I figured out a way to circumvent the nonsense. The promoters were perpetually broke, and the only thing they cared about more than pussy was money. So I established a deal with them where I would pay $1,000 for every girl they introduced me to who I eventually fucked. But they couldn't be hookers, and the promoters couldn't pay the women. I even offered a $5,000 bonus if I ended up seriously dating the girl. This changed the narrative. Now the promoter had a vested interest in talking me up instead of doing the opposite.

A Vegas promoter lined up some girls, and I chartered a Hawker 800 to take us to San Diego for a party. The party was at a mansion on Hillside Drive, one of the most expensive streets in San Diego. We walked in through a two-foot-thick iron door that opened up to an infinity pool and a spectacular view of the Pacific Ocean. The pool deck was on the edge of a cliff that boasted a 270-degree view of everything from the city to the valley to the coast.

The three-story mansion had curved walls of glass in every room. The master had a two-story closet with exotic wood and a bird's-eye view of the ocean and coastline. But it was virtually empty. It had barely any furniture and no decorations whatsoever.

The owner was a slightly out of shape country-club-looking guy named Charles. He wore dock shoes, no socks, and a polo shirt. He was loaded but prided himself on being thrifty, always working the angle, and getting a good deal. I was the opposite. I bragged about what I spent and wanted people to think I paid more than I did.

"You wouldn't believe me if I told you what I pay to rent this place," he said.

He teased me before finally revealing that rent was only six grand a month. I had been looking at San Diego real estate and knew that was absurd. The place should have been $80,000–$100,000 a month. I was completely confused. It didn't make any sense, but I also didn't think he was lying, so I kept asking him for the story until he finally spilled the beans.

"The house was built on spec, and the builder declined an offer for $18 million. Then the market crashed, and he rode it all the way down. Now he can't legally sell it or rent it because of some litigation with a neighbor over an encroaching support beam two hundred feet under the ground. The whole thing is a mess. The house was just sitting empty until he found a homeless man sleeping in the living room.

When my realtor told me what happened, I approached the owner directly. I offered to pay cash and keep an eye on the place. The house is great, but I barely use it, I'm only here a couple days a month."

"Shit, would you want to split that?" I asked.

"Probably not worth it for three grand."

"What if I fully furnished the place, made it totally livable? It would be dialed in when you came into town. We can split everything; I'll find a house manager and get it all done."

After some convincing, he agreed. I hired a property manager, housekeeping, decorator, and a pool guy. Charles got a crazy deal on a used Ferrari and stuck it in the garage. I had the Cobra transported out and bought a seventies Land Cruiser. The garage was full, but there wasn't one practical car on the whole property.

I was fucking excited about this house. I'd wanted to live in San Diego, and now I was going to do it in the nicest house in the entire city. If this place didn't scream "rich motherfucker," nothing would. This would also help my image, making it easier to get into juicy poker games. Not to mention the most important reason of all: Since Jessa and I were in the middle of another breakup, I would get a shitload of pussy living in this thing and with minimal effort.

This was my chance to come back and conquer the city that once whipped me while in the military.

CHAPTER 36

Hate Fucking

Dave Navarro texted Jessa a naked picture of himself with a hard on. Our on-again, off-again relationship had never been healthy, but celebrities really started coming after her once she became a Playmate.

Jessa and I had technically broken up a week prior, but we were still talking. She texted me in the afternoon that she missed me and asked if she could come over later. I agreed, which usually meant our breakup would be over and we would be getting back together. Meanwhile, she had made plans to meet up with a singer who we'd previously gotten into an argument over when he hit on her while we were together. She said she was going to a concert and would be over after, but she didn't mention it was his concert. A while later, she sent another *I miss you* text. I replied, *I miss you too, come over.*

An hour later around ten, she sent a selfie kissing the lead singer while giving me the finger and then turned her phone off. I sat in my apartment, livid, driving myself crazy thinking about her hooking up with that skinny asshole. Around midnight, she turned her phone back on and asked to come over. I was pissed, but my sex addiction was stronger than my ego, so I said ok. She replied that she'd be over in ten minutes, then gave me the runaround for two more hours before finally showing up completely shitfaced around two in the morning. I was fucking pissed for obvious reasons, but she'd also promised to stop drinking, and her drunken antics had been a major point of contention for our entire relationship.

I hate fucked her, came on her face, and told her to get the fuck out of my apartment. After I threw her ass out, it dawned on me that she had been drunk driving the Lexus that I was paying for, so I chased her down the hallway, asking for the keys. In the parking lot, I wasn't going to let her drive hammered, so I grabbed her purse. We fought for control of the purse until I got ahold of the keys. I put the keys in my pocket, chucked her purse, and went back to my apartment pissed.

I was heartbroken, but I was also done with that bitch. I had limits to the amount of shit I would tolerate, and she'd blown right through that. We had been almost inseparable for over two years, so it hurt, but I had no choice.

I needed to get my mind off of her, so I planned a trip to Cabo with a couple buddies. Then I called a promoter and asked him to round up some girls. He told me to come out that night, and he'd introduce me. That evening, I went out to 1OAK and he had about fifteen girls at his table. The hottest one, a girl named Tina, looked like a Persian version of Penelope Cruz with bigger eyes, a bigger nose, and much bigger tits. He introduced me, we did some shots, and I flirted with her, and her blonde friend joined in as well.

They were dancing with each other and kissing, which was pretty hot because they seemed to actually be into each other, unlike most girls who do it for attention. I was standing with my back to the booth, drinking champagne and eating chicken fingers while Tina and her friend took turns grinding on me. Whatever the promoter said to them worked because they were all about it. Tina was sucking on my ear, and I suggested we get out of there.

"Can she come with us?" Tina asked.

"Sure."

The blonde went to the bathroom, and I asked the promoter if the girls were hookers. He laughed and said, "Absolutely not, they are bottle servers for Light Group." I paid my tab, told him good night, and walked out with Tina.

In the limousine, I raised the divider, and we started hooking up. She was sucking my dick before we hit the first speed bump. Five minutes later, we arrived at Panorama. That thirty-three-floor elevator ride was the longest of my life.

Our clothes came off as soon as we entered the apartment, and she beat me to the bed. Her tits were bigger than I thought and didn't even look like they belonged on such a skinny body. More blowjobs, a condom, and thirty minutes of fucking. I took a shower and heard her screaming on the phone while I toweled off. I figured she was fighting with a boyfriend.

But after hanging up, she let loose.

"You left my girlfriend at the club!" she yelled. "You are so selfish! How could you just leave her there?"

"Shit, I forgot." It wasn't really true that I had forgotten; I just knew she was a 100 percent to fuck me, and the threesome was probably 80 percent. "A bird in the hand is worth two in the bush" is what my Grandfather Harry used to say.

"My friend is pissed, and this is your fault! I told you specifically that I wanted her to come with us."

"I don't know why you're mad at me. She's your friend; you could have waited for her. You should thank me that I fucked you good and didn't care about banging your friend, you crazy fuck."

When I called her crazy, a switch flipped. Tina went from mad to outright fuck you. She grabbed my phone, ran out to the balcony butt-naked, and threw the phone like a Frisbee into the darkness.

This was before iCloud. Everything was on that phone. All my photos, all my contacts, my entire life. I really wanted to kill that bitch.

I wasn't about to kill her, but I could five-year-old boy copycat her. I grabbed her clothes, her thong, her purse, and her phone. I hurled the entire pile of shit off the balcony. At least her crap could keep my dead phone company.

She started punching me, so I calmly picked her skinny ass up, deposited her in the hallway, and shut the door. I must admit, the thought of her having to take the elevator butt-naked to the lobby did bring a smile to my face.

I figured there was a small chance the phone memory could be transferred, so I went down to look for it. Miraculously, I found it within seconds of getting to the parking lot, and apart from a cracked screen, it still functioned perfectly!

Mark Twain once said, "Truth is stranger than fiction, because Fiction is obligated to stick to possibilities; Truth isn't." You couldn't make this shit up; I mean, I wouldn't have believed it if I didn't see it. I don't know what was crazier: her getting this upset because I didn't bang her friend or my phone surviving a 330-foot freefall onto the pavement.

My pals in the Panorama security office told me that Tina made her way to the desk, naked, and they gave her a robe. She left in a limo, in typical Las Vegas style.

That week, I partied a lot. I didn't want to think about Jessa, and the best way to distract myself was with new girls. My buddy had rented the Hugh Heffner suite at Palms, and we went there to after party one night. I was fucked up on GHB this time, and I saw a really hot girl with big tits walking toward the elevator. I stopped her and said, "Let's go smoke a joint."

"My boyfriend is downstairs waiting for me," she said with a smile.

"I gotta go down too. Let's just smoke this joint quick."

She was buzzed and giggly and said, "Sure, okay, let's go quick." She followed me into the suite. It was multiple stories with a big pool that hung over the city, and it had a glass elevator in the center of the room. I grabbed a lighter from the bar and sparked up the joint. We were smoking and walking as I showed her around the place. I saw the massage table room and figured that'd be a good place to bang. We started kissing and removing clothes. I put her hand on my dick and kicked the door closed. She wouldn't let me fuck her, but she sucked my dick for a while. I have a hell of a time getting off from blowjobs, so it ended with her licking my ass while I jacked off on her head. I got her number, and she ended up coming to Cabo.

I'd lined up around a dozen girls for the trip to Cabo. Some came from promoters, some the Playboy casting director introduced me to, a few repeats, and because I'm sick in the head, Tina, the psycho who threw my phone off the balcony. She actually came. It ended up being me, Nick Cassavetes, and nine girls on the chartered G4.

Before reaching cruising altitude, I banged Tina in the bathroom. I guess I shouldn't have been surprised when she came out topless, throwing Skittles all over the plane, and forcing the girls to do shots with her.

When we got to the villa, the girls continued drinking. A couple started doing body shots off each other. One girl was dancing on the dinner table topless with maracas, and when Tina shot her in the face with a super soaker full of tequila, it almost started a fistfight. Nick and I escalated a slap-boxing contest to bareknuckle boxing, but we called it off when Nick cut his foot open. He was bleeding all over the floor and the place looked like OJ Simpson's crime scene. My lip was split open, and we couldn't help but laugh.

"I'm getting too old for this shit" Nick said as he headed towards the fridge in search of a Corona.

We chartered a yacht, and the girls went parasailing naked. I smoked a bunch of weed and rotated through the girls below deck, none of which minded me being with the others. They only had two options, and Nick wasn't giving them the time of day. I hadn't been in a situation with such a dick shortage since college, and I didn't think about Jessa once.

CHAPTER 37

Instagram

I first created my Instagram account exactly two months after the Cabo trip, on May 1, 2012. At this point, I understood the importance of creating jealousy and competition with girls. I knew that showing something was more powerful than saying it. So I decided to show everyone that I was rich, sought-after by hot women, and doing fun shit. If done correctly, it would have a low perceived effort and wouldn't look like bragging.

Social media is a tool that allows you to communicate with tons of people at once. It's more effective than texting every girl in your phone because it accomplishes the same thing without *showing interest.* It allows you to pop into their heads via a photograph, and as they say, a picture is worth a thousand words. Those girls will see your picture and get FOMO* thinking about you doing something fun, or they'll see you with another hot girl and get jealous. This will make them want to reach out. Once they message you, it's all over. They've communicated interest; you're in the driver's seat, and getting laid should be easy. You can play the game and take a little while to hit them back if you want, or just

* Fear of missing out.

ignore them completely; but make no mistake, *you* are being chased, and that is the goal.

Social media also helped me get into better poker games, and heads-up matches that made me tens of millions of dollars. It opened doors, but the truth of the matter is, the primary driver in starting my Instagram was to get laid with less effort. I also wasn't over Jessa, and I selfishly wanted her to see me doing well.

People will talk shit, saying that is manipulative, and they aren't wrong, but I wrote this book to tell my story, not to get people to like me.

CHAPTER 38

Sam

Every Wednesday, I drove up to Los Angeles to play in Nick's home game. It was like printing money. One night, however, I was down $130,000. I'd gotten unlucky in a big hand, and I wasn't running good. It was late, and I'd accepted I wasn't going to break even. I was just hoping for a slight comeback.

Nick got a text and perked up.

"Blitz, you might just get even." He hinted a mystery player was on the way. Nick was notorious for fucking with people, but he seemed especially enthusiastic about this prospect.

A dark-skinned guy about 5'8" dressed all in black stomped in like he was King Kong. It was obvious he was wired on something because he was sweating profusely and couldn't stand still. Nick introduced him as Sam Magid.

Sam sat down abruptly and bought in for $50,000, which caught my attention. Most people buy-in for $10,000 to start. In two hands, he lost the entire $50,000. He reupped for another fifty, and before the button went around one orbit of the table, he lost that as well. He bought in for a third time with $50,000, put some sunglasses on, and shoved all his money into the middle of the table—without even looking at his cards!

"Can you beat a blind man?" he taunted the players as he slapped his shaved head.

"Is this guy serious?" I whispered to Nick.

"I told you, motherfucker."

Sam was in total kamikaze mode. A guy took the fifty grand off him, and Sam bought in a fourth time, same amount. Finally he won a hand and doubled up to $100,000 when he luckily caught a deuce to beat ace king. Unaffected he still just kept going all in. This was the most insane thing I'd ever seen in a game. There was $150 in the pot, and he was betting $100,000 without looking at his cards. In a single hand, I could get almost even. Most people folded because a hundred thousand dollars was a shit ton of money for that game. Unfortunately, someone picked him off before I could, and Sam stormed off to the bathroom.

"Is he always like this?" I asked Nick.

"Sometimes it's worse," he smiled. "But it's always a good show."

Sam returned with blow all over his nose and face. It felt like I was the only one seeing this. Everyone else played it totally straight.

Are we going to just sit here and ignore the fact that this dude looks like Tony Montana with coke all over his shit and is punting $50,000 bullets like he's pulling a five-dollar slot machine? I wondered.

Sam bought in with yet another $50,000 installment and actually started to look at his cards but shockingly played worse than when he played blind. He accidentally called a $30,000 bet on the river from actress Jennifer Tilly with no pair because he misread his hand and thought he had a straight. When the dealer informed Sam that it requires five cards in a row to make a straight, Sam simply replied, "Good point." It was fucking comedy hour, and the hits just kept on coming.

JENNIFER TILLY

Actress, Academy Award Winner,
World Series of Poker Winner

It was two in the morning at Nick's game. I had dug myself a deep hole and wasn't going home anytime soon. All of a sudden this guy Sam shows up and within half an hour I was not only unstuck but I was up for the evening. I was just getting ready to leave when I looked down at pocket Kings. I bet, Sam raised. I decided to put a stop to the nonsense right then and went all in. He insta-called. Sam flipped over 3,7 offsuit like it was pocket Aces. "Can we run it twice?" he asked happily. Sam had a childlike joy and wonder about playing poker, and most certainly a childlike comprehension of the game.

It was always a delightful thing when he showed up. Privately I called him "Samta Claus." He had the ability to sprinkle his magic fairy dust on you and instantly transform you into a winning player. After a while he stopped coming. I heard he graduated to Bilzerian's game and inklings of the legend that was Sam would surface from time to time.

Once I was in Vegas playing with Nick at the Bellagio when suddenly there was a big flurry like "The Eagle has landed!" Frantic texting was going back and forth, and then Chuck materialized behind Nick saying urgently "He's here, he's here, we're all set up!" And with a courtly gesture Nick racked up his chips and said "Boys, I gotta go. I have a previous engagement."

I was jealous. I knew they were going to play with Sam, and I wasn't invited.

Lazy Frank, Nick's assistant, approached the table and whispered in his ear.

"It appears that someone tracked mud through the house," he said.

"Clean it up."

Frank headed towards the back of the house. A couple minutes later he returned visibly flustered.

"I need to talk to you," he said.

"What do you want?" Nick asked.

"It's important. Can you come here?"

"This fucking guy is betting fifty thousand a hand without looking at his cards. I'm not going anywhere. Spit it out."

Lazy Frank leaned in near Nick's ear.

"It appears Sam took a shit, missed the toilet, stomped around in it, and then tracked it through the entire house."

"I don't care. Clean it up."

I couldn't stay quiet. I had to jump in.

"Nick, you just gonna let this dude track shit all over your house?" I taunted.

"This guy is losing $700,000 in a $10,000 buy-in game. He can shit in my bed if he wants to."

I had no rebuttal...I mean, what the fuck was I supposed to say to that?

Across the table Sam had piled up a mound of blow right next to his chips and began snorting it right off the felt. Everyone was in a good mood, except the guy that Sam smashed with his nine deuce off suit. After losing another couple buy ins, Sam finally left in disgust.

"Is he good for the money?" I asked Nick.

"Yeah, he's super fucking rich. Chucky met him at Soho House, and he said he liked to play poker."

"Nick, what the fuck was that? How do you accidentally miss the toilet?" Lazy Frank queried.

Nick, ever the film director, slowly looked at Lazy Frank like we were in a scene from a mobster movie. "That wasn't an accident...That was a message."

The next time we played at Nick's house, Sam challenged me to play him heads-up. Nick savvily claimed 10 percent of my action any time I played Sam, which was fair since he introduced us. It was damn near impossible to lose to Sam over the long haul. He didn't even look at his cards half the time and it seemed like he was more interested in bluffing and talking shit than he was in actually playing poker.

Sam's home in the prestigious Bird Streets of the Hollywood Hills had been dubbed the "*Vanity Fair* House" and was probably worth $30 million dollars. He had lined the walls and gate with razor wire like a super max prison, and koi ponds surrounded the house like a moat. The floors, tables, and marble walls all had a black-and-white theme that reminded me of the movie *Clockwork Orange*. Everything was designer and super expensive, partially due to his late-night coke-induced online shopping binges. He had $75,000 fountain pens, limited edition hand-engraved crystal champagne glasses, and Hermes blankets and pillows everywhere. There was a movie projector outside so you could watch films on the side of the house while sitting in the hot tub. The place looked more like a high-end nightclub than a home.

First time we played heads-up, I beat Sam. He insisted we play again, double or nothing. I beat him a second time, he doubled down for a third, a fourth, and kept going. We started in the evening playing for $20,000 a game and were up to $200,000 by morning. I didn't have to risk a great deal in order to win a shitload, but the problem was Sam never wanted to stop. We played until sunrise every fucking time.

Sam.

In the beginning, he gave me cash on the spot, but as time went on, collecting became more difficult. He bounced checks due to insufficient funds and even wrote checks on accounts he'd closed months prior. One time, he gave me a quarter million-dollar check with a blood stain and so much coke residue on it that I was worried if I tried to cash it, I'd get arrested. He had plenty of money; he just hated paying gambling debts.

I tried to set parameters and say, "Just one game for $30,000." But we'd always end up playing all night. After he stiffed me a few times, I quit playing with him. But then I'd hear about him losing $800,000 in a game and paying up the very next day. It was such an obscene amount of money that it was impossible to walk away. If Sam was going to lose to someone, I figured it might as well be me.

I suggested we go to Vegas, knowing we'd both have to bring money to the casino, and I'd be able to collect when I won. I told him I'd bring a million dollars in cash if he wired a million to the Wynn, and he agreed.

Sam ran around the house grabbing random shit and taking bumps every time he stopped to catch his breath. He furiously shoved designer garments into a duffel bag like they were dirty underwear. Just watching him gave me anxiety.

He had chartered a jet, and Paris Hilton and her whole family were already on board waiting for us. By the time he finally cranked up his all black G63 Mercedes SUV, they'd been sitting on the plane for almost two hours, and we were at least an hour away with traffic. The seats were upholstered in black leather with what looked like white stitching, but that was just the cocaine imbedded in the seams.

He steered with his knee while texting Paris, lying about how far away we were. On Sunset headed toward the 405, he jumped the curb and drove down the grass median to avoid a bit of traffic.

I remembered that the gas light had been on the entire time we'd been on the road and screamed, "Dude, you're completely out of gas!" To which he replied, "Good point." Traffic to the airport was bumper to bumper, and there was no way we'd make it without refueling.

At the gas station, he dumped in $20 worth, threw the G Wagon in reverse, and backed into the center unit of the pumps, scratching the entire side of his car in the process. Completely unbothered by the whole situation, he jerked it into drive and took off, but not before ripping his entire back bumper clean off the truck. I gotta give the fucking guy credit though, he didn't even tap the brakes; he just left half the paint from his door and the entire bumper right there at the pump.

He had the pedal pinned to the floor and was texting with one hand while scooping blow with the other. I double-checked that my seat belt was buckled and screamed at him to watch the fucking road.

He looked over at me, eyes bugging out, sweat dripping off his nose, and calmly said, "We're late."

"I know we're fucking late!" I yelled. "Watch the fucking road, you fucking lunatic!"

He put his phone down, placed two hands on the wheel, and acted normal for a few minutes.

"You're so fucking crazy. You left your entire rear bumper at that gas station," I reminded him.

"No, I didn't," he replied in a monotone voice, lying out of his ass.

Paris and her family had been sitting on the runway for more than two hours, but they were very pleasant and not visibly upset. I was shocked because they were way too wealthy to tolerate this kind of nonsense. After some extremely awkward small talk and greetings, Sam sat down as far away from the Hiltons as he could. I was always fascinated to observe how well-regulated, well-adjusted, normal human beings interacted with that raging psychopath.

After about twenty minutes of fidgeting, he excused himself to go to the bathroom for obvious reasons. He came out looking like he had scarfed down a dozen powdered donuts. There was white residue all over his face and black shirt. I could feel the manic vibes coming off him. He looked like he was going to burst.

I had a military backpack with a million dollars of cash in it, Paris Hilton and her family behind me, and this absolute fucking hand grenade of a human being in front of me with a kilo of blow in his lap. *What's going to happen next?* I wondered.

Walking through the Wynn, we were swarmed when people recognized Paris. Sam loved the attention because fame was the one thing his money couldn't buy, and being her friend made him important by association. He was giddy, and I admit, after seeing that, I wanted to be famous too; I remember thinking it would feel good to be so admired by everyone.

We had a section roped off in the poker room, and people were gathered around, trying to take pictures while security kept them at bay. I pulled out my bricks of cash, and Sam signed for and received chips from the million dollars he'd wired to the casino. Finally, I'd get paid when I won, I thought.

We agreed to play $100,000 freezeouts. I played aggressive and lost the first one rather quickly, which did not make me happy. There was nothing worse than suffering Sam's lunacy and effectively paying to do so. As I pulled another hundred thousand-dollar brick out of the backpack, Sam grabbed it and literally licked the cash.

I bet $25,000 on the turn, Sam smacked his head and called. The river card was a king; I missed both my straight and flush draws. I had nothing, and there was almost $70,000 in the pot. I had a pot size bet left, and I felt like he was weak, so I went all in.

Paris's mom asked how much we were playing for, and Sam told her "a hundred."

"Oh, I wanna play!" she squealed, thinking he meant $100.

"I have shit...what should I do?" Sam asked as he showed her his hand.

She wasn't paying attention and said, "He's probably bluffing." Based on her offhand remark, he called my all in with a pair of fucking fours and won $200,000. Mom clapped and cheered, and everyone celebrated while I wanted to jump off a building.

It was not a good night; I was tilted and not playing patiently. After I lost another $100,000, Sam decided he wanted to take a break and go to the club. We headed up to Sam's suite so he could lock what *used* to be my money in his safe. After securing the cash, he did a huge line of coke. I was so irritated that I did a line myself. Being around this maniac sober was just inhumane punishment.

He scooped the blow into a small metal container, screwed the top on, and we headed to the nightclub. The bouncers parted the ropes, and we walked right in. Sam ordered a bunch of champagne and handed the waitress a wad of cash. It's always painful watching people spend your money. He requested a little privacy from one of the owners, and we were escorted into his office.

I had a fully engraved nickel-plated .45 in the small of my back, and when I sat down in the wooden office seat, the gun dug into my skin. I pulled it out and laid it on the desk. It was a beautiful pistol, and I certainly didn't mind showing it off.

Sam fumbled around with his coke-filled tin can like it was a goddamn Rubik's cube. The powder had gummed up the threads in the screw off top, and it wouldn't budge. He had really worked himself into a frenzy trying to open it, and I could tell he was about to blow a gasket. He threw the container on the floor, and it bounced off the ground, hit the desk and came flying back at Paris's friend, who dodged the incoming projectile. It finally came to a stop at the base of a cabinet, lid still attached. Fueled by frustration, Sam grabbed my gun from the desk and went to shoot the can. I leapt up and yanked the gun out of his hand before he was able to fire off a round.

This was one of those moments in my life when I say thanks because of just how wrong everything *could* have gone. There was a bullet in the chamber, and if he'd clicked the safety and shot a tin can full of cocaine all over a nightclub office with a world-famous billionaire heiress present, I can't even imagine the fallout. Just discharging the firearm would have been a nightmare. But add in the drugs and a backpack with $700,000 and it was the trifecta—guns, cocaine, cash—that leads to only one place: prison.

I grabbed the tin can and smashed it with the butt of my pistol. The coke exploded on the desk like a piñata. Nobody wasted time, going in like a bunch of busy bees on a pile of honey.

An hour later, we were at the tables again. I lost $700,000 that night, and I was really pissed. Every time I beat Sam, I had to chase his ass around the city to get paid—and now he had real money in front of him, and I'd just given him almost three quarters of a million dollars. I was sick to my stomach and had to take ten milligrams of Valium to get to sleep.

Financially, the loss obviously hurt. But it emotionally hurt as well. I'd been playing with real cash, dollars that I had personally counted and banded up, so it stung more than losing casino chips. Plus, I'd done blow, drank booze, and almost died on the car ride with Sam. I was stressed the fuck out. Gambling was so hard on my body; the stress spiked my cortisol levels, breaking down muscle and fucking up my ability to sleep.

I really needed to find a new job.

I managed to win $300,000 back from Sam before we went our separate ways. However, I was still down $400,000, and he'd torched a million at the Baccarat tables. The casino was the only winner.

A few days later, I got a text from Sam.

I lick your money fag.

The guy was relentless.

At least I pay motherfucker.

Are you scared of me, I am your daddy. Are you scared of your father?

We went back and forth for a while, until I finally told him, *If I come out there and whip your ass, you better fucking pay me, same day. You are my bitch. Come to daddy.*

I'm bringing $500,000. Go get some cash and I'll be there in three hours.

I have a cashier's cheque for half a million, he replied.

I chartered a plane to LA and left immediately.

I beat Sam for $750,000. His cashier's check plus another one for the difference both surprisingly cleared. I was trapped because I hated the stress of gambling, but there was no other way to make this kind of money this fast. I knew I had to eventually find a way out or this job was going to kill me.

CHAPTER 39

Loan Survivor

I lost over a million dollars in a game hosted by the owner of Cirque du Soleil in his Ibiza villa.

We were playing big, and the game was pretty wild. Players were having million-dollar swings, and I was on a downstroke. The average net worth at the table was over a hundred million, and the room was full of strong personalities. One of the founders of Facebook offered me $150,000 to shave my beard, which was tempting. But I liked my beard, and taking that kind of bet would make me look like I wasn't as rich as I wanted people to think I was, so I told him to fuck off.

Clarence Wilson, a hedge fund manager from Texas, offered me half a million dollars of equity in his fund to go to a nightclub with him. If he offered cash, I would have happily accepted, but it was equity, and I didn't want to stop gambling. I was in full degenerate mode.

It was surreal to witness this type of wealth. We'd just taken Guy Laliberté's (the person who's house we were staying in) fifty million-dollar 178-foot sailing yacht out for the day. As we played poker in the living room of his hundred and twenty million-dollar home, I noticed a large book on a stand. I asked Guy what it was, and he said it contained all the pictures from his recent trip into space.

"How much did that cost?" I asked like the nosey bastard that I am.

"Six million," he casually replied. I'd been around money when I was younger, but not this kind of money.

Clarence pulled me aside after one of the games; he looked at me very earnestly and sincerely and said, "Dan, you're really bad at poker. I think you should stop playing and get a new hobby." This was funny coming from one of the worst players in the game, but it meant my table image was clearly working. I was, however, interested in his advice about my future because I didn't want to play poker much longer.

"I've produced some movies. It's fun. I could get you into one if you wanna try acting."

"Ok, fuck it. I'll do it."

CLARENCE WILSON *(NAME CHANGED)*

Hedge Fund Manager

I met Dan playing poker. He was described to me as an arrogant ex-military guy with some family money. I saw Dan as a fellow fish (bad recreational poker player), but he fancied himself a pro. While my observations of his play never ever had me believe he was a pro, one thing he was acutely aware of, and took advantage to make large sums of money, was that there were richer people who played poker, and their skill seemed to be inversely proportional to their wealth. Although Dan may have been a bad poker player, he had a great skill for getting in games with richer people who were worse.

I learned this lesson from Dan too late as my ego would always lead me to play against the best instead of making money or saving money playing with the worst. When I went to get my ego checked at an emotional intelligence class, I convinced Dan early in our friendship to do the same. Dan happily and easily agreed, which was contrary to what most people would have expected. We became much closer after that and with new resolve in life.

Dan's resolve was to stop giving a fuck what people thought (loss of ego) and to run an experiment to get famous in order to get girls. We had always theorized that fame was more powerful than money with respect to sex. We just didn't know it was one hundred times as powerful. As Dan unleashed the genie of fame in a whirlwind of improbable and impossible events and escapades, I witnessed and was occasionally swept up in some of the absolute lunacy.

When we returned to the States, Clarence called his buddy Lin Oeding and got me a role in the Antoine Fuqua movie *Olympus Has Fallen*. Before I arrived, Clarence said, "Don't be flashy, don't let these guys know you have money. Just show up and blend in."

"Hey, what's up with the guy with the beard?" an actor asked Lin Oeding, the stunt coordinator.

"He's a friend of a friend. I brought him on because I need ex-military guys to help train the stuntmen for the upcoming White House breach. Why do you ask?"

"I have that same watch he does."

"And?" Lin replied

"Mine is thirty grand, but his is covered in diamonds, so it probably costs a hundred grand!"

"Really?"

"Yeah, and he's over there rolling around in the dirt with it."

On the first day, I already blew it. Lin knew I had too much money to be doing stunts, but he liked that I worked hard and didn't complain. So when my uncle Big Dan died in a plane crash and I had to leave in the middle of filming to go to his funeral, he offered me a second opportunity to work on the movie.

"You gotta shave, though, if you want to play a helicopter pilot."

Union scale for bit part actors doesn't remotely equal the $150,000 I had turned down to shave a couple of weeks earlier. But shaving this time wasn't a bitch move, so I did it. Actors transform for roles.

Me in the flight suit, beardless.

When the filming ended, I went to Houston to see Clarence. We shot sporting clays, raced McLarens, and went to a strip club. Clarence's goal in life was to die with zero dollars in the bank—he even wrote a book about it—so he ran it up every day.

While in Houston, I got a call from Randall Emmett. He was a stereotypical Hollywood movie producer who went around telling everyone that he was a Hollywood movie producer. He asked me to invest a couple million dollars into his movie *Lone Survivor* staring Mark Wahlberg.

"Do not, under any circumstances, *ever* invest in a movie for financial gain," Clarence advised.

"Randall promised me a part, and they're in New Mexico now with the full cast. You want to go check it out?"

With Clarence's experience producing movies, I figured he'd help vet this potential deal. Plus, he had a brand-new Challenger 605 jet, which made getting there easy.

In a banquet hall, the cast and crew hosted a dinner for the families of the soldiers who died, inspiring the book and the film. I met Randall and Peter Berg, the director. They put on the hard sell and Pete pitched me on a role for Daniel Healy, a SEAL who died on the rescue mission.

"It's a legitimate role," he said. "A minimum of eight minutes on screen and eighty words of dialogue."

“If you can get that in writing, and you view this as an investment into an acting career, then it would be worth a million dollars,” Clarence said.

I caught a ride back to Vegas with Randall on his lead investor’s Lear jet. Randall was an asshole. He sent his assistant to return his rental car and then almost left him at the airport. He told the guy he had two minutes and made him sprint after the plane down the runway. When he finally opened the door for the winded, sweaty kid, there were two open seats, but Randall made the guy sit in the tiny-ass shitter the whole ride. Despite being a dickhead in general he was nice to me, and after a couple of weeks of hounding me, we agreed to terms on my investment in the film.

When it was time to shoot in New Mexico, I chartered a G4 and brought my assistant and a hot brunette with a perfect body. When the flight attendant went into the back to make some food, the brunette started sucking my dick. A couple minutes later when she climbed on top, I noticed the flight attendant discreetly slip into the bathroom. After banging, I desperately had to piss, so I went over to the bathroom

Flying to New Mexico.

door and released the flight attendant. It was an extremely awkward exchange. I was covered in sweat, holding my dick down, and trying to not make any physical contact with her, but the galley was pretty narrow. I avoided eye contact and handed her a wad of cash when we disembarked.

The following day, the brunette decided, in her infinite wisdom, to wear a schoolgirl outfit that could only have come from a sex shop. She had big tits, wasn't wearing a bra, and relied on the absolute minimum of buttons to keep it all together. It was incredibly distracting.

"What the fuck?" the director asked me.

"What?" I played dumb. "Want me to send her back to the hotel?"

He laughed and suggested we put her in the next scene just to see Mark Wahlberg's reaction when he walked on set. The director was a sport about the whole thing.

During a break in my filming schedule, I went to the famous Halloween party at the Playboy Mansion. As a kid, I'd always heard about the crazy parties Hefner threw, and it was a dream to visit the legendary residence. Once the GHB kicked in, I became more adventurous and ended up fucking a superhot brunette with big real tits in the crowded Grotto.

Check that off the bucket list.

I went back to New Mexico to finish filming *Lone Survivor*.

Randall gave me the inside scoop on how everything was going since I was an investor. The movie had a $40 million-dollar budget, but it only cost a fraction of that to make the film. They presold the foreign rights for around $20 million, and the state of New Mexico gave production about $12 million back as an incentive to film there. This meant production only needed to raise $8 million to get the $32 million. Surprisingly, my $1 million was an eighth of the total money actually needed to make the film.

Pete, the director, said he was frustrated because Marcus Luttrell, the "lone survivor," kept changing his story, and they had to reshoot scenes to accommodate his evolving tale. Seemed strange, but I figured maybe the guy just had PTSD or something. The next day Marcus gave me the only line of dialogue that made it into the movie, which was,

"The objective of this mission is to capture/kill Ahmad Shah." When I later found out that the mission was strictly for surveillance I remember wondering, Is *this guy completely full of shit?* Nobody forgets the objective of the mission that they write a book about.

While in "hair and makeup," I met the actor playing Shane Patton. Shane was in my boat crew in BUD/S class 239, so I gave him some insight on what he was like. Marcus got upset because I didn't announce to the actor that I wasn't a SEAL and told Pete he didn't want me to be in any more scenes. Pete told me that he was in a bind because he needed Marcus to be happy in order to promote the movie. I was pissed, but at the time I believed Marcus was a real hero, so I did the scenes they asked me to do and went back to San Diego.

CHAPTER 40

Betting a Bugatti

AG followed my Instagram and kept up with what I was doing. He saw I was back in California and had heard about my Ibiza losses, so he thought the time was right to clip me.

Alec Gores was a multibillionaire notorious for being a shrewd businessman and an ultra-high stakes gambler. I'd heard stories about "AG," and the legendary heads-up (one on one) poker matches he'd have with Andy Beal, the billionaire banker from Texas. AG had reportedly beaten Andy for over $700 million in the last year alone. So when AG first challenged me, I was as excited as I was nervous.

I employed the same strategy I did with hot girls; I didn't communicate too much interest or act eager.

Maybe after my hunting trip. Marky Mark said he wants to watch if we play, I texted. (Mark Wahlberg was Alec's neighbor).

Yes, we'll have him come n watch, Alec replied.

I showed up at his fifty million-dollar estate in Bel Air, and it was intimidating. The house reminded me of the Italian mob kingpin's home in the movie *American Gangster.* I asked him what he wanted to play for, and he casually said "A million, five million? Whatever." I didn't want to look like a piker, but I also knew I couldn't afford to lose millions of dollars in a single game. I hadn't anticipated being put on the spot like this; his girlfriend, the dealer, and even the butler were staring at me.

"Could we start off with \$2K/\$4K and a buy-in of \$500K?" I asked somewhat sheepishly.

"Sure, that's fine."

I let out an internal sigh of relief as I sat down to prepare for battle. Heads up is a whole different animal. It's a lot more aggressive, and the swings are much bigger than a normal game with multiple players.

I came out of the gates firing, raising every time I had position (meaning I was last to act, giving me the advantage) and reraising about 20 percent of his raises. He was folding too much, and within the first hour, I'd won over a hundred grand without any big hands.

I looked down at pocket queens and reraised his opening raise. He played back at me with a four bet reraise. I shoved in my remaining \$600,000 in chips, announcing I was "all in." Before I had finished pushing the chips, he said, "I call."

Shit. I knew by the way he called that he had me beat. Sure enough, he had pocket aces, the best possible hand. I felt like I got punched in the stomach, but I pretended to be unphased as I nonchalantly requested another \$500,000 in chips.

I slowed down, figuring I'd try and double up before I attempted to run him over again. A while later, I picked up pocket aces and reraised him. He didn't reraise me and just check called down with pocket kings. I couldn't believe it; he had the second-best hand in poker, and he was afraid. This was all the information I needed; I started playing much more aggressive, and it worked.

I beat him for \$1,600,000. Then a week later for \$2,500,000.

CHAPTER 41

LA

I was set up—living like I had hundreds of millions in the bank, and it wasn't costing me hardly anything.

I was spending more time in LA, and I wanted to give the city a chance, so I offered to split a nice house in the Hollywood hills with Eddie Ting. I liked the concept of sharing houses with people who were never there, and Eddie fit that description. He would occasionally come to LA to play poker and recruit new rich players for his NYC game. He agreed to pay half the rent if I'd host a poker game at the house when he came in town. Eddie said the tips alone would cover our $35,000 a month rent, so it made sense for both of us. He would have access to new players, and it would give me top tier properties in three different cities to crash in when necessary.

The poker game was a huge success. The tips from the first game more than covered the entire month's rent, and Eddie and I both won on top of that. Hosting also brought greater access to other poker games and gave me more pull in the poker world because I controlled who could play my game. In order to get a seat, you needed to be two things: really rich *and* really bad at poker. The only exceptions were guys like Nick Cassavetes, who weren't rich suckers, but provided access to other good games.

We hired models to serve drinks and give players massages at the table. The girls ended up making so much money in tips that we actually stopped paying them an hourly rate. Players would occasionally toss the waitresses $5,000 chips and word traveled fast. I had one of the juiciest games in town, and every girl wanted to work it. This brought in tons of new women, which was good for me, the poker game, and my social media. The more money I spent, or appeared to spend, the more people wanted to gamble with me.

AG would text me every so often, and I'd always invite him to my parties or my poker game, but he never came. This time he wanted to play me at his beach house in Malibu. I accepted, and we agreed to play the following day.

I sat down confident and started firing at him like before. He began reraising me, and I folded, figuring he was getting some cards. I bet the turn in a big pot, he called, and I checked the river expecting to win at showdown, but he went all in. His bet didn't make sense, which usually means a player is bluffing. I had a good hand; I wanted to call, but he'd never done anything out of line before, so after a minute, I folded. He laughed and eagerly showed me the bluff. Fuck. *If I called him, I'd be up three million dollars*, I thought to myself. He was playing different this time.

I started second-guessing my whole strategy.

My head was spinning, but I didn't have time to dissect what was going on. With him on the offensive, I found myself playing a guessing game. He was doing to me what I used to do to my old opponents. The difference was this was for staggering amounts of money, and if I was wrong, it would change my life. Before I knew it, I'd guessed wrong and was down $2,600,000.

I irresponsibly bought back in for two million dollars. As I signed for the chips, I felt a wave of anxiety, so I excused myself to the bathroom. Sweat began beading up on my forehead as I washed my hands and stared at myself in the mirror. *You aren't playing right; this isn't the spot you should be taking the biggest gamble of your life in.*

I played a few more hands before telling him I wasn't feeling good. He didn't want to stop, and I don't blame him, but this was like the battle of David and Goliath, and I needed to be on my A-game if I didn't want to get squished like a bug.

I had a queasy feeling in my stomach as I drove home. The adrenaline from the game and the stress from the loss swirled together like a tornado in my mind. *How did things go so wrong? Should I switch my strategy? What if I lose again?* I started to question everything, including whether or not I should even be playing for this kind of money.

I'd come into the match with such good momentum. I was in the best spot of my life financially with the two previous wins to pad my bankroll, but that was gone now. Momentum is important; Alec played noticeably better and more aggressive when he was winning. Even though I was much better than he was, I knew I couldn't fade the swings, and I didn't want to end up broke.

CHAPTER 42

Losing My Hair

I used poker to capitalize on my addiction to the rush of gambling. I experienced some of the highest highs and the lowest lows of my life playing poker. It's hard for a normal person to comprehend the pressure of making a decision that determines the outcome of either winning or losing millions of dollars. The level of stress it causes can actually manifest itself into physical changes in the body and even your outward appearance.

When I was playing AG, I remember running my hand through my hair, and twenty or thirty hairs would fall out. It would also kill my appetite and spike my cortisol levels, which cannibalized muscle and made it impossible to sleep. Stress is powerful; it can cause depression and give you anxiety. Plus, it's linked to six of the leading causes of death.

High-stakes gambling also desensitizes you to money. It's borderline impossible to have respect for money when you are winning and losing such massive amounts in such a short period of time. It's hard to not get jaded when the flop bet is an exotic car and the opening raise is a lawyer's annual salary.

I think the most detrimental part of poker is something that most people don't think about. It forces you to mute your emotions. When you're at the table, you can't allow yourself to get happy, excited, or upset because you will give off information. If you get a big hand, you don't smile; you sit there stone cold and emotionless. You do the same when you miss a big draw and have to fire a million-dollar bluff at the river. When poker players win a pot, they don't cheer and celebrate like at the craps table. It's terrible etiquette, and it would probably get you banned from a private game.

Every time I won a big pot, I would think of something shitty to piss myself off. I did this to make sure I didn't get happy and because being emotionally unaffected makes you appear richer. I found, the less you care about winning the money, the less your opponents will care about losing it.

All of these factors take a toll on your mental state. Not allowing yourself to be happy for hours on end while playing has an effect on your happiness when you aren't playing. People aren't robots, and they can't just turn their emotions on and off like a light switch. If you spend years of not allowing yourself to be happy, it can cause irreparable damage to your psyche. Poker is probably one of the hardest professions there is. I can't think of anything worse than going to work busting your ass and losing money.

MIKE "THE MOUTH" MATUSOW

Poker Player, Four-Time WSOP Winner

I've known Dan since around 2005 when he came in and started playing 25/50 no limit hold 'em with us at Bellagio. As time went by, we became pretty friendly and found ourselves playing tons of 25/50 together.

Having played professionally for twenty-four years, I can attest to how hard playing poker for a living is considering I've gone broke nine times in my life! After the fifth, I swore it would never happen again, only to let it happen again. In February 2016, when I lost $200K in a forty-eight-hour session, I was dead broke with zero outs to make money or pay my bills. I couldn't *sleep or eat, and I was suicidal every day for two weeks. The stresses and ups and downs in my life were crippling. It's something that very few can say they've gone through.*

We always say poker is a hard way to make an easy living. As high of limits as I've played, I've never played as big as Dan has. So, knowing the ups and downs I went through in my life, I can only imagine the stress he has playing for millions in a poker game. I would win or lose $30K a night or day and was never happy when I won but always miserable when I lost. It takes a special person to play poker for a living and an even more special woman to put up with the lifestyle.

The hardest thing of all was having to drop down in limits once I started losing. When the money gets tight, having to play smaller stakes to survive is mentally torturous and demoralizing. It's something I've struggled with my entire poker career. But today I'm back on my feet, doing well, playing high stakes, but I am very careful to not make mistakes of the past.

I love Dan as a person, and I know he always fights the good fight on the felt.

CHAPTER 43

Don't Count Your Money Sitting at the Table

My last session with AG haunted me. For days afterward, I replayed my hands, dissected the game, and kept asking myself what I could have done different. At the time, I felt like I was being bullied but after some analysis I determined AG had just hit a good run of cards. I also figured out a crucial detail: *things went south for me right after AG showed me that bluff*. That's what threw me off. He got in my head and made me question all my previous folds. It was a ploy; and a ploy recognized all-too-well since it was something I used to do. Something I used to do to suckers.

I'd fallen for my own trap.

My plan was to get back in the driver's seat and take control of this match. I'd noticed AG was more concerned with the total dollar amount bet, than the bet size relative to the pot. To him a half million-dollar bet meant strength no matter how big the blinds or the pot was. So I decided to double the buy-in and more than double the blinds for the next match. Beating me last time only served to whet AG's appetite, so when I suggested $5K/$10K blinds and a $1 million dollar buy-in, he eagerly accepted. Part of me felt like I'd stuck my head in the lion's mouth. Knowing if I was wrong—or just got unlucky—the consequences would be disastrous.

I started off slow, letting him think I was playing conservatively for the first half hour and then I began to lean on him. By hour two I was fully steam rolling the guy, raising 100 percent of hands preflop and continuation betting 80 percent of flops. On top of that, I hit some big hands so when he pushed back, it was often met with more aggression.

I brought a hot Jewish brunette named Dalia, who I'd been dating for a couple months. She'd seen me battle Sam before, but it was nothing like this. She watched in shock as we bet hundreds of thousands—sometimes millions—of dollars each hand. AG saw how the game held my girl's attention and, in an attempt to impress her, started playing without looking at his cards. Unfortunately, this actually made him tougher to run over because he started thinking about the game in terms of what I could have, instead of just folding when he had nothing. It made him pay attention to the board more and fold less. He started picking off my bluffs and I was forced to shift gears and slow down. Thankfully, after beating me for almost $2 million, he went back to looking at his cards.

As the game went on, AG decided he was now going to start betting "things" instead of money. He'd look up from his stack and casually say, "Mercedes" or "Ferrari," and that meant he was betting $100,000 or $300,000 respectively. Occasionally AG would pump it up by saying, "I raise you a Bugatti" or "a Lear Jet," and I would have a $1 or $3 million-dollar decision to make. It actually fucked with my head a bit, and I was glad when he stopped.

Battling with AG.

Green chips are $100,000, blue chips are $25,000, and white chips are $5,000.

After dinner, he got tired and began to play more passive, allowing me to pick up pots easily. The mountain of chips in front of me was growing by the hour. My bigger blind strategy had proven to be effective, but by 2 a.m., I was exhausted. There was no question I'd given good action in the match, and I was up $8,800,000 making this hands down the biggest win I'd ever had in poker. I was ready to gather up my chips and call it a night. But when I asked to quit, AG refused.

"I'll flip you a quarter if you want to gamble," I offered, "But I'm beat. I have to go to bed."

AG eyed me for a second then asked, "Wanna flip for your stack?"

My stack?! I thought, *How would I live with myself if I pissed away the biggest poker haul of my life?* I was thinking a million or two, but I figured, *I'm up 8.8 million...five and a half million is still a good win.* So I proposed we flip a coin for $3,300,000 each. Despite there being over eight figures on the table, nobody had a quarter to flip. So we agreed to high card instead. We both counted out $3,300,000 in chips, pushed them in the center, and the dealer placed the deck on the table. I spread the cards around and grabbed one. AG fished a card out of the pile. High card wins.

I looked down. A four of clubs.

Fuck.

My heart dropped and my stomach turned as my mind processed the loss. But then a thought gave me hope: *There are eight cards in the deck worse than a four of clubs and three cards that tie with a four of clubs.* That meant I actually had a 21.5 percent chance of *not* losing.

AG smiled before slowly rolling over the seven of diamonds. I played it off and gave him a fist bump before the dealer pushed him the pot. While losing a $6,600,000 flip took some wind out of my sails, this was still the biggest win I'd ever had, and I walked away with $5,500,000. Plus, AG seemed to appreciate my lack of respect for money, which had to be worth something.

Four days later, we met back at his Bel Air home. The blonde dealer smiled and asked, "How much would you like to buy in for?"

"Two million," I said as casually as possible.

"I'll take fifty million," Alec announced with a conviction I found unsettling. One thing was definitely clear: he wasn't going to be throwing jabs; he was looking for a knockout.

I'd determined the best way to play him was to have the blinds as big as possible, so we started at $5K/$10K and bumped them up to $10K/$25K within the hour. Those blinds were huge. To put that in perspective, it meant the opening raise was $75,000–$100,000. The preflop reraise was $300,000. And since AG called almost all reraises, it meant there was $600,000 in the pot *before* the flop (first three cards).

And there were still three more streets of betting on top of that.

I continued to play hyper aggressive, keeping constant pressure on him. It was like navigating a mine field because every now and then, he'd get a big hand, catch me bluffing, and beat me for a million or two. Firing multimillion-dollar bluffs worked most of the time with Alec, but when it didn't, it hurt. I'd swallow the pain and remind myself that losses would only increase the longevity of our battle. Like my Grandpa Harry used to say, "You can sheer a sheep many times, but you can only skin him once."

It was super stressful playing for that kind of money, but it was the optimal strategy. He played worse and folded more frequently when the stakes were higher. Playing as big as possible was risky, but it allowed me to win the most money in the shortest period of time, which was important because I knew he would eventually quit playing me.

I battled him until three or four in the morning. When he finally threw in the towel, I was up $8 million dollars. He always tipped his dealers hundreds of thousands of dollars when he won, and I didn't want the dealers to have any incentive to possibly cheat me, so I tipped them $300,000 and walked away with $7.7 million. It's crazy to think a dealer could make more than the yearly salary of the vice president of the United States for one night of slinging cards, but that was the world I was living in.

The wire came in twenty-four hours later; nobody paid faster than AG. He didn't even flinch about it.

It was strange winning that kind of money in a night. I felt like it should have made me happier, but it was such a large amount, it almost didn't even feel real. I think I would have been more excited about it if I'd immediately taken a break, sat down for a moment, and truly contemplated what I had just accomplished. But I didn't celebrate or stop to enjoy the view because I was focused on climbing the mountain.

Another reason I didn't celebrate was because I knew if I lost, I would go back and play AG huge again. I didn't have the bankroll to sustain heavy losses at this limit. My whole life could potentially go up in smoke, and I could find myself in a different tax bracket, grinding the low limit games if things went really bad. I was playing outside the limits of my bankroll. No responsible poker player would've taken a shot like this, but I didn't care. The edge was too big; I had to take the risk.

The last reason that I didn't celebrate the wins was because, just like Kenny Rogers taught the world, you don't count your money sitting at the table. You will almost never stop at your absolute high point, and you don't want to be playing thinking, "Damn, I was up more an hour ago" or "I don't want to call this bet because if I lose, I won't be up anymore." You should make the correct play, and the money shouldn't have anything to do with it. You don't hold on to your chips with a death grip because the game is fluid. Sometimes you have to risk to win, like drawing to make a big hand, or bluffing when its mathematically correct. You play the odds; your chips will ebb and flow like the tide, but over time, you'll win more than you'll lose.

Poker isn't like blackjack or craps where you quit after a good run. It's how you make a living; just like a stockbroker doesn't quit trading after a good day in the market. When you win, you should keep playing, because if you're winning, that means others are losing. You'll play better when winning, and they'll play much worse when losing, so this is when you have the biggest edge. The game never stops in poker; it's all just one long session.

CHAPTER 44

Transition

I had a threesome and a foursome, but group sex with a girlfriend wasn't usually great. The girlfriend gets jealous, and the other women don't want to piss off the main squeeze.

I'd been seeing Dalia for a few months exclusively when she joined five other girls and Mike the sports bettor on a quick trip to Cabo to celebrate my win over AG. I began to think that having a girlfriend was impeding my lifestyle. Dalia was smart, hot, and laid back. There wasn't anything wrong with her, so it made it difficult to decide what to do. The trip was fun, but I didn't feel free. I felt restricted.

I told her I wanted to take a week break because we'd been together for a couple of months straight, and I needed time to breathe. The first thing I did was text some girls I'd been wanting to fuck. I took a group of them to Sam's for a poker game. I fucked one girl in his movie theater, another in his guest house, and I had another meet me at my house when I left.

I had girls coming over all week. I told them I could only hang for an hour and literally scheduled them like business meetings. I didn't miss having a girlfriend one fucking bit. After a few days of this, I called Dalia and was honest. I wanted to be single; I didn't want to be tied down.

Cabo.

I'd been wanting to hook up with Victoria for a while. She was a twenty-five-year-old investment banker for Credit Suisse and was absolutely gorgeous. I was being respectful of Dalia, so I didn't pursue it. But as soon as we broke up, I invited Victoria over.

When she arrived, I suggested we get high in the Jacuzzi. Victoria said ok, but prefaced it with a warning that she didn't know how to swim, which I found hilarious. I held her up by her stomach while she kicked and paddled like a helpless puppy. It wasn't until then that I realized how amazing her body was. She always dressed very conservatively with big frumpy black dresses and sweaters, so it was impossible to tell if she was hot or obese.

After a minute of her flailing and saying she was terrified of the water, I decided we'd tackle that another day. We went to my room, and I took a shower to rinse off the chlorine. I invited her in and helped her take off the bikini. She was the perfect blend of innocent and confident. Shy enough to make you respect her, but bold enough to be sexy. I was trying to play it cool, but it took every ounce of my self control to wait for her to initiate.

I toweled off after the shower and went to brush my teeth. As soon as she touched me we started hooking up and everything was going well. She was naked and super wet when I was fingering her but unexpectedly said *no* to the sex. I did the full stop, put on my clothes, and told her to take off. This one was painful because I really wanted to fuck her, but I stayed strong and thought of dead cats as I scrolled through my phone looking for a replacement. I texted a girl that I'd previously hooked up with to come over while she was getting dressed.

Victoria later told me she would've fucked me if I persisted, and I'm sure this is the case with some girls. But, I don't reward rejection with affection. It establishes the wrong dynamic.

Don't chase women; it will make them like you less.

CHAPTER 45

Sam, Part 2

I didn't expect Sam to actually show up at the party, but there he was at the door in black jeans, Louis Vuitton crocodile combat boots, and black sunglasses. Sweat dripped off his face onto his chest.

"Did you run here?" I asked.

He grunted ambiguously.

I immediately escorted him to a hot girl who'd been begging me for cocaine and made the introduction. Then I made my rounds, saying hello and making sure everyone was having a good time. Paris Hilton and her new boyfriend lounged on the daybed. I was happy to see her; she was always nice, and it's good to have celebrities at your events, especially female ones.

A hot girl with great tits stopped me as I walked to the bathroom. "Are you Dan?"

She complimented the house and asked for a tour. There are a few things I've learned throwing parties. One is that there are certain code words or pass phrases.

"I'm so drunk."—Universal mating call

"Are you Dan?"—I know who you are, and I want to have sex with you.

"Is this your house?"—Let's have sex

"Can I have a tour?"—I'm interested in sex

"Where's your room?"—Let's have sex now

I led the girl to my bedroom and opened the door.

Sam was seated at my desk, screaming, blood pouring out of his hand. A hot blonde struggled to hold his arm down. And a doctor in full scrubs hovered over him with a big-ass needle.

"What the fuck?" I yelled.

"You need to leave," the hot blonde said.

"Bitch, I live here. What are you doing to my friend?"

"Can you help me hold him down?"

Sam shoveled coke into his nose with his free hand while they wrestled with the other. Seeing him covered in blow actually made me feel a bit better. It would have been far more bizarre if Sam were sober.

The girl who wanted to fuck me was done. "I'm sorry, this is too weird for me," she said and took off.

Now, equally irritated and confused, I yelled, "What the fuck are you doing to my friend?"

"Sam tried to remove a champagne cork with a machete. He missed the bottle and took off half of his thumb," the doctor replied. I could see his thumb dangling, and there was a large pool of fresh blood beneath his hand. "We need to numb him up so I can stitch his thumb back on. Can you hold his arm?"

I grabbed Sam's injured arm with both of my hands and pinned it to the desk. It was like fighting the Kraken. He was screaming and motherfucking the doctor. The doc injected his thumb with Lidocaine, and Sam hissed like a vampire burned by daylight.

The blonde who I'd incorrectly assumed was a nurse was tall, thin, and superhot. I inquired how she found herself involved in this unfortunate scenario. She told me her name was Angel and that she worked for Sam.

Meanwhile, Sam was burbling and making strange noises like he was underwater.

"Okay, let's get him stitched up," said the doc.

The doctor pushed through the curved needle, and Sam screamed and jerked his hand, ripping the suture out and sending the cocaine pile everywhere. White powder floated through the air, punctuated with red blood droplets. The doctor didn't factor in Sam's tolerance for drugs, so the numbing injection hadn't done a thing. He gave Sam another shot of Lidocaine, and we finally managed to get him stitched up.

I couldn't have Sam running around my party looking like Freddy Krueger, so I kicked him and the trauma team out of my bedroom. I got Angel's phone number on the way out the door.

I got

Your money

Come

Over, Sam texted me a few hours later.

I had begun to notice a direct correlation between the nice things I did for Sam and the speed of his debt payments. I had to capitalize on his momentary willingness to settle his tab.

Sam's gate was open, so I drove all the way up to the house. The front door was ajar, so I walked in.

Just when I thought the day couldn't get any weirder... Sam's pants were down below his ass, and he was running around the living room. The same doctor was following him but with an even bigger needle this time.

"Stay back! Stay back, you butcher!" Sam yelled.

"What kinda Michael Jackson shit is going on here?" I asked.

"He called me over here for a testosterone shot so he would heal faster. I came all this way, but now he won't take the shot."

Sam paid a slew of concierge doctors exorbitant amounts of money to give him whatever he requested, but he usually chickened out when it came to needles. I grabbed Sam and held him down while the doctor did his thing. Sam kicked his legs like a five-year-old boy the entire time.

After it all calmed down, I went to the bathroom. When I came out, Sam and the shady doctor were seated at the table, playing heads-up poker for $50,000. Immediately after winning, the doctor began grabbing the cash and stuffing it in his bag. Sam, meanwhile, retrieved the machete and came back, hissing at the doctor.

"You should leave," I advised the doc.

He listened and rushed out the door.

CHAPTER 46

Sam, Part 3

Sam and I would arrange a time to play and then call a bunch of girls because there had to be at least one or two to deal. He'd offer the girls up to $5,000 to do stupid shit like get naked and smash glow in the dark golf balls into his neighbor's homes at two in the morning. The girls would also make anywhere from $500 to $3,000 for dealing cards depending on how much was won.

I was up around $700,000 when Sam made a comment about liking my new Ferrari. I'd just bought the second Lamborghini Aventador roadster in the country; I was running out of garage space, and I figured it would help me get paid, so I said, "You can have it." He was shocked, which was impressive because very little surprised Sam. When I tossed him the keys, he said

he wanted to go to Soho House, a members-only club for Hollywood parasites to network with each other. It was just down the hill, and I thought, *What's the worst that can happen*?

Sam slammed on the gas, and I frantically grabbed for my seat belt. We unintentionally drifted through the first corner, and it dawned on me. Not only was Sam a terrible driver, but now he was trying to impress me.

"Slow the fuck down!" I yelled over the roar of the engine, which, of course, made him drive even faster. I felt like I was on a rollercoaster from hell with Satan at the controls. We broke eighty miles an hour on Doheny Drive. The hill and the steep decline made us accelerate faster and the brakes less effective.

Out of nowhere, a dump truck pulled out in front of us.

I couldn't even get my vocal cords to work to yell the words, so I just pointed, and Sam stomped the brakes. The car skidded down the road, and I was certain we were going to die. Time slowed down, the whole world stopped. Sam turned hard right into the side road the dump truck had just vacated, and we missed hitting him by what seemed like inches.

"Stop! Stop! Stop!" I yelled, and Sam slowed down. I leapt out of the convertible to safety.

"Come on, Blitz," Sam whined. "I'll drive slower, I promise."

"Fuck you! You're unfit for the road!" He pleaded for me to get in the car, but I wasn't hearing it and took an UberX home. Sam must have felt bad about the whole thing because he wired $700,000 off his debt into my account that afternoon.

A few hours later, Sam called about going to a hockey game. He had seats on the glass, seven hot girls, and he promised me that his bodyguard would be driving. Of course, Sam ran late, so we didn't even arrive at the arena until there were only twenty minutes left in the game. People had taken our seats since the game was basically over.

"Please remove the peasant squatters from our seats," Sam instructed the stadium staff.

As we shuffled towards our seats, Sam got into a verbal altercation with a middle-aged dad sitting with his daughter. Sam said something abrasive, and the guy knocked off Sam's hat. Sam threw about fifteen punches, none of which landed. I watched in horror as the stands converged on Sam. There were all these season ticket holders who sat next to each other game after game, one of which was a massive three hundred-pound corn-fed white guy who pinned Sam on the glass with his forearm.

I jumped out of my seat and put Cornfed into a rear naked chokehold. It was tough because the guy had almost no neck; it was as if his shoulders just attached directly to his head. I was thinking he was gonna turn and rip my head off my neck, but he kept his attention focused on Sam. I was under his chin, so the choke was in deep. I squeezed tighter and tighter until he finally released Sam.

Security came and broke it up. After asking a few questions, they took Sam. He assured us that he'd be back and told us to stay in our seats. I saw security ask for his ID and a cloud of blow went into the air as he retrieved it from his pocket. I thought, *Oh man, he's finally done it. He's going to jail.*

We continued watching the game, wondering if Sam would go to jail or if by some act of God they'd let the lunatic loose. After about five minutes, I went to check on him. He was in cuffs and by every indication, he was going to be arrested. There was no way he didn't have at least an eight ball of blow on him, so I was really worried.

He went to jail but somehow got out the same night. I learned afterward that there was evidently a pattern of Sam arrests that inexplicably resulted in no charges. My theory was that he had some sort of diplomatic immunity or that he was a government informant. The government informant seemed the most likely, but the thought of coked-out Sam working with the feds made me laugh out loud.

Earlier in the year, I told Sam that he was hopeless and that I wasn't going to play him in poker anymore because he was so bad. After I quit him, Ilya, a high-stakes gambler/bookie, sent Phil Ivey in to play Sam and started booking all his big sports action. When Sam didn't want to pay, the word on the street was people were sent to talk to him. I was told they took him off for around $80,000,000 and got paid $50,000,000 before a federal indictment brought the syndicate down. The indictments went all the way to New York with Russian mob ties.

Ilya got locked up, and we found out that our phones had been tapped for at least six months. I was part of the investigation, so I was privy to the evidence in the case, which included everyone's text message history. It made for quite an interesting read.

The government froze $2,500,000 of my money, and Wells Fargo shut down my private banking. The $2.5 million was money Ilya had wired me a few weeks prior as a deposit, and anything he sent was frozen. When he asked me to sign it over as part of a settlement agreement with the government, I said no problem. This wasn't the first time I paid a ransom to the government to get someone out of jail.

CHAPTER 47

Bet Everything

Mike was a super sharp guy who saw all the angles. He figured living next to me would be worth more than the rent he was paying and he was right.

After a few months of splitting the house with Eddie Ting, I realized I was spending the bulk of my time in LA. Ilya and Phil Ivey were paying $45,000 a month to rent a house with an insane view up the hill on Blue Jay Way. After the Ilya indictment, Phil agreed to sublet me their house at a slight discount.

Mike, the sports bettor, rented a house across the street from me in hopes of doing business. He proposed that I get some big sports betting accounts and let him bet on them. Mike said he would give me 30 percent of the profit and agreed to pay 100 percent of the losses. That is what gamblers call a freeroll, and I like freerolls, so I said yes. I had a reputation for being rich, gambling hard, and paying my bills, so it wasn't hard to get major accounts established.

Mike came out of the gates firing. He was betting a hundred thousand a pop on sixteen different things. I thought five TVs in my living room was enough, but I had to get two more racks brought in just so I could sweat all the fucking games. It was fun to watch sports for the first time in my life because now I had a reason to care. We won around

$17 million on the first account before they shut it down, and we won more on others.

This was around the time when the Wynn Macau opened up, and the big Asian whales were wandering into the poker room looking to gamble. The savvy American pros made short work of them, and they responded by banning white guys from the big game.

I found an Asian American pro at the Bellagio who spoke fluent Mandarin. He couldn't afford to play the big Macau game, so I said I'd put up all the money and agreed to split the profits with him 60/40 in my favor. I set everything up and sent him over there.

We spoke almost every day, and he kept me up to speed on what was going on. So when he informed me that the big Macau gamblers were coming to Vegas that summer, I started making arrangements. I knew about all the good games before they happened, so I bought pieces of the best players and made sure they got seats. I was also able to help some of the Internet whiz kids play above their bankroll and got them into juicy games that they otherwise would've been shut out of.

It was extremely profitable. One of the players I had a piece of won $14 million that summer in Vegas. I won almost $2 million in a single game myself, and the Asian in Macau was winning millions as well. Rick Salomon (the guy from the Paris Hilton fuck tape) was beating Andy Beal for around $50 million that summer, and I had 25 percent of that. I had so much fucking money coming in, I honestly didn't know what to do with it. Too much of anything is bad, except for money. There is no such thing as too much money, or so I thought.

RICK SALOMON

High-Stakes Gambler

Rick, right before he married Pam Anderson.

Tampa Dan told me he was going to be really famous, more famous than Paris Hilton. I laughed my ass off...thought to myself, Zero chance. I still don't know how this hillbilly got so famous. Somehow, he got girls before he was famous even though he admits he was a giant nerd. I remember being in the Rhino trying to take this stripper home, and she wouldn't go home with me, telling me she was in love with Tampa fucking Dan. I was def horny on some good cocaine, and this was not good news to me. You will not go home with me because you're in love with the king of the nerds?

He used to run around the Bellagio with all these kids who never left the house and were the most socially awkward humans alive. He staked them all and made a lot of money, and I had to watch and listen to their fucking nerd laughs that have now ruined poker. Poker used to be gangsters and cowboys. Now it's Blitz nerd camp with timing tells.

CHAPTER 48

Victoria

Despite me kicking her out of my house, Victoria and I remained on good terms, and a few weeks later at my pool party, Angel, the girl I thought was a nurse, approached her about having a threesome with me. I knew Angel was bi, and we'd been fucking for a month, so I suggested she ask, figuring this approach could only help, and it did. Immediately after Angel asked her, Victoria came up to me and said she wanted to fuck me, but without Angel. I felt a little bad having Angel set it up and then not including her, but I'd wanted to hook up with Victoria for years.

Victoria hadn't been with a lot of guys, and the sex was phenomenal, so we started dating. I'd learned my lesson from Jessa and Dalia, so I made it very clear from the start that this would be an open relationship. She agreed and quickly became my main girl. Victoria was extremely loyal and refused to even look at another guy.

She was my perfect body type, her face was flawless without makeup, and the sex was some of the best I've ever had in my life. She would talk dirty and do anything I wanted. She didn't have any drinking problems; she was smart and wasn't materialistic at all. If I were to design a girlfriend in a lab, I would come up with *almost* exactly her.

I like submissive girls, but Victoria was too submissive. She didn't have her own opinions or a strong sense of self. I felt like she was always who she thought I wanted her to be. That was her only flaw. Honestly, if we'd had great conversations, I probably would have just married the girl.

When you like someone too much, sometimes you'll act differently and try too hard. You'll sacrifice your authentic self to appear more desirable, and this usually has the opposite effect. This was the problem with Victoria; she liked me too much, and as a result, she wasn't comfortable enough to just be herself. I had no idea at the time, and it caused me to push her away, which only further exacerbated the problem.

One of the reasons women are attracted to assholes is because assholes project a strong sense of self. Assholes are selfish, and they do what they want, so they always appear confident. If you try too hard, it makes you seem weak and less authentic, and that gets boring in a hurry. To be clear I wasn't an asshole, I always treated people with respect, but my brutal honesty and unapologetic behavior was commonly misconstrued.

No matter how much stupid shit I would do, Victoria would never try and make me jealous like Jessa did. That said, I knew she didn't like that I was sleeping with other women, and after a while, she demanded monogamy. She deserved it, so I tried it for a week or so, but I couldn't give up the other girls. I'd been waiting my whole life to be in a position like this, and I'd worked so hard to get here. I didn't want to be restricted, so I was honest and ended things with her.

Soon after, she came back and said she wanted to be with me and didn't care, but asked that I lie to her about other girls if she asked. I agreed, but then she'd ask me a bunch of questions to try and catch me lying and get mad if she did. It was very strange, but she loved me, and I loved her back, so I tried to make it work.

It was difficult because I constantly had girls around for poker, parties, and the living documentary I was making of my life on social media. The more girls that were around, the easier it was to get laid, and having a main only made them try harder because it was a challenge. Vaginas and money are similar in that; when you don't need it, everyone wants to give it to you, and when you desperately need it, nobody wants to give it to you.

CHAPTER 49

Sam, Part 4

I was in bed one night with Victoria when Sam called. This was very strange because Sam never called. His normal communication style was to send seventy-five one-word texts because he had such terrible ADD and did so much blow that he couldn't formulate a coherent sentence.

"Come over, come over. You gotta come to my house right now."

"I'm in bed with a girl, what's going on?"

"I bought you a present, and it's amazing. You gotta come over here!"

"Look, buddy, I'm in bed. I'll come over tomorrow."

"No, no, you gotta come right now. It's a surprise. You'll love it, you gotta come over right now."

I had given Sam a lot of gifts over time. Cars, Tom Ford jackets, fifty thousand-dollar watches, you name it. So I knew if he got me a present, then it was something badass. But I couldn't imagine what couldn't wait until the morning.

"I'm not coming until you tell me what it is."

"I got you a tiger shark, and I got me one, and they're like brothers, and they're gonna be like you and me, and they're gonna live together forever."

Sam was the embodiment of cocaine; like if cocaine was a human being, it would be Sam. Extreme highs and lows, always seemed like a good idea but never was, started off fun but always ended terribly. Victoria knew this and wasn't thrilled about going; she referred to his house as a black hole. Once you entered those walls, time no longer existed. You could get trapped for hours, sometimes days, and you never knew when you'd get spit out. The only thing you could be relatively sure of is you'd be leaving richer.

On the way over, all I could think of was *Where did he put these sharks?* He was infamous for doing crazy things in his house. At one point, he claimed to have spent $3 million on Versace tile that he was going to line the house with. I figured he was just talking shit, but I'll be damned if it didn't arrive. He put it on the floors, in the shower, the backsplash in the kitchen, everywhere. He even had it inlaid on the top of his poker table over the felt, which completely destroyed it. The chips and cards flew all over the room, slipping off the slick tile surface.

Days later, Sam went on a bad sports betting streak and decided the tile was bad luck, so he had it all completely ripped out and thrown in the dumpster. He was capable of anything—hundred thousand-gallon fish tanks installed in the walls, multimillion-dollar aquariums outside, whatever.

We walked in the front door, through the kitchen, and into the backyard. I suspected that he had been exaggerating, but these were fucking tiger sharks. The real thing. Maybe six feet long, complete with the dark stripes on the side. And they were in his swimming pool.

Sam glowed and grinned from ear to ear. He was so proud of himself.

I noticed one of the sharks just chillin' in the shallow end with a half-eaten fish floating beside him. When I got close enough, I tapped the shark's fin. He didn't move a muscle. I grabbed his tail and pulled him back and forth; blood seeped out of his gills.

"Sam, this fucking shark is dead."

"What?" He looked shocked.

"Dude, they're saltwater animals. What did you think was going to happen?"

Sam looked at me like I was mentally deficient. He lowered his tone and hissed, "You don't think I thought of that?"

I noticed debris at the bottom of the pool. Some were smaller, clear, glass-looking objects. Others were bigger, cylindrical, with logos. Then it hit me—that crazy motherfucker had thrown all of his household saltshakers and canisters of Morton table salt into the pool. In Sam's coked-out, convoluted brain, he figured that would turn his pool into a saltwater aquarium.

"Who would have known?" he muttered, clearly perplexed by the situation.

"I dunno, Sam. I probably could have guessed they wouldn't survive. Probably your housekeeper, your landscaper, your assistant, and the homeless guy who tries to sell newspapers on La Cienega. They could have predicted this as well."

I think it was some form of cocaine-induced psychosis, but Sam had really spun completely off the planet. I didn't even argue with him; I just left.

As I walked out, I noticed another dead shark had fallen over the infinity edge of the pool and was trapped in the recirculating mechanism. Sam let them rot for weeks until the stench was so bad that he had no choice but to call the pool cleaning company. They reported Sam to the police, but somehow his invulnerability to consequences protected him yet again.

CHAPTER 50

Movie Roles

I was getting kinda tired of poker, and I thought being a movie star would be a much cooler job.

I knew I'd have to build my reel before getting any big parts, but I played poker with a bunch of directors and producers, so I put the word out that I was looking to get into acting. Nick Cassavetes was directing *The Other Woman* starring Cameron Diaz and offered me the part of "handsome man at the bar." I had to read for the role as a formality, so I showed up at the casting director's office with my lines memorized.

I stood in the middle of the room and was instructed to read my lines to the guy operating the camera. This was very awkward since I was effectively hitting on him while he read Cameron Diaz's lines. I was doing a horrible fucking job, and this, in turn, gave me anxiety, which only made it that much worse. I left the office feeling like a complete fucking retard. Nick rescheduled a fresh read with a woman, and I managed to read the lines without imploding.

I went out to New York a couple months later to shoot the actual scene at a bar located close to Times Square. I had a couple girls meet me at my hotel the day prior. We got high and ate room service between threesomes. I set my alarm, and the next day, I woke up, ate breakfast, put on a custom Tom Ford suit, and walked to the bar. I had my lines memorized, but I was nervous since Nick was my buddy and I didn't want to fuck this up, especially after my initial meltdown.

I showed up at the bar, and Nick and Cameron Diaz were sitting there waiting. Nick introduced me, and as I shook her hand, I noticed she was towering over me. We're the same height, but her 5" heels made her 6'2". Nick, who was 6'6", asked if they could put boosters in my shoes, which instantly made me feel like a midget asshole and second-guess if I was the right guy for the part.

Nick Cassavetes.

Diaz asked the prop guy for a credit card and complained when he handed her a shitty Visa. This was back in 2013 before every dentist with a BMW had a black card. So, thinking this was my time to shine, I proudly tossed over my American Express black card, hoping to get some kind of recognition. She couldn't have looked less impressed. *Fuck. This is going to be a disaster,* I thought.

As we rehearsed the scene, she looked at me like she wouldn't sleep with me in a million years, which totally threw me off. My lines landed flat, and Nick told me to just improvise and hit on her like I normally would in a bar. That went even worse since I am not the guy who goes to a bar or hits on a girl—ever. Nick had me do a couple shots of tequila with him to loosen up, and I could tell Diaz was getting frustrated.

Nick was confused; he had watched me fuck tons of girls and knew I got pussy all the time. He'd witnessed superhot girls competing to bang me and must have assumed this role would be like playing myself. What he didn't realize was, I wasn't the guy who hits on girls; I'm the guy who gets hit on by girls. My success was due to *setup*, not my one-liners at a bar. I hadn't hit on a girl since college, and this whole situation was so opposite of what I normally do that I felt like a fish out of water.

I fumbled around and fucked it up until we went back to the original lines. After about nine more takes, we finally wrapped. I did such a shitty job he ended up cutting the entire scene from the movie but didn't have the heart to tell me until it came out. Thank God he did. The last thing I wanted to be remembered for was looking like a flailing try-hard, attempting to hit on a cougar at a bar.

Shortly after this disaster, Lin Oeding, the stunt coordinator on Antoine Fuqua's *Olympus Has Fallen*, had teamed up with him again to work on a new film called *The Equalizer*, starring Denzel Washington. Lin suggested me. "He's got a good look, I like the beard," Antoine said, so I was on the next G4 available for charter, heading towards rehearsals in Boston with one of my favorite actors of all time.

Every day on set, the makeup artists put fake tattoos on me and made sure everything matched the previous footage. My primary scene involved a heavily armed gang of mercenaries who invade a Home Depot to kill the unarmed Denzel character.

In hair and makeup.

Rehearsal with Antoine Fuqua.

I met my death walking down an aisle and being confused by dirt and sand on the concrete floor. I looked down and then a barbed wire dog collar caught around my neck like a noose. Heavy bags of cement were kicked off an upper row of shelving, and the weight pulled the noose tight and lifted me fifteen feet off the ground. My character hung suspended as Denzel stood on the upper shelf, staring me in the eye, coolly watching me choke to death. He stared straight into my eyes, his face only two feet from mine as I spit blood and died.

There had been a lot of rehearsal for the scene. I wore a "jerk vest" attached to a metal wire fed through a powerful pulley system. Those movie scenes where someone flies backwards after a superhero roundhouse kick are filmed using jerk vests. In the first rehearsal run-through, they didn't have the weights and motors calibrated properly, so I was jerked all the way to the Home Depot roof until my head crashed into the metal. I was lucky that I wasn't paralyzed. Mistakes on action film sets can be bad news. On one movie I worked on, they waited too long to activate the pully on a stunt guy's jerk vest, and he had half his face burnt off in an explosion.

After my scene, Denzel complimented my death. The part was small, but he's one of my all-time favorite actors, and his compliment really made me feel good.

Small gestures like that impact people. It's something I tried to remember when I started to get recognized shortly afterward. If someone wanted to take a picture with me, I always said yes. I have almost never declined a photo unless I was getting bombarded. It's an insignificant, fleeting moment for the public figure, but it could be a huge deal for a small-town kid with big dreams.

CHAPTER 51

Smushball Lawsuit

Michelle was a human Barbie doll with huge tits, big eyes, and a tiny waist. Though she acted ditzy, she was no idiot. She knew exactly what she was doing. Michelle was one of those women who oozed sexual energy and used it to her advantage.

Every time I saw her, she was wearing something low cut with no bra and had a champagne glass practically glued to her hand. She had been dating a poker player named Tom Dwan for a couple of years. He and I had hung out a few times, and we had mutual friends. He was usually referred to by his poker moniker "durrrr" and was a legend in the online poker world.

I thought about banging her, but I never flirted. I was always good about that. I wouldn't even make eye contact with a friend's girlfriend. Tom had been playing in Macau for a long time, and Michelle frequented the poker room in Vegas. Her tits seemed to get bigger and bigger while her tops got smaller and smaller. She wore a lot of Spandex, and you could see her nipples from fifty yards away. I don't even think she owned a bra. She would flirt with Bobby Baldwin at the poker table before heading out to the club. We'd always look at each other after like, "What the fuck was that?"

One night, I was going out with some girls to meet a promoter at a club in the Wynn. Michelle texted and asked what I was doing. I invited her to join us, which was kosher because another girlfriend Lacy was coming and they were friends. Lacy was seeing a former Victory poker player named Keith, who I was staking in Macau. So they could sort of chaperone each other.

At the end of the night, Michelle and Lacy ended up at my place in Panorama. I could tell Michelle wanted to stay, but Lacy didn't want her to. They sat there for over an hour until Lacy finally gave up and left.

"I haven't spoken to Tom in a month," Michelle told me before saying they were going to break up. I wasn't tight with Tom, but we had done some business, and I knew I should refrain from nailing his girlfriend. But she put on the hard sell. I was capped up on GHB, and she was superhot, so we ended up banging that night and then the following day at her place, which was also his place. They lived together.

"This is pretty fucked up," I told her afterward when the guilt kicked in. "You're really breaking up, right? I don't like screwing over guys I know." She assured me they were done, that it was all over but the final goodbye. I suppose I also rationalized that he was better off without her if she was the cheating kind. And she was; I later discovered that I wasn't the only guy she was banging.

Lacy said something to Keith, who said something to Tom, who promptly started texting and leaving messages on my phone.

"Don't tell him," Michelle begged. "We're going to break up. We haven't even spoken in forever. But I don't want to fuck with his head while he's in Asia. And if you tell him this news, he'll be super tilted."

The worst thing you can do is play poker in a shitty headspace. You're basically guaranteed to lose, and Tom had already racked up some big losses in Macau. If their relationship was on death's door anyway, then what difference did it make? It's not like he was coming home and crawling into her bed every night. He was halfway around the world, and they weren't even speaking to each other. So I lied to Tom. I felt like shit telling him that we didn't hook up, but I couldn't see any better solution.

Four days later, he asked again.

By now, I was starting to get suspicious about Michelle. After all this, she *still* hadn't broken up with him. It was at the point where I would be doing him a favor by telling him what kind of woman he had back at home. I could have continued the lie and saved myself the headache, but if I was living with a girl who fucked other people in my circle the minute I left town, I'd want to know.

In a place like Las Vegas, there was always some meathead who wanted to fight any male who so much as looked at his girlfriend. That's backwards. The meathead and lady meathead are the ones with the agreement. Some random stranger doesn't owe either of them anything. Unless you have an ugly girlfriend, someone somewhere is always going to try and fuck her. And even then, someone still probably wants to fuck her. It's her obligation to decline the unwanted attention. If she flirts back, then it's only a matter of time before she will fuck one of them.

There is nothing worse than dating a girl that you don't trust. In spite of all that, Tom unfortunately did not seem to share my philosophy and didn't receive the honesty well. He went off the deep end and told everyone what a scumbag I was for the next year at least. I can't say I blame him, and I suppose I am a scumbag, but in the end, I would argue he's better off.

That said, Michelle did have some damn good cats. She had these amazing little longhair Persian cats that looked like mini-lions after grooming. I offered her $10,000 for the calico one, but she wouldn't sell. However, she did promise me the first one if her cats ever had a litter. Michelle kept her word, chartered a plane, and brought me the calico baby girl as a present. She wouldn't take any money for the kitten but allowed me to give her $7,500 for the plane.

The kitten had a limp, and Michelle said she had fallen but would quickly recover. After a day or two, I took her to a vet who did an X-ray.

"She's been stepped on," he said. "That leg is seriously broken and has mummified."

He suggested euthanasia.

"No fucking way," I said.

"It's going to be a $5,000 surgery, and the leg won't make it," he said. "We'll have to amputate it."

I got a second opinion, and there was no saving the leg.

"Do it."

Which is how I ended up with my first handicat that I named Smushball. And I sued Michelle for the veterinary bills. It wasn't about the money; she had lied to me and stepped on my animal. I was beginning to see traits of my father's principled nature shining through in my actions. Writing this book, I was laughing, thinking what kind of asshole sues a Little League, and here I was being a bigger asshole, suing a girl over a cat.

BOBBY BALDWIN

Former President and CEO of City Center and 4-Time Winner of the World Series of Poker

Shortly after this episode, I told Dan that I just saw Tom Dwan at the bar. He was having a scotch and soda and seemed distraught, and I asked him, "What's wrong Tom, did you lose a lot of money in Macau or something?"

"No. I had a good trip in Macau, I actually won money...But I lost my girlfriend."

"What do you mean you lost your girlfriend? You talking about Michelle?"

"Yeah, Michelle."

"Well, how did you lose her?"

"While I was in Macau, Dan Bilzerian fucked her."

And I said, "Tom, that's not possible. I know Michelle, she's a first-class girl, she hangs out with other girlfriends while you were outta town, but she always shuns the advances of other men, so that's not possible. Who's the idiot that told you that Dan fucked your girlfriend?"

Tom looked at me in his demure way and said, "Dan told me."

So, having nothing further to say, I told him, "Well, Tom, if you live long enough, you see it all. Good night."

CHAPTER 52

Better to Give Than Receive

I had made a ton of money but hadn't been as philanthropic as I wanted to be.

I used to take care of my grandmother by paying her bills, hanging out with her, and trying to do nice things for her as much as I could. I got her a giant TV and would hide five grand in her sock drawer every now and then. She was a crier, so whenever I did anything for her, Grandma would start weeping, and it felt good to know she appreciated it.

I had been giving her granddaughter money for the past decade as well, but that came from her asking to borrow money and me telling her I would give her the money with one condition: that she never ask for money again. I learned a good policy from my father. He told me, "Don't give loans to friends or family. If you are going to help them out, make the money a gift, or you will just end up ruining a relationship and causing nothing but animosity."

It didn't quite go as planned; she kept asking for money. Granted, she was in a difficult position being a single mother, and at the end of the day, she was family. So rather than have her go through the process of continuously asking, I just set up a direct deposit in her account every month. I noticed that doing things for people made me feel better than buying shit for myself. So I began searching for people I could help locally. I found a cancer patient who needed financial assistance and gave him twenty grand.

I saw a news article about the rapper The Game launching something called The Robin Hood Project. I messaged him to get involved. He came over to the house and told me his story, about being shot and how he had come up in life. I wondered if he was doing the charity for publicity, which a lot of celebrities do, and I always hated. But after speaking with him one-on-one, it seemed like he wanted to help people. So I decided to give away $100,000 in cash to people in need before Christmas. We worked together on a few projects, and I even got Mike the sports bettor to join in a couple times.

One family I found was a husband and wife in Las Vegas who'd adopted six children, all of whom they said had some challenge that made it unlikely they'd be adopted otherwise. Two of the children were born from a drug-addicted prostitute, and they'd suffered lasting effects. One boy had leukemia, and they were seeking $10,000 for his medical treatment. There are a lot of opportunists who lie for money, so I did some digging and grilled the father. When his story checked out, I gave him $20,000 instead. He broke into tears, and it felt really great to make such an impact. It was a relatively trivial amount of money for me, but it was almost a life-and-death matter for their son. Afterward, I felt more happiness than when winning one hundred times as much money. That was a big lesson for me.

When I was a kid, Dad had fed me the old "it's better to give than to receive" cliché. To that, I responded, "That's perfect because I love to receive, so you can just give me a bunch of presents, and we will both be happy." I didn't believe in that sappy bullshit back then, and no amount of talking could have convinced me otherwise.

Like many lessons in life, sometimes the only way to learn is through personal experience. This type of learning can lead to some real pain as you will soon see.

CHAPTER 53

Puerto Vallarta

John Racener asked me to stake him in the 2012 World Series of Poker Main Event, and I agreed to do so. But for some reason, he never came to retrieve the stake money. As a result, I didn't get my 70 percent of his $5.5 million win, and it cost me $3,882,168.

A year later, when a similar opportunity came up, I didn't take any chances.

"Hey, do you want to buy a piece of me in the Main?" a player named Jay Farber asked. "I'm selling 20 percent. How much do you want?"

"All of it," I said adamantly.

"Cool, I'll get the money when I see you next."

"No, I'll meet you right now. Where are you?"

"At Aria."

"I'll see you in thirty minutes."

Jay wasn't known as being a great poker player, but I didn't care. He went on to beat out more than 6,300 other players and took home second place in the WSOP Main Event, earning $5,174,357. My $2,000 investment netted me over a million dollars.

I sat in the front row to watch Jay play the final table of the tournament, and ESPN caught Victoria cuddling and stroking my beard. She loved beards and would absentmindedly run her hands through my bristles for hours. People later suggested that I had hired a beard petter for the event, which would not be out of the realm of possibility, I suppose. But I never saw a section for that on Craigslist.

I bought Jay a nice Audemars watch and chartered a G3 to Puerto Vallarta to celebrate the great showing. I brought a bunch of girls, two friends, and a promoter who invited even more girls. I was in the front section of the plane with a hot, tall blonde and a hot brunette with big tits. The blonde was sitting on my lap, making it clear that she and I were hooking up.

We did some shots, and the brunette, not wanting to be left out, announced that she was bisexual. This quickly led to them making out, which led to them sucking my dick. The girls got naked, and I took turns fucking them on the couch. The stewardess walked in on us, did an about-face, and walked back out. I looked over and realized everyone in back could see us because I'd forgotten to close the drapes.

I was switching condoms between girls, and blowjobs while doing so was the natural order of things. I had one foot on the seat and one on the floor as I was fucking the brunette girl's face at a downward angle while unwrapping the new rubber when the stewardess walked in again. I think she heard it get quiet during our little intermission and thought we were finished. Visibly traumatized, she stumbled back to the front, and I didn't see her again for at least an hour.

Jay told me later that he asked the stewardess if she had ever seen anything like that previously.

"Absolutely not!" the lady answered. Then she said, "But there was one time when a client asked me to cook him a meal, and when I came back, he was having sex!" She paused for a second and said, "And you know what? It was the same guy!"

There must be thousands of stewardesses working private flights. What were the odds that I would end up with the same woman catching me fucking twice? She turned out to be the same flight attendant who had worked my charter to the *Lone Survivor* set.

Our Puerto Vallarta villa was on a cliff, perched four hundred feet above the ocean with a beautiful infinity pool that seemed to just disappear into the sea. We went ziplining, chartered a yacht, scuba dove, and drank. Well, mostly we just drank.

Jay Farber in our PV villa.

The next day, a $10.8 million wire transfer from AG for my last poker win posted to my account. I was sure he was gonna pay, but I never celebrated until the money was in the bank. It made me happy, like a big warm blanket of financial security. One less thing to worry about, and one step further away from normality.

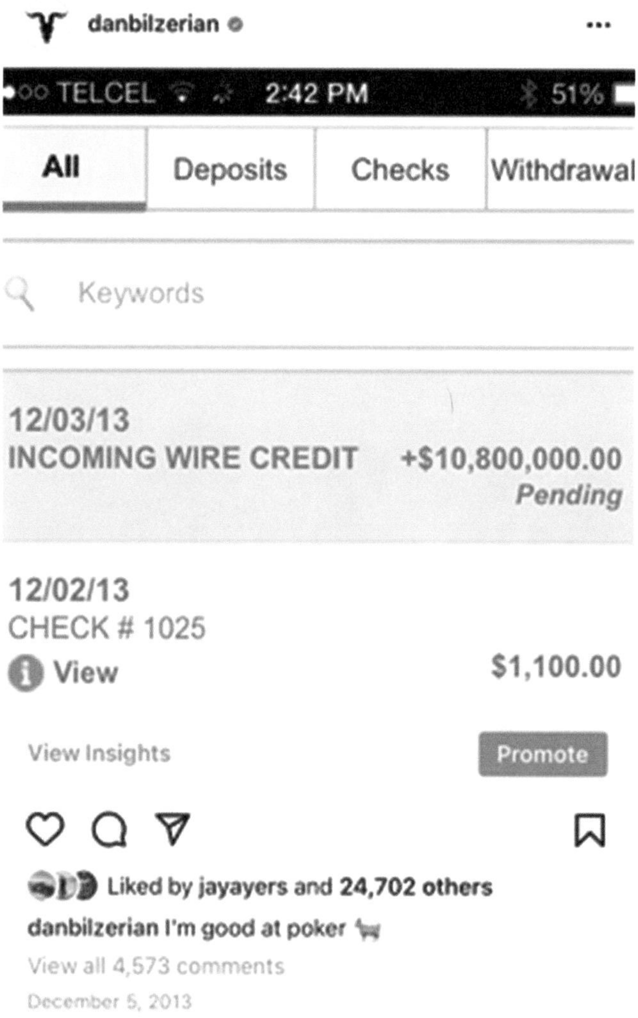

Wire from Alec Gores.

I'd been grinding super hard all year. I made stupid, ridiculous, crazy amounts of money, but I hated being stressed out all the time. Gambling is one of the most tense, nerve-wracking jobs on the planet. So I had to take trips to get away and force myself to relax, to enjoy being on top of the mountain. It was always short lived, though, because when I got to what I thought was the peak, I'd see it was only a false summit and realize I had so much further to climb.

CHAPTER 54

Five Million Minimum

The billionaire wanted to battle again, but this time with a five million-dollar minimum buy-in.

I walked into AG's house and, much to my dismay, found poker pro Mike Sexton seated next to AG.

"What's he doing here?" I asked.

"Your guy is with you." AG smiled. "I want my guy with me."

My "guy" was a casino pit boss who I'd brought to watch the dealers, not to coach me. AG wouldn't cheat, but his dealers certainly could. I should have told Mike to fuck off, but I mistakenly let him stay.

After eight hours, I was up around four million. Mike had been watching and studying me the whole time; at first it wasn't so obvious, but as the night progressed, I was the only thing he was looking at. I knew he'd be coaching AG after, so I wanted to get out of there as quickly as possible.

"I'm tired, how much longer do you want to play?" I asked.

"It's only eleven. Let's play till three or four."

"I can't. I'll do another thirty minutes. We can play again this week."

AG was pissed—I could see it in his face—but playing with a poker pro staring at me and dissecting my every move was bullshit.

"I don't want to quit, but if you want to freeze the chips, we can continue the match later," AG proposed.

This meant he wouldn't pay me the four million, and the next game, I would start with $9,000,000 in front of me. I'd beaten the guy for around twenty-five million at this point, so I said sure no problem and went home to regroup, figuring the longer I stayed, the more information Mike would give AG.

Sure enough, when I returned, the billionaire was playing better. Mike had given him the answer to my hyper aggressive strategy; AG was now fighting back, reraising me and bluffing. So I had to shift gears and play more defensively because I couldn't afford to play a game of chicken for ten million dollars. I was back playing the guessing game like in Malibu. On top of that, every time we got into a big pot, AG peppered me with questions or offered deals to try and get information. Normally in a casino, I would just ignore this or tell the guy to fuck off. However, this was a more delicate and complicated dynamic, being that we were both pretending to be playing a friendly gentleman's game while secretly trying to take each other's heads off with the added caveat that we were playing on credit in his home, and I wanted to get paid.

Toward the end of the night, I had over $18,000,000 in front of me, and AG had me covered with his usual $50,000,000. I was on edge because I knew if AG said, "all in," then I would have an eighteen million-dollar decision to make.

I was dealt ace six of diamonds. I flopped a nut flush draw and raised AG. He reraised me back to $2,000,000, and I called. The turn was a diamond, giving me the nuts, the best possible hand. My heart was racing when he bet $3,000,000 into me. I didn't want the board to pair or another diamond to kill my action, so I made it $6,000,000, leaving me with $10,000,000 behind. *Holy shit* I thought, *this will be a thirty six million-dollar pot if he goes all in.*

I waited quietly for AG to act; instead, he started in with the questions again.

"I have a really strong hand; I think I'm going to have to go all-in. Do you want to do a deal?"

"What is your offer?" I replied.

"You can take your bet back and give me the pot."

"No."

"I have a strong hand. I can't just call. I might just have to go all in," he said, clearly posturing to negotiate a better deal. "Would you run it out for what's in the pot and not do any more betting?"

I declined all his offers. But he kept blitzing me with nonsense for about twenty minutes, asking me to show him one card. He seemed really weak, and I thought he would fold if I didn't show. I also knew this was a good spot to bluff with a naked ace of diamonds. So after he hounded me forever, I showed him the ace. If I had shown him my six, I figured he would know I had a flush. It turned out to be a bad show because he flipped over a king high flush. I couldn't believe it!

In poker, when you are playing heads-up, there are certain spots when you just gotta get the money in the middle. Kings preflop and second nut flushes are hands where if the other guy has the one hand that beats you, you just gotta give him the money. It's referred to as a cold deck or a cooler.

I thought he had two pair or three of a kind. I never in a million years considered that he would be scared with a second nut flush. If I had his cards, I'd be dying to get my chips in the pot. I never dreamed he had such a strong hand. It was crazy how *scared money* this guy played, being as rich as he was, but that's also why I was able to run him over. I literally won almost every dollar off this guy bluffing; he folded *way* too much.

AG struggled with the decision about this one hand for so long that I left the table and sat in the bathroom. As I sat on that toilet, all I could think was *You dumb bastard, you just cost yourself $13 million dollars showing him that ace*. It took almost an hour before he finally gave in and folded. I felt like an idiot for screwing up the biggest hand of my poker career. But it was hard to be too mad because I still ended up winning $12 million. Plus, I think he would've folded regardless. At least that's what I tell myself so I can sleep at night.

The wire hit the next day.

CHAPTER 55

A Sign

We were seated in Jack Nicholson's famed floor seats watching the Lakers.

At halftime, my friend and I walked around the court to go to the bathroom. The floor seats were always lined with rich guys and celebrities. I saw the film director Antoine Fuqua sitting in the corner by the basket, so I went over to say hello.

"Hey, I was a stunt guy in *Equalizer*, good to see you again."

"Yeah, I remember," he said. "But who the fuck are you?"

"I'm Dan. We met through Lin Oeding."

"Yeah, yeah, I know." He kind of squinted his eyes. "But who the fuck *are* you? I've never met a stunt guy who wears a three hundred thousand-dollar watch and has better seats for the Lakeshow than I do. What do you really do for a living? And don't tell me a stunt man either." He started laughing.

"Well, I also play poker."

"Shit! I gotta start playing poker then." He chuckled.

Right as Antoine and I shook hands and said goodbye, a guy who had been waiting came up and asked me for a photo, then a couple others did the same. Antoine's eyes got big, and I remember the look on his face; I've never seen someone more confused and curious. I hardly ever left my house since the chefs and assistants ran all the errands, so this was the first time that fans had asked for photos. I figured it was a fluke, but it was a sign.

That whole interaction was surprising; I didn't realize Antoine had picked up on all those things, but it felt good to be perceived as important. I was also usually so busy bragging to the world that this was the first time I had a slow reveal with someone. It reminded me of something my mother told me when I was younger. She said, "It's much more impressive to find out someone is rich when they haven't mentioned it." Needless to say, it was too late; that train had left the station, and it was about to really start picking up steam.

PART 4

Fame

CHAPTER 56

The Plan

We win 42 mil was the text I received from Rick Salomon. I had 25 percent of his action, so my share was $10.5 million.

I was on a ski trip with Victoria when I saw the text. We were watching a movie with Bobby Baldwin and his girlfriend in the theater room of a log cabin in Montana. The excitement hit me hard. I was finally allowed to get happy and fully take it in; I wasn't in a poker game, and I didn't have to mute my emotions or worry about losing it back. It felt amazing to win money and not suffer any of the stress. I had made over $23 million in the last couple of weeks and didn't even have to play one game.

One thing I regret about that time in my life was that I didn't pause to appreciate it. Success should, ideally, be like climbing a mountain. Take a break every so often and really absorb the view. Appreciate that progress, then climb higher, and savor the next view even more. I didn't do that. I climbed and climbed as fast as I could for ten years, and I didn't stop to look at shit. On that vacation, when I got that text, I finally stopped. I took it all in...

I was in very rare air.

I felt like Johnny Depp in *Blow* when he ran out of rooms to store his cash. I had giant safes in all my residences and safety deposit boxes at all the banks and Vegas casinos. Everything was full and couldn't handle another stack. I had so much gold stored in one of my boxes at Aria that the female cashier on duty legitimately hurt her back when she pulled it out. They had to pay her worker's comp for her injury. One safe had $5 million in cash in it, and it's not like in the movies where that fits in a big suitcase; $5 million takes up a ton of space.

I bought a Gulfstream jet and spent a million dollars just on the Wi-Fi and custom interior. I had a multimillion-dollar watch collection, millions in gold, guns, and Bitcoin. I'd bought a Lamborghini, a couple of Range Rovers, a Bentley, a Ferrari, and the first $900,000 Mercedes-Benz Brabus G63 6x6 in the country. I had so many cars that the garages in all three homes were full, and some had to be parked on the street. I literally bought anything and everything that I'd ever wanted, and it didn't even make a dent in my bank account.

By now, most of the high-stakes gambling world was on to me. They knew I was winning huge amounts. It's hard to act like you aren't making your living playing poker when you play all the time and make tens of millions in a night. I didn't care; I was sick of the stress and tired of pandering to the suckers. I'd made enough money. It was time to take on a new challenge, climb a different mountain.

I saw how a super-rich, jaded degenerate like Sam reacted to Paris Hilton. I saw how a billionaire like AG reacted to Mark Wahlberg. I saw how the women at my pool parties behaved whenever a celebrity entered the property. Fame was access. It was validation. It was power. And it had the added bonus of compelling women to fuck me with less effort on my part. Fame was a whole *setup* in it of itself, and the only thing I didn't really have.

I'd had a taste of it, and I mentioned it to my father since he'd had his time in the spotlight. In the '80s, he was on the cover of all the major newspapers, for good and for bad. So I was curious about his thoughts on the matter. Our relationship had improved as I got older, and I would regularly ask for his advice. I wouldn't usually take it, but I always listened. He told me, "Son, you either want to be totally anonymous or super famous. Don't ever get caught in-between like I did. Being well known will put a target on your back, but it won't give you immunity. Only serious fame can provide immunity. The Feds don't want to take down household heroes like Denzel Washington or Brad Pitt."

It was too late to be anonymous and that sounded boring anyway. My father was right, this wasn't something I wanted to half ass. I'd already started down the road, now it was time to see how far I could go.

There were many ways to go about this, one being the standard dumbass reality show. A lot of production companies were reaching out pitching ideas, but like the shows you see on TV, everything is staged, none of it is real. I knew this was a guaranteed recipe for fame, but sacrificing my authenticity to get attention felt like selling my soul.

I would not be fake.

I would not be politically correct.

I would not sell out, and I would not apologize for who I was or what I was doing. I was going to do it, but it was gonna be on my terms.

I always wanted to be a rock star when I was a kid, but I never wanted to learn to play guitar.

It was bucket list time. I was gonna buy all the toys I ever wanted, travel, do exciting shit, and fuck a lot of hot girls. Basically, everything I had dreamed about as a kid. And I would post it all on social media for every other guy with a similar fantasy to come along for the ride.

I hired digital media strategist Ben Stevens to secure digital press and coverage. Then I hired a hungry talented camera guy named Jay Rich who'd been relentless about working with me.

"Here's what I want," I told Jay. "Get candid, authentic fifteen-second highlight reels of what I do. I'm not going to set up shots, and I'm not doing any retakes. You'll have one chance to get it." I also warned him to avoid interfering. My life took precedence over a video of my life.

I was about to kick things into a much higher gear and money was going be the catalyst.

JAY RICH

Photographer/Videographer

How did I link up with Dan? Well, I kept harassing him until he finally answered one of my emails and told me to come on over. At this time, Dan only had ten thousand followers, but he reminded me of a young Hugh Hefner. Coming from a preacher background for twelve years, having a bitter divorce, and not going to my first nightclub until I was thirty years old, this was very different than the church world I came from.

It was fascinating when I first started with him because he blew up quick. He's been in a few films, but he wasn't a superstar, he can't sing, for sure can't dance...He didn't even have the biggest house. So why did he cause so much chaos on the Internet? Why was he getting more attention than any actor or athlete? It was simply because he was very intelligent and had this "I don't give a fuck" gift. It's a gift that I've only seen a few people have, like the Kardashians, Kanye, and Donald Trump. He just doesn't give a fuck about what people say. I remember, at times, I would tell him, "You should delete that comment, you should change that caption. You're offending people."

He'd always tell me, "Fuck 'em. Never allow anyone to control your thoughts, voice, or vision." He always told me, "As long as they talking, you're growing."

We've had many viral videos and photos, and he never wanted me to Photoshop him—he just wanted me to capture moments. I saw so much fake shit in LA that I learned quick you can't compare people to things you see on TV, except Dan. Dan is just Dan.

Let's talk about girls for a second. He wouldn't say much when the truckloads of girls would come in. So I'd talk to most of the girls first. Some girls would come just to see what the hype was about. Some would come to get a career overnight. Most wanted revenge on an ex. And others actually physically just liked him. Now I know a lot of people, but I've never seen truckloads like this. At the time, the biggest ticket was if he posted you on his IG—a girl could all of a sudden have a million-dollar career overnight. They'd get shit from their ex-boyfriends, current boyfriends, from their families, and friends, but if they could stomach it, they'd become an Instagram success overnight.

Unlike most of the girls, I got a chance to have a lot of great conversations with Dan and also a lot of arguments. I found out quick that Dan is a very intelligent man. His psychology and the way he views things was definitely on a different level than what I had encountered before I met him. Him being a white man, me being a black man, and him still taking me in and showing me the ropes about business, content, and marketing was something I wasn't used to. I got lucky enough to be in a lot of business meetings and to watch him break down situations and deals to a point where the other person just had no rebuttal.

I wasn't happy all of the time I was with Dan, but he was so real, and everything he did on IG was real. He was so bluntly honest. I was tired of hanging around people who just lied all the time, so I could admire that side of Dan. He would call me fat, and these days, people get offended. He would always say, "You can't change how tall you are, you can't change the size of your feet. If you can't sing, if you have no rhythm...but you can change the way your body looks." He would tell girls the same. Some would take it personal. Some changed their life for the better. In my mind, he was always looking out for my health, but I'd always clap back at him and say, "I'm a lot healthier than you. You've had two heart attacks."

Those are the things I liked about Dan. The brutal honesty. The late night talks. The biz advice. The spiritual conversations.

I've always been an underdog my whole life, and I've heard so many people talk shit about Dan. It made me want to understand the psychology. Many people will write many different things about Dan. But if you ever got a chance to get close to him, there's nothing that he wouldn't do for his friends. He never posted any of the charity work he did; it's almost like he wanted people to think he was a bad guy. All in all, why Dan never allowed anyone to see the real side of him, I'll never know. Because I think that's the person you'd really, really like if you hate Dan.

CHAPTER 57

Racing Exotics

I chartered a helicopter to take Sam, Victoria, and me to a private track day at Thermal Raceway in California. As soon as we left the ground, Sam pulled out a crumpled hundred-dollar bill that contained a mound of cocaine. He spilled the blow all over the seat and his black jeans, which highlighted the residue like a black light reveals semen. As he lifted the bill toward his nostril for a snort, the cold air from one of the overhead vents got hold of it, and instantly the mound disappeared. He looked like the *Peanuts* character Pig Pen with a big dust cloud of cocaine swirling around him in the air. The pilot turned to see what was going on.

"This aircraft is filthy!" Sam yelled. "There is blow all over the place! What kinda show are you running?"

The pilot wasn't fazed. He ignored the question and continued to fly.

At Thermal, we had to sit through a safety briefing. They were pretty anal about track behavior, unlike Willow Springs Raceway where you could do whatever you wanted. Last time we went to Willow, I hired ten poker girls to be our cheerleaders, complete with pom poms, crop tops, and tiny skirts. We ignored them; they were just there to make the video better. Everyone focused on racing. In fact, the girls received so little attention that one of them ended up fucking a track employee in the bathroom.

I started my day with a few warm-up laps to learn the track. While I was trying to memorize the apexes and braking points, the rest of the guys just went full retard. It was a total shit show.

Tony, the loudmouth tattooed Persian who'd set up the track event, drove Sam's Porsche Carrera GT and almost collided with Sam in his vintage 1969 Shelby GT500 on the first turn before spinning it off the track. Sam screamed at him.

“You almost crashed two of my cars at once. You almost cost me two million on a corner!”

A few minutes later, Tony’s buddy Vinny, an actual male gigolo, put the half million-dollar Aventador his sixty-five-year-old sugar momma bought him into the wall. He bent the rims, ripped the paint off, and filled the entire car with rocks. This didn’t go over well with the track management, and they pulled us aside to explain that our behavior was completely unacceptable.

Clearly, the lecture went in one ear and out the other because a few minutes later, Sam was attempting to do burnouts in the pit lane where the speed limit was five miles per hour. Sam was a terrible driver who didn't really understand the mechanics of a manual transmission. He'd rev the engine, but instead of dropping the clutch, he slowly released it, causing the car to lurch forward. Sam immediately slammed on the breaks, and the cycle repeated. It looked from afar like his car got jacked by a teenager suffering from cerebral palsy.

After five minutes of doing his best to burn up his clutch, Sam, in all his infinite wisdom, came blasting down the track going the wrong direction at over sixty miles an hour in reverse with his head hung out the window like Ace Ventura. This was the last straw; the safety officer lost his mind and shut it down.

Sam had destroyed both of his cars. He'd completely blown the motor on his Porsche. The GT500 had smoke billowing from under the hood; the clutch was fried, and it would only drive in reverse.

While my assistant was trying to figure out what to do with the undrivable vehicles, Sam retired to the club house to do blow. The owner of the track walked in, and instead of hiding the coke, Sam told him that he'd built a track for women and Priuses and explained that he would never come there again. To which the owner replied, "If you don't get off my fucking property, I'm going to call the police."

I posted a good video from the track day, and people like to see guys actually racing exotic cars instead of just showcasing them, so it was well received.

CHAPTER 58

Steve Aoki

I met Steve Aoki around the start of Victory Poker when he was an up-and-coming DJ, and very quickly we became friends.

STEVE AOKI

Two-Time Grammy Nominated DJ, Music Producer

One thing you should know about Dan is we're cut in a lot of the same ways. On the outside, it might look like we live big, exciting lives, and in a lot of ways, we do. But in a lot of ways, we're also pretty private. A lot of folks don't know this about me because of the way I am onstage, but I wouldn't say I have too many close friends, and I'm betting Dan would say the same about himself. We're both always on the lookout and move around with our guard up. That's how it is when people always seem to want something from you. It's hard to know who to trust.

But I trust Dan. He has my back. I love the guy to death. I feel more connected to him than I do to almost anybody outside my family.

He pushes me in ways I'd never think to push myself. What people see is how he pushes me in a thrill-seeking way, chasing adventure, although what I really appreciate is the way he challenges me to think. Like with poker. That's how we first met—in the poker room at the Wynn, 2009 or so. I'd come to Vegas to DJ. I had a small following back then but was beginning to make a name for myself—a long way from making the kind of noise I do today. I happened to sit next to Dan at a small stakes table. I was just learning the game, but Dan was used to playing for higher stakes. We got to talking.

Now, you meet a lot of people at the poker table. Over the years, I've met a bunch of cool people from all walks of life, only it's not like you actually become friends with these people. They're your poker buddies, that's all. But with Dan, it was different. We clicked. At first, it was mostly about poker, but then we started hanging out, and it was about chasing these great adventures, challenging each other.

I played my first big-time poker games because of Dan. It was four or five years after we'd met, and I was still feeling my way around the table. I went to watch Dan play at the Phil Ivey room in the Aria—a $100/$200 game, but the blinds don't really mean that much. Right away, the straddles ramp up to $400/$800, $800/$1,600. I didn't think I'd ever be at that level, but after a while, Dan turned away from the table and said, "You should play. It's a good game."

I said, "No way, man. Not my speed."

He said, "I think you'll crush it. These guys are terrible!"

No way was I ready to play at this kind of table. Almost everyone had a million bucks in chips in front of them. I was intimidated by that kind of money, but Dan thought I could handle it. He stood from the table and said, "Take my seat, man. I'm gonna sit out a while."

You have to realize, this was an invitation-only table. I had no money on me. I'd only come down to hang with Dan, but he *must have figured it was my time. He knew I was ready before I knew I was ready. The money was a problem, though, because there was a $20,000 minimum. It worked out; one of the guys with the big stacks said he would loan it to me.*

He said, "If you win, you can pay me back now. If you lose, pay me back later. We'll figure it out."

Dan just kind of disappeared. I assumed he was hanging back, leaving me alone to do my thing, so I didn't really think about it. I trusted his trust in me—only I couldn't see my way to playing a hand. I folded Ace-Queen. I folded a small pair. I folded my big blind. Everyone was raising all around the table. If I played a hand, I thought I'd get eaten alive.

Finally, I was dealt King-Queen, so I called the $800 straddle, thinking I'd at least see the flop, but then the guy behind me raised to $5,000. Another guy called, and the betting came back to me. I looked around to see if I could spot Dan, secretly hoping a look from him would tell me what to do, but he was nowhere, man. It was crazy! So I breathed deep and called.

At this point, the pot was over $15,000. The flop came Queen-Four-Six. It felt to me like my Queens were good, but then the guy to the right of me pushed all-in, with over $1 million in chips. I only had about $12,000 left at this point; I'd been bled out by the blinds and a couple calls. I was pot committed, and the only move was to call. Then the action was on the guy to my left, who took a long, long time to act. He was thinking about it and thinking about it and finally folded Ace-Queen. Thank God.

Once again, I scanned the room for Dan, but he'd left me on my own. Later, I'd find out he was watching from a distance to see how I'd handle the pressure, but I was on my own, heads-up against the guy who'd gone all in. He turned over a Three-Five—a straight draw. He didn't make his straight, and I took down the biggest pot I'd ever seen, and I had Dan to thank for it. When I caught up with him later, he didn't buy that he'd had anything to do with it.

He'd seen how it went down and said, "That was all you, man. You were ready."

Maybe I was, but here's the thing: I don't think I'd have ever realized it if Dan hadn't stepped away from the table like that and handed me his seat.

Like I said, he pushes me. He believes in me—and, yeah, he's competitive as hell, but he can dial it down and play poker with my mom and my sister and my niece who's just learning the game for $1/$2 stakes. Those games seem to mean as much to him as when he's playing for big money.

Same with chess. He's got years of experience. He's good... really good. Me, I'm still learning, and Dan screws me hard—just kind of bitch-slaps me around the board. He beat me every time, until one night, late, we sat down to play at my house, and I threw him an opening he wasn't familiar with. He gave me this kind of look that said, "What the fuck is that?" It threw him off, and I set up my pieces in a way that put me ahead by a little, and I hung on to win. I couldn't believe it. And the thing about Dan is he can be crazy competitive, but he didn't seem to mind losing to me that one time. It was like a Mr. Miyagi moment. The student becomes the master...That's how it is with us, you know.

What people see is the stuff we put on Instagram: midnight bicycle rides at Red Rock...taking Can-Ams through the desert to a small bar in the middle of nowhere... doing flips into his stunt pillow or my foam pit...living on the edge, you know. And that's a part of what we share, a big part, but if you look beneath all of that wild, adventure-type stuff, you see this thirst to live life bigger, louder...smarter. To think more deeply, more confidently. That comes from Dan. He's always telling me I should slow down my DJ-ing and start doing fun shit with him all the time, and maybe he's right. Or maybe the key is finding a better balance. Either way, he helps me to live life to the fullest, and I am so damn grateful for his friendship.

A lot had changed in the last four years; I'd more than 10Xed my net worth and garnered a couple million followers on social media in the process. Steve had blown up too and was now pulling down $100,000 a night at Hakkasan. He invited me to his show, but before taking the stage, we met up in his hotel room. When I walked in, I was surprised to see Waka Flocka and Flavor Flav hanging in the living room. But that's Steve; he is always collaborating with artists and honing his craft. We did a couple shots before the club security escorted us through the Hakkasan kitchen and into the DJ booth.

Steve and I crouched down in the booth as the opening DJ got the crowd hyped for the headliner. When the bass dropped, Steve and I popped up, and the crowd went nuts. I jumped up and down with him for a bit and then quickly moved into the corner to watch the show.

Steve climbed up on stage and said something on the mic about me being there, and the crowd cheered. All of a sudden, the lights turned to me. Steve reached his hand out and told me to come on stage. This was totally unexpected, and I was nervous about going up there with no purpose. I wasn't a performer, I didn't really like crowds, and all I could think was *What in the fuck am I supposed to do, just stand there and look like an idiot?* This was Steve's job, and he was clearly good at it, so I just trusted that he had a plan.

I reached out and grabbed his hand. Steve pulled as I climbed the speakers to get on the stage. I looked at the crowd. People were yelling my name, and there was a sea of phone lights pointed at me. I smiled and held my arm out to the people, wondering what the fuck I was supposed to do next. He quickly handed me a magnum bottle, and I followed his lead, spraying down the crowd with champagne. They gave us cakes to throw at his fans as well. We pegged grown men with full birthday cakes, and they were super happy for the experience. The anxiety was gone, the people were stoked, and I was having fun.

I noticed an inflatable life raft being passed around by the crowd. "Jump in that!" Steve yelled at me.

"Are you serious?"

"Hell yeah, get in there!"

I wasn't sure how this was going to go, but stage diving was on my bucket list, so I figured fuck it. I took a flying leap off the stage and dove headfirst into the raft, just like we used to do in BUD/S minus the ice water. I stood up and held onto the front rope with my left hand in the air like a bull rider. The crowd carried me around the entire venue. It was some real rock star shit.

The goal for the past years of my life was to get in games, which required some bullshitting and trying to look like a loser. Now that my goal was to have fun and enjoy life, I was finally able to be authentic and be myself. It felt good. These were some of the best times of my life—I was doing amazing shit, getting laid was seamless, and my plan was working well.

The talent agency ICM started representing me, and they threw me some cool opportunities here and there. In April, they called with a pitch from *Hustler* for an article on me and a photo shoot with porn stars.

Sounded like fun...

CHAPTER 59

Throwing a Porn Star Off My Roof

The crew from *Hustler* rolled up with two porn stars, a camera crew, and a reporter. The producer had a bunch of cheesy ideas for pictures, most of which I declined. They got a shot of me cleaning one of my engraved Colt .45 pistols with Victoria in a bikini while the porn girls played ping-pong butt-naked in the background. There was a photo of me dealing cards to the nude girls at the poker table. For the climax of the shoot, they wanted me to throw a skinny porn starlet named Janice Griffith into the pool. They asked me to put her on my shoulders and throw her over my head, but that seemed dangerous from eighteen feet in the air.

"I think that's a bad idea. What if I hip toss her from my waist?"

Janice agreed, the crew liked the idea, and so up to the rooftop we went. They didn't teach porn star tossing in my judo classes, so I wasn't entirely sure how to go about this. But we played around and decided that I would hold her back with my left arm to stabilize and use my right arm to shotput her as far as I could. I experimented with hand placement, and basically, I had to throw her by the pussy. It was exciting,

Hustler *photo shoot.*

and she seemed to be having a good time, given that she was strangely wet. I don't think I've ever felt a girl that drenched. I'd like to blame the accident on a lack of grip due to the lubrication, but that wasn't the case.

"If you grab me, you're going to pull us both over the edge," I said. "Whatever you do, don't hold on to me." She understood, and we did a couple *dry runs* to rehearse. Everything went well until the very last second. In the video, you can see her arms in the air, but suddenly as I was throwing her, she freaked and grabbed my shirt. I almost went over the edge. It took every ounce of my strength to throw her hard enough so she would clear the concrete edge of the pool. A nine-inch chunk of fabric she'd torn from my shirt floated down. As Janice neared splashdown, her foot clipped the edge of the pool.

The crew dumped their gear and rushed over as Janice climbed out of the water. She said her foot hurt, and we urged her to go to the hospital; I even offered to drive her. But she declined and said she was fine.

My buddy Alan posted the video, and it went viral. Every news outlet in the world picked up the story. That bad press got me a lot of international attention because once one major outlet runs a story, everyone else picks it up and regurgitates it. TMZ wrote about me for the first time, leading its article with the snide line: "Instagram's Biggest Playboy can add Instagram's biggest dumbass to his resume." The headlines were misleading—"Dan Bilzerian throws porn star off his roof"—giving the impression that I'm just chucking bitches off my roof for no reason. But in twenty-four hours, I gained over five hundred thousand additional followers on Facebook, almost a million on Instagram, and somewhere in there became Instagram's biggest playboy.

Once all the media attention poured in, along with references to my net worth in each article, Janice suddenly had to go to the hospital because she was hurt so badly. Despite posting a picture of her on Twitter with three dicks in her two days later, she found an attorney who claimed lost wages as a result of being unable to work. In actuality, she should have been arrested for attempted homicide. You can clearly see her try and kill me in the video.

Good thing I was poker buddies and racing pals with crazy-ass power attorney Tom Goldstein, Esquire, legal mind extraordinaire, arguer of almost fifty cases before the United States Supreme Court.

He wrote the porn star's attorney one of the most infamous legal missives ever written. It dripped with sarcasm and disdain, and Tom now says it is his most well-known piece of work. Go ahead and read it for yourself.

GOLDSTEIN & RUSSELL, P.C.

202-362-0636 | 866-574-2033 (fax) | goldsteinrussell.com

May 12, 2014

Shoham J. Solouki
Solouki Savoy, LLP
316 W. 2nd St.
Suite 1200
Los Angeles, CA 90012

Dear Mr. Solouki,

I represent Dan Bilzerian and received your letter on behalf of Janice Griffith.

I am genuinely sorry that your client was hurt. No one wants to see anyone injured. But the suggestion that Mr. Bilzerian is responsible for that injury is embarrassing. I'm sorry she made you suggest it in writing.

The whole tragi-comic thing is of course on tape. Given that you agreed to send Mr. Bilzerian a threat to sue, I can only assume you must not have seen it.

It shows facts your client always omits: she was under contract to Hustler and agreed with Hustler's request that she be photographed while being thrown off the roof. I always thought that this kind of thing was Photoshopped instead. Perhaps Hustler's editorial standards would not permit it. Perhaps she insists on doing all her own stunts. I really do not know.

In all events, she agreed. Very few people I know would make that choice. But there it is. And chronologically, she's an adult competent to make it. Hustler and your client asked Mr. Bilzerian to be the thrower, and we can all agree that was the better end of the deal.

So like your client, the facts of the claim won't, quite, fly. The tape shows the two carefully practicing this flight of fancy under Hustler's direction, and your client expressly agreeing to go ahead. In legal lingo, she assumed the risk.

But maybe I'm not creative enough. Maybe your client's theory is that Mr. Bilzerian negligently violated the established standard of reasonable care for one who throws a porn actor off a roof into a pool during a photo shoot for an adult magazine. I'll let that one sink in for a moment.

But there's more. The tape shows that she did the one thing that she had been explicitly told in advance would stop her from making it to the pool: she grabbed Mr. Bilzerian's shirt. Now, I'm no physicist. And it won't surprise you that I don't have any relevant personal experience. So I don't know the precise amount of thrust it takes to heave someone across to a pool a floor below. But I'm also not blind. And it is apparent that Mr. Bilzerian's *shirt* did not reach out and grab *her*.

As I said, I don't doubt your client was genuinely hurt when she clipped the edge of the pool. But there are some natural questions about just how awful those injuries were. Her prompt text to Mr. Bilzerian's assistant demanding $85,000 for her hurt foot inevitably leaves the regrettable misimpression that she is nothing more than a crass opportunist.

Thankfully, she does seem to be getting on. I don't run in the same circles, but like a lot of people, I do have Twitter. And with all due respect, she overshares. I can't bear to describe most of what is on her eponymous account, thejaniceXXX. I will save you the embarrassment of looking for yourself. Just trust me that her recent missives with the hashtags "#deepthroat," "#fatpussies," and "#NSFW" (the others are SFW?) suggest that her career is gangbusters. Indeed, I doubt the exclusive interviews with TMZ that have come from these events could have hurt.

Maybe your client will think this letter is unduly harsh. After all, I've never met her. I'm not at all familiar with her oeuvre. If my life depended on it, I could not tell you what phrase she has tattooed on her left breast. Nonetheless, I feel my tone is justified. I didn't send a letter threatening to sue her on an obviously ridiculous claim.

So if your client sues Mr. Bilzerian, she will obviously lose. But please don't let her believe that since you may well have a claim against Hustler, there's no downside to tacking him on as another deep-pocketed defendant who might settle just to make her go away. Mr. Bilzerian will never, ever permit the case to be resolved prior to the inevitable judgment in his favor.

If she sues, the complaint will be sanctionably frivolous. Your client should just box up almost every last bit of her property (please exclude all videos and photographs, as well as the seemingly inevitable small yappy dog) and drop it off with you in safe-keeping for Mr. Bilzerian. After he receives the judgment in his favor, he will have it all delivered to him. Then he will probably blow it up with a mortar in the desert.

I enjoyed our brief correspondence.

Very truly yours,

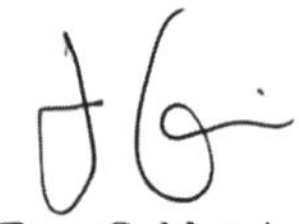

Tom Goldstein

I can't say it helped my case, but it was certainly worth the laughs.

TOM GOLDSTEIN

Supreme Court Litigator, Teacher at Harvard Law School

I've argued almost fifty cases in the Supreme Court. But Janice Griffith's infamous failure to launch is how I came to write the thing I'm best known for in the law.

The pages of Dan's are filled with dozens of stories that are at least as bizarre as that one. I suppose my perspective is different from most people in these pages because Dan and I go back to way before he was famous (to when he was just "Tampa Dan") and because I always skipped the crazy parties.

But a bunch of times I came by the next day—to make sure nobody was dead. And nobody ever was, so far as I'm allowed to say. And he's never been convicted of a serious criminal offense that hasn't been either expunged or sealed by court order.

Over the decades, we've done plenty of desert driving, firing automatic weapons, paintballing, and playing poker (net winner) and chess (I'm hopeless). I'm lucky enough to say that he's one of my best friends.

This book legitimately takes you behind the scenes of the crazy days and nights that Dan creates with the snap of his fingers. But if I have a criticism, it's that the book doesn't give you a sense of just how smart and loyal Dan is. That's true for several reasons. Filling pages with the details of business negotiations and hours-long calls talking buddies through their problems just isn't sexy. Dan also knows how to work his image and celebrity maybe better than anyone in the world. And he isn't interested in getting you—or anybody else—to like him. Almost the opposite.

The book also reads as if Dan has been the same weed-smoking, gun-toting, multiple-girl-banging dude from the day he slithered out of his mom's womb as @danbilzerian with a fully-grown beard. In reality, he evolves more than anybody I know. That's good because some of his early thinking was honestly really stupid. But he is always thinking. And when he says "I'm no smarter than you"—that's the one and only part of the book that's bullshit.

CHAPTER 60

Flipping the Fame Switch

Hamza, a rich Arab, invited me to Cannes for the famous film festival. He claimed his mother owned a hundred-million-dollar mansion right next to the hotel that serves as the epicenter for the festivities. If we got there and split up clubbing costs, he'd take care of all other expenses. Sounded good, but the trip got off to a rocky start.

My plane was getting a custom interior installed, so I decided to save the three hundred grand and fly commercial for the first time in years. I figured, let someone else deal with pilots, flight plans, and the offended stewardess who always seemed to catch me fucking on chartered jets. What's the worst that could happen?

Upon arrival, I discovered the airline lost all my luggage. I wildly swung between furious anger and panicked shock. The lady at the counter couldn't have cared less. She acted like it was no big deal to be stranded halfway across the world without so much as a Quaalude or a clean shirt. There was over five hundred thousand dollars in watches alone in that luggage, and she was talking five hundred-dollar travel vouchers.

The next thing I found out was that Hamza's mother wouldn't allow us to stay in her mansion because of renovations. Things were not going as planned.

"We can stay on my yacht," he suggested.

His vessel was an eighty-foot speedboat, not something suitable for several dudes to share for two weeks. I told Hamza this was horseshit and he'd better figure something out. He found a 154-foot yacht that'd cost around a million plus the cost of gas, food, etc. for the two weeks. Seemed expensive, so I texted Mike the sports bettor to see if he wanted to come. He was in, and we agreed to split the cost three ways.

We went to dinner that night at a restaurant/lounge on the water. To my surprise, people began coming over asking, "Can I make photo with you?" to which I replied, "Sure, no problem."

Then an American guy introduced himself as an entertainment manager. He said he represented the actor Ron Perlman, the star of *Hellboy* and *Sons of Anarchy*.

"Would you mind if Ron came over and said hello?"

"Sure, send him over," I replied.

Ron was super cool and said he wanted me to be in a new movie about three generations of soldiers: a grandfather who was a World War II vet, a middle generation as a grunt who was in 'Nam played by Ron, and he was pitching me to be his son who served in the Gulf War. Our conversation was repeatedly interrupted by people wanting a picture with me, which was completely new and bizarre. I took the pictures for a few minutes until someone finally asked Ron for one.

"Are you sure you want me and not him?" Ron asked the fan jokingly.

We finished talking, exchanged numbers, and Ron headed out. "What the fuck just happened?" I wondered. An A-list celebrity was sitting here, and people only wanted to interact with me. It was like a *Twilight Zone* episode. I had about 2.5 million followers on Instagram and half that on Facebook, but people were going crazy. I was usually in my bubble and never went out in public, so I had no clue that I was becoming this object of interest in real life.

All the press that I thought was bad, like throwing the porn star off the roof and her suing me, had actually served me. The media was now calling me the king of Instagram, which sounded really fucking lame, but people relentlessly telling me that I was their hero felt good. Either way, the plan was working.

We took some European models back to the boat, and I hooked up with one of them and then her friend thirty minutes later. Zero effort.

We went out virtually every night, and I had the same experience each time—guys wanting to shake my hand or take a selfie with me and girls smiling while migrating closer. Even Rick Ross knew who I was, which was wild because I'd been listening to his music for years. It was like I flipped a switch, and all of a sudden, everyone knew who I was.

Rick Ross.

Hamza took me to a twenty-five thousand-dollar a person black-tie event, which only reminded me what I didn't want to do. This "old money" crowd was all about rules. There were rules about what to wear, what forks to use, where you could sit, and what kind of language was appropriate. I wanted no part of that nonsense. After an hour, I went back to our yacht and threw a real party. We invited a few guys and had a couple promoters bring a ton of European models.

The luxury fashion brand Roberto Cavalli hosted their yacht party the same night a few boats down. I'd guess it was a similar vibe to the black-tie event because a lot of their models left and came to our boat. I walked down the dock with Justin Bieber and watched the paparazzi swarm him. I'd started getting attention, but it was nothing like what that kid was experiencing. The paparazzi were very obnoxious. I didn't envy that; I felt bad for him. So I gave him a Quaalude and got the boy laid.

Justin Bieber.

It was a memorable evening because I lived a lifelong dream of mine: having sex with a stranger without saying a word. The girl was an Eastern Bloc high fashion model with high cheek bones and a perfect jawline. I saw her standing at the bar, staring directly at me with these big blue eyes. I stared back at her. When she didn't look away, I walked over, took her hand, and led her upstairs. Only for a moment was there any awkwardness because she said something, and I didn't respond. I wanted to see if I could pull this off. And I did. I didn't say one word until we were finished.

I'd fucked a couple girls prior and had backups on the couch, so I didn't really care if it failed, and that's probably why it succeeded. I've found the less you care, the better you'll do.

The more shit I did, the more confident I became. I started pushing conventional boundaries. A girl flirted with me at a beach club in the middle of the day, and I fucked her in the men's bathroom with both of us stone sober. Then I hooked up with her sister. A few years prior, I would have never attempted such ridiculous things, but you never know what you can accomplish until you try.

I've found that the more attractive a woman is, the more unconventional your approach should be. Beautiful women get hit on all the time with the same bullshit. So be outrageous; try something different. Make it exciting for her, but do not reveal too much interest or attachment to the outcome. And always have a backup. Having a sure thing takes the pressure off, it makes you less needy. Neediness to women is like garlic to vampires.

I had so many things going on with so many different girls that I truly didn't care. If you don't have this abundance in your life yet, act as if you do, and it will come.

I eventually grew tired of Cannes and decided to check out St. Tropez. I'd heard people talk about it and wanted to see for myself, but like most super expensive places, it's impossible for hot girls to afford to go unless they're being sponsored. The beaches were nice, but I wasn't a fan of hookers and old dudes, so we left rather quickly.

After St. Tropez, we went to Monaco to watch the Grand Prix. I flew a group of girls out and rented a slip front and center to the race so we could watch the whole thing from the back of the boat. As our yacht sailed out of the marina for points south, my phone buzzed.

BRETT RATNER

Director of *Rush Hour*, *X-Men*, etc.
Producer of *Horrible Bosses*, *The Revenant*, etc.

I first reached out to Dan Bilzerian when I was with Edward Norton in Cannes during the film festival staying on a friend's yacht. We definitely were having a great time ourselves, but we heard Dan was on a yacht parked very close to us. So I got his number and texted him, letting him know how much Edward and I admired him and how he was trouncing all of us in the game of life.

I was hopeful that one day I would be invited to one of his legendary parties. That day came several years later. I was so curious to figure out—why him? Why is this guy so popular with women? I had spent many years hanging around Hugh Hefner at the Playboy Mansion and knew that Hef was not only educated and cultured but a perfect gentleman and had the utmost respect for women, which was why he was so successful with them his entire life.

I must admit Dan is not quite the person that we all believe him to be. He is bright, has real humility, is incredibly down to earth, and just an all-around cool guy. As I sized him up as one cocksman to another, he is shorter than I expected but more buff than I expected as well. It could've been because his clothes are probably two sizes too small, and as a result, I couldn't help but notice he had a sizable package in those short shorts of his. That must be it, I said to myself. Could this the secret? Is this why all these beautiful women adore Dan?

As I stood next to him on his sprawling lawn at his mansion with no less than one hundred girls in bikinis and just the two of us, I quickly realized I needed to work out. Then again, maybe not. I'm popular with women, most likely for my successful movies and less likely because of my svelte body, but Dan, on the other hand, is a real sex symbol, and I'm not being facetious. He's constantly working out, obviously takes good care of himself, and has the most masculine beard I have ever seen. Dan is a man's man! Guns, ammo, smoke, abs, exotic animals. Of course, I get it. It's the whole package. But is it? Is there more than we all see? Is Dan Bilzerian a walking contradiction to what all of us thirty-two million plus Instagram admirers see every day? Is he the next Hugh Hefner, or Charlie Sheen, or maybe even Wilt Chamberlain? Does he have something real to say or is it just all smoke and mirrors? This book will surely give us some of these answers.

During my two weeks in Cannes, I had hung out with more celebrities than in my entire life combined. None of them seemed any different than anyone else I knew, but it was still interesting and my bucket list was getting smaller by the day.

That trip cost a total of $1.4 million, which Mike, Hamza, and I chopped three ways. A far cry from the "we'll just split the cost of booze" excursion I had been promised, but it was worth every penny in terms of unique life experience. I witnessed the power of fame firsthand; I saw what it did to people's perceptions of me and the effect it had on women. The seed was planted. This was just the beginning; I knew I could do this bigger and better, and that's exactly what I planned on doing, for better or for worse...

CHAPTER 61

Becoming a Cop

Before I left for France, I'd purchased a nice house on the golf course in Las Vegas. When I returned, a bunch of free SilencerCo silencers were waiting for me and a request to judge a Tropic something bikini competition. Notoriety was starting to pay off.

I flew to LA to make a video at a shooting range with a bunch of girls in exchange for some free guns. I'd been making a decent effort to document my adventures on social media, and it was working. My numbers grew rapidly, but capturing the moments wasn't as easy as I thought. I wasn't able to convey one-tenth of what was happening.

This time, because it was a planned shoot instead of a trip, things worked out easily. We had an assortment of pistols and a rifle with an optic that employed the same tracking technology as an F-16 fighter jet. You could lock onto a target up to a mile away and pull and hold the trigger, but the gun would not fire until it was the perfect shot. It was hilarious watching topless blindfolded girls shoot steel at five hundred yards. We made a cool video, and it was fun.

Just a couple of hours later, I was back at my Hollywood place, in the Jacuzzi with the girls smoking a joint. Somehow, the topic of goats came up, and one girl refused to believe that I had any on the property.

"You wanna bet?" I asked.

"Yeah. If you actually have goats on this property, I will suck your dick right now. But if you're lying, you have to take me skydiving."

"How about if I win, you have to drive me and my two buddies to Lake Elsinore tonight so we can skydive in the morning. If I lose, then I will give you $10,000."

"Deal!"

Now, obviously, I knew for *certain* that goats were sleeping on my property because I had just lined their house with some really nice

Lovesac fake fur blankets earlier that same day. My buddies and I had already made plans to skydive in the morning. I just didn't want to have to do the driving.

"All right, put some clothes on. We're taking a road trip."

I led the girl down to see my pet goats, and then we started packing the car.

Lodging was pretty sparse at Lake Elsinore, and the finest accommodation was a Motel 6. I got a room with two queen beds and gave no impression that I was interested in sex. I took a shower, got into bed, and turned off the lights. She showered, made it clear she was not putting any clothes on, climbed in my bed, and then got on top of me. We fucked, and since I have a hard time sleeping after sex, I took a sleeping pill.

I begrudgingly woke to an eight in the morning alarm, still groggy from the pill. I rallied my friends, and we all went to the drop zone.

Skydiving was one of the things on my bucket list, but I refused to go tandem. I was originally going to buy a parachute on eBay and charter a plane or a hot air balloon and just send it. But my assistant did a little research and discovered I could legally bypass the tandem jump if I completed some training.

He got an instructor to come to my house, and I completed the six-hour course. It had been a few months and I'd since forgotten everything. The only tidbit that I remembered was that a parachute failure couldn't always just be cut away. Instead, you had to identify the problem first. For example, if it was a double open, and both chutes were deployed, then you'd better try and unfuck them because that's what you're landing with. If you cut away the primary, it would almost certainly collapse the secondary. There were a ton of other scenarios, most of which I didn't recall.

I put on my jumpsuit and headed to the runway. For some reason, I had a bad feeling about the whole thing, but I wasn't going to turn back now. When I dove out of the plane, I felt a spike of adrenaline, but it wasn't as scary as I had imagined. Having the ground fourteen thousand feet beneath me made the fall seem much slower than bungee jumping or cliff diving. Even though I was falling much faster, it was hard to tell, being up so high with no points of reference.

I pulled at four thousand feet, and fortunately my chute opened with no issues. I hit the ground super hard because I flared too late, but I was able to "leg it out" in a dead sprint. It was fun; I posted a pic, and it was one of my least liked photos. I was quickly learning that pictures with hot girls and expensive shit always outperformed interesting action adventure. This didn't mean I was going to change what I was doing, it meant I would adjust what I was sharing. Having fun was still my first priority.

A week later, my friend who took me shooting in LA introduced me to a police chief in New Mexico who ran a special program deputizing ex-military guys. He primarily wanted former SEALs and Special Forces operators to help serve high-risk warrants alongside the U.S. Marshals. But my pal put in a good word, and the Chief suggested I come down.

The police chief turned out to be an ex-Marine, a little over six feet tall, probably weighed about 220 pounds, and was solid coiled muscle like a pit bull. His armory put mine to shame, which wasn't easy to do. He had belt-fed machine guns, seven police cars, piles of body armor, and a shipping container full of ammunition. Marine battalions in Iraq weren't as well equipped.

I came in the prescribed uniform, which consisted of a plain black collared shirt, tan tactical pants, a police duty belt, and a tan plate carrier. The first thing on the chief's agenda was breakfast burritos and huevos rancheros that he ordered smothered.

At the range, I did both the pistol and rifle qualifications pretty easily and then went out that night on patrol. Coincidentally, one of the reserve cops was Arik Burks, who had been my First Phase proctor in BUD/S. He'd retired after twenty-five years in the SEAL teams and was doing the reserve cop thing for kicks.

"You only have to work four days every four to six months to stay current," Arik told me. "Last trip, I raided a meth lab and served a few murder warrants. It was three straight days of door kicking. But other times, it's just sitting around."

On my last day, the chief swore me in, printed up an ID card, and bam, I was a law enforcement officer.

Right before serving a murder warrant in New Mexico.

CHAPTER 62

Belligerent Midget

When the King of All Media asked me about sexual statistics, I answered honestly.

"I fucked fourteen women in twelve days," I told Howard Stern about my time in Cannes. Victoria was at home, listening, and she was furious. I felt bad, I really did, but I wasn't going to lie, and I certainly wasn't going to hide from who I was.

His show was my first live interview, and I was a little nervous. I probably should've prepared but instead spent the night partying and having sex in my hotel room. I couldn't have slept more than two to three hours tops.

I was pounding coffee while speed walking to the studio as the sun was coming up. I kinda had to piss going in, but I was late, so I didn't bother. After an hour, I couldn't hold it any longer and asked to take a bathroom break. He said he was almost done and to just hang tight. Thirty minutes later, I couldn't think straight, I was sweating, and legitimately worried I might piss myself when he shook my hand and thanked me for coming on. Howard was a pro, and he made the whole interview flow seamlessly. After his show, life got even crazier.

At first, the nudes trickled into my Instagram inbox. But as my notoriety grew, the flood gates opened. Hundreds came in every day, sometimes thousands. I posted some of the more creative ones, which generated even more followers and even more nudes.

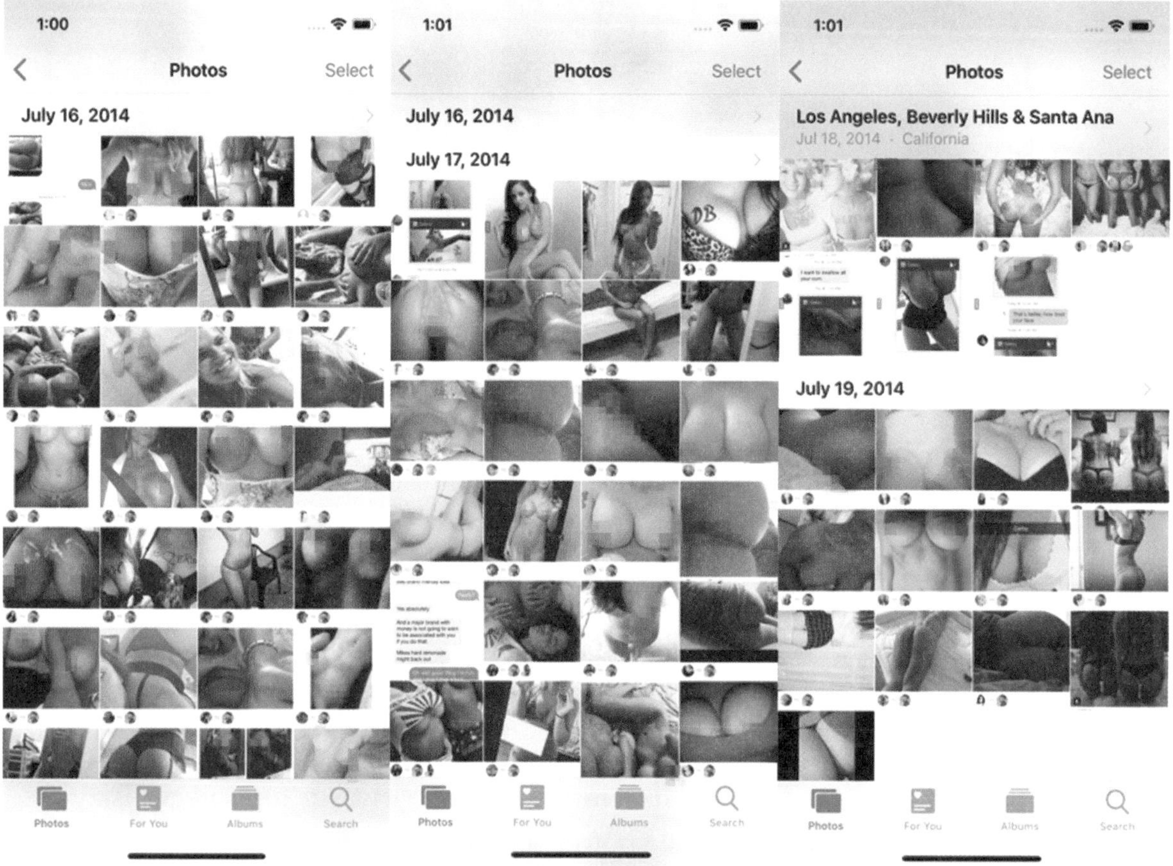

Three days after the interview, I met up with Arik Burks in San Diego for Comic-Con. He hadn't seen me outside of BUD/S or New Mexico, so he was surprised to see me getting stopped all night long. People constantly wanted pictures, and I kept my vow to take pictures with anyone who asked. No one was being rude or trying to start shit, but there were so many people that it took half an hour to walk fifty yards. The security guys helped manage the onslaught of mostly male fans.

Women were less aggressive, but they always found a way through. They would observe a crowd, pick out who the center of attention was, and zero in. It didn't even matter if they knew who I was or not. All they knew was that the guy in the center of the swarm had status—and as a guy, high status will get you a lot further than physical attractiveness. There is a scientific study that showed when the female goldfish is trying to decide who to mate with, and since all male goldfish look alike, she goes with the male goldfish that has the most females around him. Interesting how human psychology works on a primal level.

Sometimes if a hot girl was really visibly interested, I'd give her as little of my time as possible. And that made her seek my attention more desperately. That's an important part of *the setup*: If you can get a woman to chase you, give her subtle push away, then when you're ready, it's game over. The sex is always better when they've had to put in effort to fuck you.

An hour later, I took a girl into a porta potty. After a couple minutes of getting my dick sucked sitting on the side of the urinal, we got to fucking. It took a while because, no matter how hot the girl is, it's hard to get off in tiny spaces that smell like shit.

When it was over, I busted out of the door covered in sweat, looking like I'd just run a marathon. One shitty thing about being famous is that people notice you and will take unsolicited pictures as if you're a zoo animal. "Why is he so sweaty?" I heard people asking. Before all of this, if I spilled something on my shirt or looked like shit, it didn't matter, but now there was no hiding.

A teenager came up and asked for my first autograph. He was young and nervous but seemed like a nice kid. He said he was a big fan. I gave him back his notepad, took a hundred-dollar bill out of my pocket, and signed it for him. "Let's see how long you can *stay* a fan," I said. Looking back now, I wonder if he still has it.

After that, I went back to New Mexico to get in some police hours. I'd received my actual badge and wanted to see what the real cop shit was like.

We linked up with the U.S. Marshal, and I got to breach a door, and by breach, I mean I kicked it right off the fucking hinges with my boot. I was the first guy in to serve a murder warrant. After we cleared the house, one of the cops stomped his dirty-ass boots on the dude's white couch whilst yelling, "Fuck yo couch." We didn't even look like police.

With all the plate carriers and machine guns, we would have been more at home in Afghanistan than rural New Mexico.

I had never been on this side of the siren before. Usually, I was the one in trouble for one thing or another. But now I was the cop. I could feel the power that came with it. We would walk into a gas station with body armor and badges, and everyone would just move out of the way. It was surreal.

A couple of days earlier, I'd fucked a girl in a portable shitter at a comic book festival, and now I was serving murder warrants in the desert, driving a police car. This didn't feel like real life.

From there, I sped to LA to throw a birthday party for Victory Poker founder Dan Fleyshman at my Hollywood house.

DAN FLEYSHMAN

Founder and Former CEO of Who's Your Daddy

Over the years, Dan and I threw some legendary parties together at his various homes. His main rule was "Don't invite dudes." So if you look back at videos of our parties in 2013 and 2014 before his Instagram had really taken off, we had two hundred to four hundred guests in attendance, often with a eight to one girls to guys ratio. The parties from 2015–2020 just kept escalating as his homes got larger and the network of models, celebrities, and friends kept expanding.

People often ask me, "Does he really play poker?" I usually laugh out loud and tell them quick stories about how he beat one of our mutual friends for $10,800,000 in one session and posted the wire transfer screenshot on his Instagram a few days later. Dan ultimately beat that same guy for $53,000,000. I also tell them how many games we played together where I watched him win six and seven figures in a session. Of course, there are losses along the way as well, but overall, he's really good at game selection and causing players to make bad mistakes.

In closing, as I reflect on the last decade, we've really been through a lot together. We've had friends pass away, watched countless people come and go, but just like when he called me to get him bailed out of jail at five in the morning, Blitz is the first person I would call if there was a civil war or a zombie apocalypse.

Fleyshman suggested a theme of "CEOs and Secretary Hoes," which gave the women an excuse to dress as slutty as possible. I invited my usual proportion of at least seven girls to every one guy, and my new-found fame put the odds even more in my favor. I could hook up with three to five women a night when I hosted a party and generate leads to keep me busy for weeks afterwards.

It was a great scene. The highlight was a midget fucking two girls in the entryway bathroom. A random girl walked in on it and started filming, causing a fight to break out between the girls. After, he was found chain-smoking cigarettes in my living room. That midget really didn't give a fuck about anything. When I had someone inform him that he couldn't smoke in the house, he refused to stop, and I had to have his ass thrown out. I fucking hate cigarettes.

Even with all the debauchery, there was a really enlightening moment that had a major impact on my life perspective.

I had been flying combat-wounded veterans to all my parties. This time, I brought out a Marine we'll call John who'd lost both of his legs in combat and now worked as a motivational speaker. He was super nice and appreciative and just happy to be doing something so out of the ordinary.

Around two in the morning, I found myself talking to a brunette that I really wanted to fuck, but I talked up the Marine to her, told her he was a war hero and that he worked helping others. I set it all up and then introduced her to John.

The next day, I was hung over and staggered to the table for my afternoon breakfast. The Marine sat bolt upright, enjoying a fruit bowl and pancakes. I put on sunglasses because it was bright and I had a headache, but he couldn't stop smiling.

"I saw how much you were drinking last night," I croaked. "How are you so fucking happy?"

"Man, I feel great! Life is good. I couldn't be happier."

"Every time I talk to you, you're in such a great mood. How do you do it? Don't you get bummed out?""Why? Because I lost my legs?"

"Yeah. I guess I'd be pretty salty if that happened to me. What's your secret?'

"Shit, losing my legs was the best thing that ever happened to me!"

Now, I was still partially drunk. I was fully hung over. And I felt like I'd been run over. So admittedly, I was not at my most intellectually astute. But how in the hell could this guy say that getting his legs blown off in Iraq was a positive development in his life?

"Before I was blown up, nobody gave a fuck about me," he explained. "I was just some Marine sleeping in a tent, living in a convection oven of a sandbox called Iraq. If I hadn't been injured, I'd be back home working some shitty job, probably never leaving my home state, and never doing anything interesting. But look at me now. I'm eating breakfast in the Hollywood hills with Dan Bilzerian, I went to the best party of my life, I hooked up with the most beautiful woman I've ever seen, and I get to spend my time helping people. Plus, I get paid a shitload of money to do it. Honestly, I've never been happier."

Then it hit me; I'd paid that girl three thousand dollars to bang him last night, but still. I took off the sunglasses and looked out into the view. I was on top of the world—literally—I had a view of the entire city of LA laid at my feet and a garage full of exotic cars. I had millions in the bank and enough adventures ahead of me to fill three lifetimes, and my guy John was happier. It was time to get my head out of my ass and be more thankful.

I will never forget what he said and how he looked at things. That was such a powerful example of the importance of perspective and taking control over your own happiness. I will say, knowing I had a little part in contributing to his happiness, did in fact make me a little happier. There is nothing better in this world than doing something for someone and having that person be truly appreciative.

Give a guy a sincere compliment, and he's grateful for a day. Give a guy a stack of money, and he's grateful for a year. Give him a beautiful woman, and he's grateful for the rest of his life.

CHAPTER 63

Ink

"Come on, man," I said. "You're drunk. Leave me and my girl alone."

He snapped something silver off his wrist and held it out to me.

"This watch is worth three grand. Hang on to it until I get back with a tattoo gun. I'm dead serious! If I don't come back in five minutes, you can leave and keep the watch."

I was headed back to my villa with a girl. We'd just left a Miami nightclub after celebrating Guy Laliberté's birthday. People had asked for pictures, which wasn't strange anymore. But this was something new.

This guy wanted a tattoo of my signature. Not only that, he wanted *me* to actually give the tattoo. I'd heard of people getting a magic marker autograph and then running off to a shop to get it permanently inked in. But this loon thought I could hold the needle gun and mark him for life.

"Kid, I have never given a tattoo in my life. I've never even seen someone get a tattoo."

"I don't care!"

By this point, I was down because it would definitely be something I hadn't done before and a funny story if nothing else. I told him that I'd probably fuck it up, but if he was willing to live with the consequences,

I'd give it a shot. He ran off into the night as other people started asking if they could watch. A small crowd gathered as the kid jogged up with a backpack. He pulled out the tattoo gun along with little cups of ink. He got the machine running, and I freehanded my signature. Thank God, it turned out well. Everyone cheered, and then some girl asked me to tattoo her as well. Her fiancé was encouraging it too, which I found equally bewildering.

"Okay, but this is the last one," I said. I still wanted to get laid, and I wasn't trying to get stuck doing tattoos all night.

I wasn't about to tattoo my name on another man's wife, so I told them to think of something else. Something small and simple, and she landed on a heart on her foot. I inked her up and then kicked everyone out.

The girl I'd met at the club took my hand and led me up the stairs. The whole spectacle downstairs proved to be more effective foreplay than Ron Jeremy's tongue work. She was ready to go and clearly enthusiastic about banging me, which made the sex great. As we laid in bed smoking a joint, I couldn't help but laugh at what a circus my life was starting to become.

CHAPTER 64

Lindsey

Hollywood power agent Michael Kives invited me to a party. His home was pretty normal, but the guest list was absolutely not normal. Virtually everyone in attendance was a well-known actor, director, or agent. I considered myself more of a novelty than a celebrity, but I was certainly gaining momentum.

Michael Kives, Goldie Hawn, Kate Hudson, Danny McBride, and my date.

Danny McBride introduced himself and said he was a fan, which was a riot since *East Bound and Down* was one of my favorite shows of all time. I tried to act nonchalant when he asked if he could get a picture, but it took every ounce of self-control to not tell him what a fan I was of him. I should have told him, but I was new to this fame thing, and I didn't know if that would be weird. If my date had any questions about sleeping with me, seeing how the celebrities welcomed me put those to rest.

The next day, I had the picture framed.

Attending the Playboy Halloween Party was different this year since people recognized me. The last time I was at the mansion, I fucked a girl in the Grotto, and no one paid much attention. Now, people noticed me doing nothing. There was a blonde in lingerie with enormous natural tits; she approached *me* and started a conversation. Usually girls would come closer, look at me, or drop subtle clues that they were interested. But having women blatantly hit on me was a new experience.

I learned it was still good to make them work a little bit so they could feel like they accomplished something. Plus, it was a different dynamic than they were accustomed to, and different is always good.

The blonde's name was Lindsey Pelas, and she modeled for *Playboy*. We tried to fuck at the mansion but there were too many people so we went back to my house instead.

LINDSEY PELAS

Playboy Model

Hmm. Dan Bilzerian, where do I begin? I guess I should start with a "thank you." Thank for introducing me to Los Angeles. Thanks for the Internet fame. Thanks (and you're welcome) for my first and only threesome.

It's hard to choose a memory that stands out the most when they're all pretty standout. Our poetic first-time meeting at the Playboy Mansion. The time your plane caught on fire. Snowmobiling in the Colorado mountains. Vin Diesel and Ludacris partying at your house (loved that)...or maybe the time you were filming that PSA for the government because you blew something up that you shouldn't have. That was funny.

I guess my favorite thing about you is that it's so hard to believe you're actually a real person. People always ask me, "Is Dan really real? Is all that stuff he posts really true?" I can confirm the weapons, the women, the pyrotechnics, the wild animals, the sex, the weed, the fun, and the fantasy are all true.

One time we were on a plane landing strip in snowy Colorado. The plane had two faulty takeoff attempts, and we were stuck waiting for the fire department to see if the plane was too hot. As the firefighters came to take the temperature of the aircraft, the brakes caught on fire. Everyone on the plane ran out in a frenzy...the pilots, the chef, models, and friends. As we stood watching the plane get hosed off, Dan was nowhere to be found.

"Where's Dan? Where is he? Why isn't he coming out?" Everyone was rightly startled by fire and the freezing cold and even more so by the fact that Dan Bilzerian must've had a death wish. What kind of human being wouldn't immediately run out of a burning plane? Was he stuck? Did he get lost? Did he have another heart attack?

And then, after what felt like three hours but was probably three minutes, Dan emerged. There he was at the top of the G4's stairs wearing a long coat, his signature combat boots, and a black tee. Only now he was holding a bag of chips. It became clear to the rest of us at the same time that while we were outside scared and shaking, Dan had gone back further into the burning plane for a snack to appease his hunger. He took a slow gaze to the left where the firefighters were putting out the flames, gave a disapproving nod, and ate a handful of chips.

It was at that exact moment I realized Dan was fearless. Like fearless fearless. Not just fearless in the way people already knew about—like his affinity for blowing shit up or making bets that would cost normal people their homes or retirement funds. But the kind of fearless where death isn't even scary anymore. A man who's seen it all, done it all, and is afraid of nothing.

I had totally forgotten about the two high-speed aborts we had leaving Aspen. My pilots at the time, who have long since been fired, failed to remove a pin that allowed the plane to take off, or that is how it was explained to me. The brakes caught fire because stopping a seventy-five thousand-pound plane at over a hundred miles an hour on a short runway results in a ton of friction, which causes heat.

It wasn't really that I was fearless; I was worried the plane could explode, being that it was on fire. I was just so irritated and embarrassed by the situation that my pride trumped my self-preservation. I figured, like the captain who goes down with his ship, I would stay on, and if God wanted to shit on my head, then so be it.

Flying with Lindsey.

CHAPTER 65

Getting Paid

I started getting paid to do things that I would have gladly done for free.

BGO Gaming paid me $250,000 for a six-hour commercial shoot featuring my 6x6 Mercedes, a gorilla, Verne Troyer from the *Austin Powers* movie, and five models. The studio sent a screener copy of *John Wick* and paid me $50,000 to post a picture of me watching it the day before it hit the theaters.

Marquee paid me $75,000 to appear at their club for an hour. They put twenty models at my table, $10,000 worth of alcohol in the center, and reserved a nearby bungalow so I could slither off and bang girls. Most of the rich guys I knew from the poker scene would have paid the club $75,000 for that type of setup. The club even hosted a Dan Bilzerian look-alike contest with a $10,000 grand prize.

I thought a girl hitting on me was crazy, but I hadn't seen anything yet. Shortly after arriving at my table, a girl walked up, looked me in the eyes, and said, "I want to fuck you." I had a couple girls grab my dick; it was competitive and aggressive. Things started to snowball. The more girls were coming after me, the more it made others want to do the same. I wanted more attention when I was a kid, but in my wildest dreams, I never imagined a scenario like this. And things were just getting started.

Look-alike contest. I'm on the far left.

CHAPTER 66

Samantha and Friends

I was making around $80,000 a night in tips hosting a weekly poker game at my LA house. The game would come about when a particularly bad player wanted to play, and the rest of the seats were filled with mediocre recreational players. I say mediocre, but in a casino, if any of those players sat down, the bat signals would go off; pros would sell their sisters for a seat. The initial buy-in was only $50,000–$100,000, but guys would regularly lose a million or more in a night. Massage girls in bras and twelve-inch skirts served drinks and rubbed guys' shoulders while they played.

Ashley was gorgeous, and she gave fantastic massages. I was enjoying her handiwork whilst sending nudes to Samantha, another poker girl across the table who had a perfect body and big tits. Life was good, and I was getting lazy in terms of the game I ran on women. Ashley saw me sexting Samantha and joked about it.

When the poker was over and all the players left, Ashley asked if she could stay at my house until she sobered up.

"Sure, take the room down the hall on the right."

I did a final chip count, settled the books, and then went to my bedroom. I opened the door, and Ashley was sprawled across the bed with a huge grin on her face instead of sleeping it off in the guest room. I took the hint.

She was on her knees with my dick in her mouth when Samantha appeared a minute later in the bedroom doorway.

"Oh, my," Samantha said, surprised.

I went to the door, grabbed Samantha by the hand, and led her into the mix. She started kissing me, but she wouldn't suck my dick or have sex. So after a minute, I told her to leave. She walked out of the room, and it was back down to just Ashley and me. But now she wouldn't fuck either. She had the audacity to mention how important her faith was to her while blowing me. After manufacturing this whole hookup with her "too drunk to drive" excuse in the first place, she wouldn't even remove her skirt. She continued to suck my dick until Samantha re-entered the fray. They started kissing, but Samantha refused put my dick in her mouth because she said she had a boyfriend. With that, I'd officially had enough of the games. I kicked Samantha out for the second time and called Victoria.

"Come over here," I told her. "I'm going to fuck you, and there's a girl here who is going to watch."

Victoria stormed in ten minutes later, turned all the lights on, and blurted out, "Who's the whore?" I told her to chill and dimmed the lights a bit. She went down on me and then commanded Ashley, "Suck his dick, you slut." Ashley did as ordered while Victoria got naked and then shoved her out of the way. Victoria talked shit the whole time we were fucking.

"Do you like watching my boyfriend fuck me, you whore?"

When we switched positions, she grabbed Ashley by the hair and said, "Suck his cock. I want you to choke," and forced her head down. It was really aggressive but hot, and Ashley was surprisingly into it. Suddenly, Victoria shifted tones, got all innocent and coy, and sweetly asked, "Please fuck me, Daddy, I've been a good girl."

When I came out of the shower, Victoria was giving Ashley hell. She really didn't like her, and I realized that the whole threesome had been her version of hate fucking.

"Get off our bed," Victoria yelled. "Go sleep on the floor." Then she ordered her out of the house entirely. I told Victoria to chill the fuck out and explained the girl needed to sober up before driving. She wouldn't stop, and I didn't want to deal with this shit, plus it was a good reason to kick her out so I could fuck Ashley later. I walked Victoria to the door, told her I'd call tomorrow, and headed back to bed.

Ashley was already under the covers by the time I returned. I don't share my bed with anyone, but my gut told me she didn't want to sleep. Sure enough, the minute I climbed into bed, she scooted her perfect ass into me. I could feel that she was completely naked. Evidently she changed her faith that day because this church girl climbed on top and rode me like a porn star.

If you are thinking to yourself that women are crazy and irrational after reading this, look a little closer. The girl's behavior in this story was completely predictable if you consider the psychology. Ashley saw Samantha sexting me and, as a result, decided she also wanted to fuck me, so she snuck into my room. However, after Samantha rejected me, Ashley second-guessed her desire to bang me. Ashley didn't come into my room to just suck my dick, and had Samantha wanted to fuck me, I have no doubt Ashley would have jumped on top of me too. But the moment Ashley didn't feel like I was in demand, she all of a sudden didn't want me either.

I read the situation right and did probably the only thing I could've done to save it after Samantha cockblocked me. Once Ashley saw how much Victoria was into me, she went back to wanting to fuck me. If this situation doesn't clearly illustrate the power of competition, supply and demand, and jealousy, then you're hopeless; stick to jerking off.

Samantha texted me a while later, inviting me to a poker game at the home of fight announcer Bruce Buffer, the "It's Time!" guy. It was a small game, and once I figured out that her boyfriend was in attendance, I took off. A week after, I told her I wanted to hire her as a pussy coordinator. Her job would be to manage the girls I was talking to and introduce me to others who were interested. She booked a lot of poker girls for games and had an amazing Rolodex, so I thought it would be a good fit. Plus, I knew we were going to eventually, at some point, fuck. It was only a matter of time. I mean, she came back after I told her to get the fuck out of my room with my dick in another woman's mouth.

We met at BOA steakhouse for dinner, and it was weird. I never go out on dates, and it felt strange to be with a girl I hadn't fucked. I was sober, and people were staring at me. I tried to have a conversation, but I hadn't been on a normal date in so long that it was awkward. I started sweating because the whole thing was giving me anxiety, so I excused myself to the bathroom to eat a Quaalude and take a piss.

Quaaludes were huge hits in the sixties and seventies, commonly referred to as disco biscuits or 'ludes. In the seventies, 'ludes were the most commonly prescribed sedative in the country. They were taken off the market in 1984 because so many people were taking them recreationally. 'Ludes were great, they made you happy, didn't produce hangovers, and made you not give a fuck about anything.

"I think I might break up with my boyfriend," she said.

"Why?"

"Because I should not have a boyfriend if I'm having these urges to have sex with you."

"Do you want to fuck in the bathroom?"

"No."

The date was an absolute disaster, and I just wanted to get the fuck out of there.

A couple of weeks later, she told me she had finally broken up with her boyfriend and asked to come over. I told her I couldn't have sex because I had prostatitis. I'd been having so much sex lately that it actually inflamed my prostate (the small walnut-sized gland that produces seminal fluid) and required me to take a few days off of banging. She was pissed because she had just moved out of her boyfriend's house and was expecting to fuck me.

A week later, I was at Sam's house, and Samantha texted to hang out. I gave her the address, and she came over. I took her on a tour of the opulent madhouse that ended with sex in the guest room. I took a shower while she got dressed and headed to the kitchen. Downstairs, Samantha ran into a woman who'd been an actress on *Baywatch*.

"How do you know Dan?" the Hollywood lifeguard asked.

"I work poker games, and I've been talking to him a little bit," Samantha replied.

"Does he fuck all the girls?" the actress asked.

Samantha was a little shocked. "What do you mean?"

"Well, he had sex with me before you arrived, and I feel like every woman I meet is sleeping with him."

I showed up, and they stopped talking, which was a little awkward. After we left, Samantha recited the convo, but I didn't waiver or apologize; I just behaved like it was perfectly fine for someone single to do whatever they wanted. Samantha was superhot and wasn't used to a man not chasing or catering to her.

Ultimately, it fueled Samantha's desire to get me to like her. When the foundation of a relationship is built on the girl doing whatever she can to make the man happy, she will, by default, put up with a lot more crazy shit. And the more she did to get me to like her, the more she became invested in our relationship.

The following week, Samantha brought out four hot models to my Vegas house. Three of the girls were fresh out of long-term relationships and wanted to let their hair down, so Samantha suggested Vegas.

"The girls drank all the champagne on your plane," Samantha warned. "We should be landing in fifteen minutes." I was sitting on my couch, chillin', when I got the texts, so I drank some coffee and braced myself for impact.

The girls boisterously entered my house, laughing and immediately requesting music. They'd clearly come to Vegas to party, and I wasn't going to hang around these lushes sober, so I popped a Lude and took a shot. I fucked Samantha upstairs straight away, and we didn't bother to put our clothes back on. The girls barged into my room twenty minutes later, and they weren't being shy about seeing us naked. I got up in a rare show of modesty to put on a towel, and they all ended up in my bathroom Jacuzzi.

Samantha remained naked and encouraged her friends to do the same. A couple stripped down to their underwear while the other two kept just their tops on and sat on the side of the tub. As the water was filling, Briana, a tall blonde, bent over in front of me. She had one of the nicest asses I'd ever seen, and she stayed in that position, prominently displaying it. She looked back and grinned, but I always start orgies with the girl I've hooked up with before, so I grabbed Samantha by the hair and had her suck my dick.

Briana had her back arched and her ass in the air like a cat in heat, so I put a condom on, pulled her thong over to the side, and started fucking her. The girls sitting on the side of the tub drank champagne and watched, but it was a little distracting fucking in front of girls who weren't involved, so Briana and I eventually moved to the shower.

The girls got in the tub and appeared to be talking, but I could see them watching us. I had Briana's face smashed up against the glass as I fucked her from behind. She requested a facial; I obliged and then handed her a towel.

I finished showering, turned off the water, got out, and saw that a petite sexy brunette named Emma was standing naked in front of the towel rack. We kissed, and she dropped down to her knees and started sucking my dick. I pulled her up and promised to fuck her but explained that I needed to eat some Cheerios first. I went downstairs, ate my cereal, drank a protein shake, and smoked a joint before going back up to her room. She had changed into some lingerie, but it didn't stay on very long. She was super tight, and the sex was good.

When I opened the door to my bedroom, I found Samantha and her friend Caroline passed out in my bed. In the morning, Caroline woke Samantha up by going down on her. Samantha pushed the girl off and said, "No, but Dan will have sex with you." She wasn't my type, so I kicked her out by saying I wanted to sleep. And then I fucked Samantha.

People always ask how I fuck so much, and the answer is simple, Cialis and synthetic testosterone.

I texted the chef that I was awake, took a shower, ate breakfast, and then slithered into Emma's room. The sunlight was streaming in, and I saw Girl Number Five sleeping on the left side of her bed. Emma and

I started fucking quietly, but Girl Number Five woke up after a couple minutes. At first, she just watched, pretending to sleep, then she grabbed my arm and gave me a look. I've had this happen a lot; a girl will look at me, and it's shocking how much can be communicated with no words.

"Lemme go get another condom," I said.

I walked back into my bedroom, Samantha was still in bed, and I was butt-naked with a condom on, grabbing a handful of extras. By that point, she'd seen enough shit that I didn't feel the need to explain myself. I went back and alternated between Emma and Girl Number Five.

The reason I always switch condoms before fucking another girl is so they don't get BV (bacterial vaginosis). I found out that if you fuck a bunch of girls with the same condom, it will throw off their PH, which can make their pussies stink. I'm not really a hit it and quit it type of guy, and I try and keep my girls' vaginas in good working order.

The girls all went out that night, but Emma snuck away early and came back to the house. We smoked weed, fucked, and watched movies until eventually they all returned. I got pretty high, so I can't exactly recall which women I hooked up with or in what order, but I tended to the flock.

The next night, we landed in LA, and all the girls Ubered back home or to their boyfriend's houses from my plane. I sometimes wonder how many women sell their boyfriends good girl stories but have some drunken backstage orgy in their past that even they rationalize away as "not counting" since the dude is famous, or she was drunk or whatever.

It was almost two in the morning by the time Samantha and I got back from the airport. The chef had dinner ready for us when we walked in the door. We were eating at the dining room table when she told me she wanted to watch me fuck another girl.

"It makes me jealous," she said. "But it's a turn-on."

"When do you wanna do it, and who do you wanna watch?" I asked.

"Whenever. And I don't care who the girl is as long as she's hot and has big tits."

This was perfect because I'd just texted Lindsey Pelas a few minutes prior, and she said she'd be over in thirty minutes. I was actually trying to figure out how to tactfully tell Samantha, and this made it seamless.

Samantha was surprised that it all came together so quickly. She wanted to hide and watch the show, but the only place was under my desk. So I hung a blanket over the desk and put a pillow on the stone floor.

When Lindsey pulled into the driveway, Samantha crawled into her nook. Lindsey didn't waste any time getting naked, and we had sex for a good thirty minutes. My first thought afterward was *I have to get Lindsey out of here so Samantha can escape.*

I suggested to Lindsey that we take a shower, but she didn't want to move. I went to the bathroom by myself, wondering what would happen if Samantha just burst out of her cubbyhole like a fucking rapist. When I finished showering, I went back to the room, kissed Lindsey, and made a face.

"You need to brush your teeth."

She smiled and said, "Asshole."

As soon as Lindsey rounded the corner, Samantha shot out of the cubby and made her break. Fifteen minutes later, Samantha strolled back into the room, completely naked, holding two glasses of champagne.

"Would either of you care for a drink?" she offered.

Lindsey didn't bat an eye. I still to this day can't comprehend how little it fazed her that a butt-naked chick just magically appeared in my house when we'd been there seemingly alone all night.

"No, I'm good, thanks," Lindsey replied.

I had just smoked a joint, so I thought this was the most hilarious thing I'd ever seen, and it took all of my self-control to not burst out laughing. She went into the guest room and sent me text messages about being horny and masturbating. I didn't see them until after a second round with Lindsey, and by that time I was tired, so I ignored them and passed out.

Samantha later told me that she felt like the scenario kind of backfired because she didn't think I could find a woman more beautiful than her to come over on short notice at two-thirty in morning. I think they were both equally hot. But women can be insecure.

SAMANTHA
(NAME CHANGED)

Medical Doctor

Imagine the world's largest magnet and on the ground were paper clips. Everywhere this magnet went, the paper clips were sucked up by the magnet's strong force. The magnet is Dan, and the paper clips are the girls, the girls being anything from the most innocent girl who has never had sex to porn stars. They were all drawn to him like nothing I've ever seen. I was one of those paper clips, and now that I am removed from that environment, I can look back and analyze more accurately than I could when I was in it.

When you look at Dan's Instagram, you would think that he is this loud, boisterous man, but in person, he's actually really humble. He doesn't talk a lot, but when he does, it's something meaningful. How is this guy who just sits there and eats a lot and has sex a lot drawing in so many women at such an unbelievable rate?

My theory is that when you are going to hang out with Dan, it would be asinine to expect anything different than you see on his Instagram. His personality is unlike what you see on Instagram, but him having sex with multiple women—that part is accurate. So when these girls hang out with him, and he's having sex with multiple women, nobody gets mad because that is what you go in expecting.

There is a lot of adrenaline involved in hanging out with Dan because he is always having outrageous events, doing crazy things with guns, and there's celebrities around. You're in mansions and flying on private jets, so you always have this surge of adrenaline that is fogging any type of logical thought process of what is normally socially acceptable. And with this excitement and all of these girls throwing themselves at him, it almost feels like you're in an alternate universe.

However, there is something subconsciously going on with the women he is constantly surrounded by. He will often give attention to one girl here or there, and it makes all the other girls feel as if they are inferior. Most of the girls who are around him were the hottest girls from their hometowns and had never experienced such indifference from a male. This leads the girls to feel inadequate and insecure, which then breeds a desire for more superficial attention from him. What's actually going on is he's giving the girls what is called intermittent positive reinforcement. Basically, just giving them sex or attention arbitrarily, making them feel special for a moment in time and then when that moment passes, their dopamine crashes, their need for attention peaks, and the cycle repeats itself.

Hanging out with Dan probably isn't what my mom or my future significant other would hope for, but I learned the most from my experiences with him. I learned that private jets, exotic locations, chefs, etc. aren't that great. I could've spent my entire life in search of this, and I was able to find out through my experience with Dan that it's not something I want to strive for. Having gratitude for the little things that I have and having peace of mind is most important to me. I would've never found this out without actually experiencing it firsthand. So I would encourage anyone to have new experiences and step outside the box that society is keeping you in because only through trial and error will you find out what really makes you happy.

Samantha is clearly very astute. I knew she was a smart woman—most doctors are—however, she was more objective and perceptive than I expected. I created an environment of competition, and because there were multiple women vying for my limited attention, they by default received intermittent positive reinforcement. Intermittent positive reinforcement results in strong behavioral conditioning, and it's extremely resistant to change. You will find intermittent positive reinforcement in gambling, and it's built into social media algorithms, hence why these things are so addictive.

"Intermittent reinforcement does have one important quality—it produces robust responding that is significantly more resistant to extinction than when continuous reinforcement is used."

FERSTER & SKINNER, 1957

CHAPTER 67

Tannerite

It was like Christmas morning, but Santa usually doesn't drop off a hundred pounds of Tannerite. It's a good explosive and pretty safe to handle because it takes a high-powered rifle round to detonate it.

Most people and shooting ranges use a quarter of a pound to produce a satisfying boom. I saw a guy on YouTube obliterate a fifteen thousand-square foot barn with fifty pounds. Another YouTuber, FPSRussia, used fifteen pounds in a truck, and the door flew past him at like two hundred miles an hour and almost cut him in half. Today, it's illegal to have a hundred pounds, which the ATF says is equivalent to sixty pounds of C-4.

I bought a semitruck and had it delivered to a place out in the desert where many Vegas locals go to shoot. We filled up a giant Igloo water cooler like they use on the sidelines of football games with the Tannerite and buried it under the cab.

Then I borrowed a 20 mm cannon from an acquaintance. I'm not using slang here or being dramatic. It was literally classified by the government as a cannon. The largest firearm is a .50 caliber, and this thing shot a round more than twice as large and at a higher velocity. We carted that ridiculous gun into the desert and set it up on a table.

20mm Cannon.

I zoomed the scope to max magnification, placed the crosshairs on the cooler, and slowly squeezed the trigger. I braced myself for the recoil equivalent of a Mike Tyson punch. I wasn't sure how much trigger pull there was on the weapon, so I pulled. And pulled a little more.

No click.

Nada.

Turned out that my boneheaded buddy had never even fired the thing, and the firing pin was broken or had been removed. Not to be deterred, I picked up his Barrett M107, a .50 caliber sniper rifle that was resting nearby, put a couple of rounds in the magazine and racked it. Normally, I don't check the barrels of long guns, but something didn't sound right. I had a feeling this guy didn't actually know shit about his own weapons, so I took the magazine out, racked the action, and looked down the business end of the rifle with a flashlight. Sure enough, there was a squib (unfired bullet) lodged in the barrel. Had I pulled the trigger on that sniper rifle, it probably would have blown my face off and injured others nearby.

This adventure was not going as planned.

It's a weird feeling knowing that you just saved your own life. I felt like the universe was telling me not to do this, but I'd paid for the truck, buried the explosives, and everyone was waiting for the show. Stopping wasn't really an option.

We tried a 300 Blackout, but at that range, the bullet had slowed down too much to detonate the Tannerite. The last thing we had was a 5.56, but we were too far away to use that as well. Our short, fat, bald friend Slinger volunteered to go closer and put the old truck out of its misery.

Semi-truck explosion.

He waddled down the hill, slipping a couple of times in the loose gravel and dirt. And then *BAM*! He sent the semi's engine block into the clouds like an intercontinental missile. The explosion was deafening and essentially disintegrated all but the frame of the semi. If there were any Nevada old-timers within a mile, they probably thought the government was testing nuclear bombs like in the fifties.

"This might cause a problem," someone said. For once, we all agreed and didn't dick around. We calmly and quietly got the fuck out of that canyon.

CHAPTER 68

Art Basel

Landing in Miami for Art Basel, my crew on the plane was digital strategist Ben Stevens, my assistant Jeremy, a dude named Claude for security, and two women named Brittney and Christine. Brittney was a skinny college girl with huge real tits who happened to live with her fiancée. We had been hooking up for almost a year but kept it quiet. Christine was gorgeous but a monogamous-type girl, so we decided after hooking up a few times to just be friends.

A Ferrari, a Range Rover, and a Rolls Royce were waiting when my plane landed. In the past, I would've paid for regular rentals, but now exotics were coming to me completely free—another perk of fame. We checked into the hotel. I smoked a joint, ordered room service, and went a couple rounds with Brittney.

I was eating breakfast around noon in my suite with the girls when Ben knocked on the door. He said that Patrick Schwarzenegger, Wiz Khalifa, and Miley Cyrus were in town and wanted me to stop by their hotel to get high with them. There was a garbage bag full of weed on the table when we walked in because Miley had instructed her staff to never be caught with less than a full pound at any given time. Wiz rolled a couple joints, and the three of us smoked on the balcony.

The Art Basel events were boring as shit, so we left and went to LIV. Ten minutes after arriving, I met a hot blonde and quickly took her upstairs to fuck. The club was inside our hotel, so it was easy to sneak out and catch an elevator. Brittney and Christine noticed that I was gone and wanted to come looking for me, but Ben was a good soldier, and he kept the troops in line. I finished with the blonde, took a shower, and was back in the club before too long.

Critics make fun of my wardrobe, and I'll admit that maybe I don't present myself as the pinnacle of sophisticated GQ fashion. But what those people don't understand is how nice it is to be able to fuck, change, and still have on the exact same outfit. I don't like to shower and put on clothes that aren't fresh. So imagine the shit I would have to deal with if I changed into five different outfits in one night. By sticking to a consciously restrained wardrobe of cargo pants, T-shirts, and swim trunks, I can look the same every time I return to the party. Plus, it makes packing easier, and it's one less thing I have to think about. Most people don't see all the angles; they see the surface and make assumptions.

Leonardo DiCaprio told a mutual friend that he wanted to meet me, and I was thrilled. But between the impossibly loud music and the Quaaludes I had eaten, I couldn't communicate for shit. I felt like a slurring retard. Not knowing what to say, I offered him one of my few precious Quaaludes. He politely declined after telling me he'd never tried them before. We yelled, smiled, and raised our eyebrows like we were communicating for about thirty seconds. I gave him a fist bump and headed back to my table. I couldn't help but find it ironic that the guy who informed the younger generation about Ludes had never even eaten one.

I wish I had a better DiCaprio story, but a woman did tell me that a few months prior, she was in a club with him when he was growing out his beard for *The Revenant*. She told me he jumped on the table and shouted, "I have this beard and all these women! I'm like Dan Bilzerian!" I didn't believe her at the time, but he knew who I was, and it'd be a strange thing to make up. If you were to tell my younger self that Leonardo DiCaprio would be impersonating me in a nightclub, I would have told you to lay off the crack pipe. But strange things were happening.

German, a Miami promoter, told me a billionaire client of his had a yacht and wanted to party with me. German had lined up a yacht filled with girls every time I went to Miami, and every time, I was fucking in one of the staterooms within an hour of getting on the boat. One time I came out of the shower in a towel, and two girls I hadn't even spoken to just ripped the towel off of me and both started sucking my dick. It was like that when you're on a boat with forty drunk girls and only three or four guys. I would rarely close the door, and girls would sometimes come in while I was fucking and ask to join or just jump in uninvited. I was never a big fan of group sex because I found it kind of distracting, but getting your nuts or ass licked while you're fucking or getting a blowjob is nice.

On a boat in Mian

That night, we were back at LIV, and lots of Art Basel people where there. It was December 6, 2014, and I was about to turn thirty-four in a half an hour. A friend handed me a magnum of Dom Perignon, and I started drinking right from the bottle. Brittney the college girl and my friend Christine were to my right.

A worked-up brunette yelled at Christine, "You can't stand next to him all night!"

"Yes, I can. I came here with him."

The brunette said to get out of the way, but Christine wouldn't budge. Frustrated, the girl sucker punched Christine in the face and yanked her off the booth by her hair. Christine fell five feet onto the concrete floor, and the lunatic pounced on her and started punching her in the face. It all happened fast, and I couldn't pull her away since I was on stage, so I tried to kick the crazy bitch off, but she was too far away. I was at least able to help Christine up and back into the booth, only to find that Brittney had been knocked off as well.

Claude called the club security over and explained what happened. Christine was pretty banged up and wanted to press charges, so the cops were called. When they arrived, we all went into a quiet room in the back of the club.

"Miami code states if two people get into a fight, and one of them wants to press charges, we have to take both parties involved to jail," the police officer explained.

Understandably, Christine didn't want to go to jail, even though she was the victim. So she decided not to press charges. The other woman didn't have a scratch on her and acknowledged that she wasn't actually hit by anyone. Everyone was free to go.

Someone in the club sent a grainy video to a gossip site. On the tape, you can see me kick out into the air, and the site posted that I had kicked the woman in the face. The site was run by a scumbag who went by the name Nik Richie. Nik reached out to the girl and told her to sue me and got her an ambulance chaser attorney who worked on contingency. He told her to go to the hospital. A full forty-eight hours after the incident, she went to the emergency room and then called the police, claiming that I'd kicked her in the eye. That bogus story was posted again on the site and then picked up by newspapers. They reported that I fled the club before the police arrived, which was ridiculous because I spoke to both officers and the conversation was documented in the report. Moral of the story: Never trust what you read in the media unless you were there.

Fueling this bullshit inferno was Nik, who started the fire in the first place by misrepresenting a poorly-shot video. He wanted to be famous and wrote a book, but no one bought it. He married the daughter of an actor and tried a reality show, but no one watched it. So he focused on a website to call out hookers and spread nightclub gossip. He had tried to attach himself to me in any way possible over the last year. And after this incident in Miami, he claimed to be so troubled by my alleged behavior that he planned to donate to a women's charity.

Nik, though, was more concerned with looking like he supported women than actually supporting them. The false information he posted about people led to a lot of pain, to women getting fired, to women attempting suicide. Instead of changing his ways, the power went to his head. He extorted women, public figures, and nightclubs for money if they wanted the incorrect and defamatory articles removed. And one of those people was me. Months prior, he told a mutual friend, Justin Smith, that he would remove my articles and not post about me if I paid him $5,000. It was an inconsequential amount of money, but I told him to fuck off on principle. He was accustomed to people giving in to his threats, so it pissed him off when I said no. He attacked me and everyone around me, including Victoria, making her life very difficult.

Nik constantly posted about me until one day he fucked up. He posted that a woman had come forward stating that I'd given her chlamydia. His usual strategy for avoiding repercussions is that he would claim he wasn't the author of the post. He said he just provided the forum but that individuals posted the content so he couldn't be held responsible. However, the woman publicly stated that she had never been to the website or made the posts he attributed to her. Plus, I had five years' worth of clean medical records with monthly STD checks. And of course, Nik was unable to provide an IP address of the supposed poster because he wrote it himself. I had him dead to rights. I sued him and the site for two solid years until he ran out of money, the owners of the site fired him, and he had to slither back to the desert from whence he came.

But at that moment in Miami, with the crazy nightclub scene, he started a deluge of bad publicity. And as a result, the police opened an investigation into the Miami nightclub incident, which infuriated me to no end. That crazy bitch had attacked my friend unprovoked, and I would have been fully comfortable kicking her and facing the appropriate consequences. But to face this much heat for a swing that did not make contact was almost unbearable.

"Fire up the jet, I'm going to Nassau," I told the pilots.

The plan was to fly to the Bahamas, relax, and disappear for some quiet. But I still read the articles and saw the online comments, so being in a tropical paradise didn't really put me in a better mood. No place is far enough from the Internet anymore. I've been hiking in remote mountains and still had five bars.

This was the first real negative experience in my rise to fame, and I learned another lesson: When the press runs with a story that isn't true, there is little you can do to stop it. It's your life, but you are no longer the expert on it. You cannot address the lies because you just bring more attention to the false story as well as the shitty publication or website. That exposure is exactly what they want. My attorneys advised a simple "no comment." This was painful because I wanted to set the record straight. I have no problem getting hate for things that I've actually done. But to get shit on for fiction? That's brutal.

We flew back to Los Angeles, and I was lying with Brittney on the pull-out couch while Christine sat on the other side of the plane, still sporting a black eye from the assault in Miami. We began the descent to the LAX airport, and I couldn't help but wonder if I was going to have any issues. Everything seemed normal as the plane taxied down the runway and stopped in front of the customs office. I climbed out of bed, put on my shoes, and grabbed my passport and customs form from my assistant. I walked down the aisle, turned the corner left, and looked out the door of my plane. I stopped, frozen in my tracks.

There was a sea of flashing red and blue lights; at least twenty police officers and federal agents with guns were there waiting for me. I couldn't believe my pilots didn't warn me. *What in the fuck did I just walk into?* I wondered as I walked down the steps. An ATF agent approached me and asked if I was armed. I said no. He frisked me and put me in cuffs. I asked why I was being arrested; he laughed and said, "You know why."

I was arrested right there at the airport on federal bomb-making charges for "possessing and manufacturing illegal explosive devices." At the LA county jail, I told the female cop at processing that I was a police officer. She looked at me like "Yeah, right, motherfucker." I gave her my police ID, her face changed, and they put me in isolation.

The A/C was cranked up in my cell, and I regretted not grabbing a sweater, but when I got outta bed, spending the night in jail didn't register as a possibility. I closed my eyes, but the bright fluorescent lights shined through my eyelids. As I laid there in that small cell, my mind was racing. The whole thing didn't make sense. I did not have any explosives in my possession when they surrounded my plane. The destruction of the semi-truck in Las Vegas was months ago.

When they finally gave me my phone call, I rang Tom Goldstein, and he enlisted well-known Vegas criminal defense attorney David Chesnoff, who had represented celebrities like Mike Tyson, Britney Spears, David Copperfield, and Shaquille O'Neal. Tom said he was flying to Los Angeles and for me to just sit tight while he figured everything out.

Meanwhile, the press was going crazy. From the headlines, you'd swear I was planning on blowing up the airport. Another downside of celebrity: If you appear larger than life, there's a certain type of person who wants to cut you down to their size.

The dynamic legal duo got me out the following day. Goldstein informed me that my security guard had left the box of Tannerite at the site with my address on it. That explained how they knew it was me, but it didn't change the fact that I was totally innocent, and the charges were complete bullshit. At the time, there was nothing illegal about purchasing Tannerite in any quantity, and you're allowed to destroy your own property. But there is always a risk when facing a jury. They could be biased, idiotic, jealous of my lifestyle, or annoyed by my image. Anything can happen in a courtroom. Even elementary school kids can recite that our legal system is based on the premise that people are innocent until proven guilty. That's in theory.

I was a gambler. I made millions calculating risk and reward. And I'd seen what had happened when my father was in this same position and miscalculated. So I took the deal.

I had to plead guilty to the misdemeanor of "failure to extinguish a campfire," pay a fine, and make a public service announcement on social media telling people that blowing up semitrucks is not the intended use of Tannerite. The whole ordeal cost me over $250,000, a night in jail, and my second amendment right for a few months. It could have been worse, but it's never fun being punished for something that isn't illegal. I understood the game: When the government goes after you, the prosecutor cares about winning, not about right and wrong.

CHAPTER 69

School Girls and a Giraffe

A few weeks after my arrest, *Lone Survivor* hit the big screen and the movie was well received. My part, however, was a far cry from the eight minutes and eighty words I was promised. The one line that remained was something Marcus fabricated, which as information surfaced, proved to be a reoccurring theme.

In the book, Marcus claimed there were two hundred Taliban fighters, but the after-action report and ground intelligence indicated only eight to ten.* Marcus claimed they "killed fifty or more"; however, there were no reports of any enemy casualties. Mohammad Gulab, the Afghan villager who saved Marcus and housed him until he was rescued, told *Newsweek* Marcus's book was inaccurate. "While Luttrell wrote that he fired round after round during the battle," Gulab says, "the for-

* R.M. Schneiderman, "Marcus Luttrell's Savior, Mohammad Gulab, Claims 'Lone Survivor' Got It Wrong," *Newsweek*, May 11, 2016, https://www.newsweek.com/2016/05/20/mohammad-gulab-marcus-luttrell-navy-seal-lone-survivor-operation-red-wings-458139.html.

mer SEAL still had eleven magazines of ammunition when the villagers rescued him—all that he had brought on the mission."

True story or not, a deal is a deal. Director Peter Berg didn't give me the screen time he'd promised even though I gave him the million dollars he repeatedly asked me for, so I had to sue Randall Emmett—who Peter also fucked over—because he was the one that I had the contract with. Before I had my day in court, they paid back my original $1 million investment plus $500,000 for interest. Even though the movie has brought in over $150 million, they still have not paid me a single dollar on the 3 percent backend I own. I should have taken Clarence's advice: Don't invest in films. Movie studios maintain multiple sets of books, and they almost always fuck over investors. Even though I did it for the acting role and not for the money, they managed to screw me over on that too.

Randall was unbothered by the lawsuit and offered me a role in a movie called *Extraction* with Bruce Willis in exchange for a personal Instagram shout-out (the guy has no shame). He did a lot of super cheap flicks in states that offered 30 percent rebates for shooting on location. Let's say the movie had a $10 million budget; Randall would pay a big name like Bruce Willis $4 million to shoot all of his scenes in one day. They would put the star's face on the box and presell the foreign rights for $7 million. After the state issued the $3 million rebate, Randall would have recouped his entire investment and have a freeroll on domestic sales. The movies were usually shit and too many could sink an actor's career if they weren't careful. But guys like Bruce Willis still did a bunch of those, hoped for the best, and tucked some cash away, figuring fuck it, $4 million for a single day of work is good pay.

I played a CIA agent with some fight scenes, including one with Kellan Lutz from *Twilight*. Bruce's one day of work was a disaster. He hadn't memorized the lines, so he had to read off a teleprompter. At one point, he accidentally read the stage directions.

"I'm not going to let you take the chip!" Bruce barked and then continued, "John looks nervous and turns to the right..."

Everyone was watching as Willis got more and more flustered until Randall took him into the trailer. After a couple bottles of wine to calm his nerves, he finally came back out and finished his scenes.

I grew up watching Bruce Willis movies, so it was interesting to watch him on this side of the screen. He obviously didn't take the movie seriously, but it made me feel better about my shit performance on Cassavetes movie, now knowing even the biggest actors can have bad days.

When I got back to Hollywood, I threw a party to let off steam. Every time I had an event, I tried to outdo the last one. And the last one had alligators, topless mermaids, porcupines, and hundreds of hot half-naked girls. But summer was coming, and it was time to crank it up. This time I got a giraffe, Steve Aoki to DJ, and literally had yellow school busses full of college girls showing up at the gate. I had set the theme for this party: body paint or schoolgirl outfits only.

The guy who plays Vince on *Entourage* showed up, and it felt like an episode of the show. At one point, I was in my closet getting my dick sucked by a couple girls, and I looked over, and an A-list celebrity action star was getting his dick sucked too. It was funny because he was still wearing his sunglasses in my dark-ass closet. I didn't bother to put on clothes when I finished.

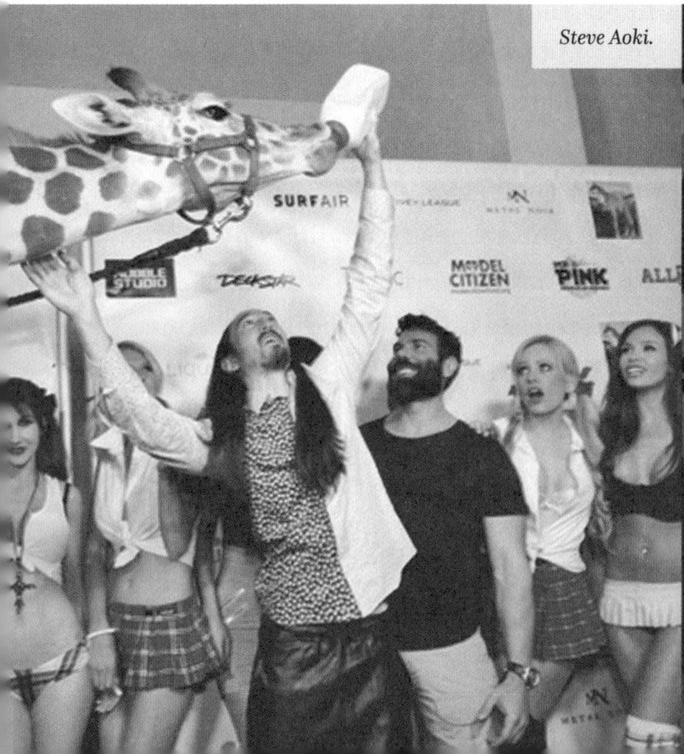

Steve Aoki.

The bus.

My bed had a bunch of girls in it, one being Lindsey Pelas. She had seen so much at this point that she didn't even flinch when I walked by her butt-naked. On the way to my shower, I passed a couple of topless girls talking to Ludacris. I grabbed a towel, and he reached out for a handshake. I wasn't quite sure where my hand had been, so I gave him a fist bump and stumbled by.

Steve Aoki, Vin Diesel, and Ludacris.

After my shower, I put on a robe and went to the kitchen to eat something. There were girls walking around wearing eight-inch skirts, heels, and nothing else; others were just wearing a little bit of body paint, and there were a few that weren't wearing anything at all. Almost every girl there was centerfold-worthy; even the bartenders were agency models. I don't know who hired them, but there were body-painted girls with lamp shades on their heads standing where my lamps used to be. It was a hell of a turnout, and everyone seemed to be having a good time.

When I went back to my bedroom, which had morphed into a VIP section, I saw a long line of girls waiting to get in. The line was wrapped all the way down the hall to the front door. I cherry-picked a few of the hottest ones, and security stepped aside, letting us in.

My bedroom was all reflective glass windows, so we could see the whole party but they couldn't see us. There was so much going on, it was hard to decide who or what I wanted to do. Tina, a tiny little brunette with huge tits and a bubble ass, was calling me over, so I climbed into bed with her and about five other girls.

I fumbled around on my nightstand for my bong and filled the bowl with weed. Tina went under the covers and started giving me a blowjob while some of the other girls started migrating over. I smoked a few hits of Tangerine Dream and tossed my robe on the floor. Tina got on top of me while two girls I didn't know made out with each other to my right.

After a bit, I pushed her off and let the two make-out girls suck my dick, and then I started fucking Tina again. I saw some girl with great real tits at the base of the bed watching, so I pulled her over, and we started kissing. I was playing with her enormous tits while banging Tina. Her tits were so damn nice and I planned on fucking her, but I didn't get around to it.

You may have noticed that most of my hookup stories are similar, and you aren't wrong. Almost every time it's kissing, hand on the dick, blowjob, and then sex. I never eat girls out; I rarely finger them unless I'm in a relationship. I know that might sound fucked up, but I figured if a girl doesn't get wet sucking my dick, then she's just not into me enough. Also I'm really good at fucking and not much else, so I'd rather just get to that.

There were at least fifty girls at the party that I'd hooked up with before, so there was no shortage of options. I usually tried to get new ones at the parties, but the girls were all so hot, it didn't matter too much to me at this point. I found that as long as I rotated between girls, I could go months or years hooking up with the same girls and never get tired of it. Plus if I waited long enough, it was like fucking a new girl since I'd forgotten what the sex was like.

When I woke up, the house was a mess. There was everything from cake in the pool to a fresh pile of shit by the side of the house because evidently someone thought the bathroom line was too long. It usually took a full day to clean up the house, but this one took two and a half. It was the biggest party I'd thrown yet, and for days afterward, I received crazy text messages reminding me of what I had done.

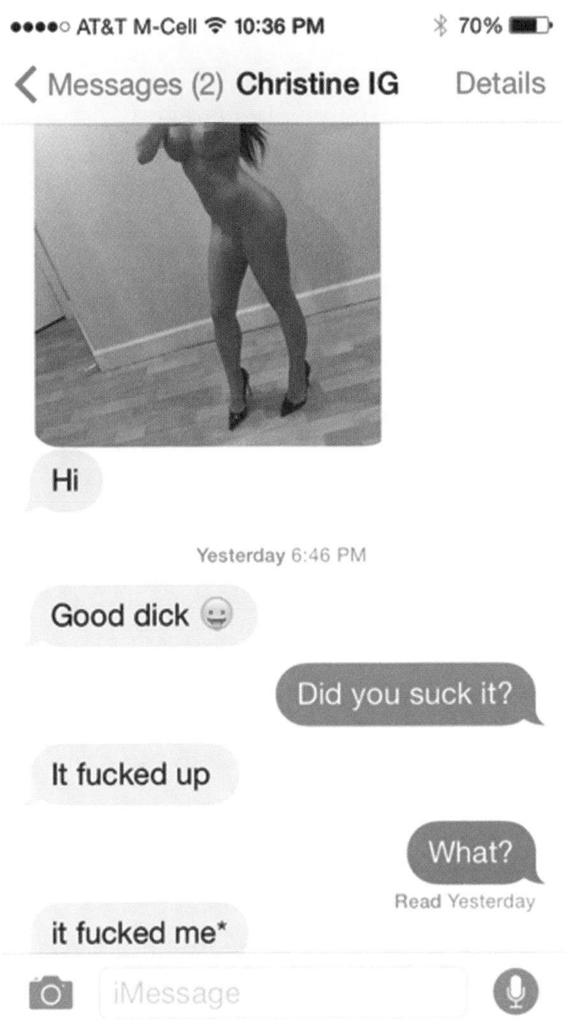

BJ BALDWIN

Professional Auto Racer, Two-Time Baja 1000 Winner

Dan's parties were always over-the-top fun. There were always awesome people there. Very interesting. Always friendly. And the women—let's just say I didn't know they made women that gorgeous.

One of many examples was a charity poker party packed full of celebrities. It became so packed that the people he was tight with ended up migrating to his bedroom, which was usually exclusively reserved for Dan's spectacular experimental sexual encounters with incredibly beautiful women. Most men would cut their finger off for a chance to have one of these women kick them in the nuts. And some of these women acted like they would walk through a wall of bullets just to have the opportunity to drink Dan's piss. Lmao. I'm sure it was problematic at times, but given the caliber of women in pursuit, I think that's a problem all men would like to have.

That night I was looking for Dan, and I found him in his closet being sexually assaulted by five of the most beautiful women I have ever seen, and all of the most favorable activities men pray for, were being done to him...and all at the same time. There was no room for additional lips or mouths to be placed anywhere on him. I opened the door, asked him the question, he answered like nothing was happening, I thanked him, closed the door, and immediately forgot what he said because I was still processing what I just saw. Four years later, I'm still processing. Lol.

Over the years, I would go to events where I was very well known for winning Baja 1000's, off-road championships, and my firearm proficiency. At every one of these events, people would ask about Dan, the bulk of the questions being "What's Dan up to?" I got it frequently enough to where my standard response evolved into "Just got off the phone with him. He's having sex with models."

CHAPTER 70

"Fame Brain"

I was invited to attend the White House Correspondents' Dinner, and I needed a date since Victoria and I had broken up. My lifestyle and the open relationship were making her miserable. I knew we were at a crossroads: Either I had to get exclusive with her or set her free. And since I wasn't capable of doing the first, I decided to stop dragging her though so much heartache. My videographer Jay Rich suggested that I take Jessa because not only was she beautiful, but she was also well spoken and she carried herself well. Jessa accepted as long as it would be just the two of us attending.

After we had separated for good, Jessa moved to Los Angeles to pursue her modeling career, and we hadn't talked much since. When Jessa pulled up to the plane, I could tell she was impressed but didn't want to admit it. She sarcastically gave me shit about being ostentatious while flashing me her signature smile. I replied by lighting a blunt held in a long quellazaire (cigarette holder), and we both started laughing like no time had passed.

On the flight to D.C., she told me she was on a photo shoot, and the photographer instructed her to "do it more sexy, like Dan Bilzerian style." She stopped immediately.

"What did you just say?"

Jessa.

"There's this guy on Instagram with an amazing lifestyle. He always has beautiful women around looking sexy. See, look." He'd pulled up my social media profile and tried to educate her.

"I know who he is, asshole. Dan is my ex!"

The photographer peppered her with questions about me until she stormed off the set. The pain and frustration in her voice when she recounted that story was, I will admit, enjoyable. Jessa had, in my opinion, chosen modeling, LA, and her own pursuit of fame over our relationship. That had always bothered me. So I moved to her city, and I became so famous that she couldn't even do her job without hearing my name. Meanwhile, I'd also fucked the majority of the big-name models she had to work with. She couldn't avoid me. I had officially accomplished all my goals for creating the Instagram profile. I'd gotten big enough that no one could ignore me, even her. In short, I Gatsby-ed her ass.

Although I sometimes responded to the women pounding my Instagram DMs (direct messages) with naked pictures, I never initiated contact, barring three exceptions. One woman that I made an exception for was Sarah, a model who provided sports updates with fruit rollups on her tits or strategically ripped up dresses. We'd spoken at length, and she was a really intelligent woman who used to be a boxer.

She lived on the East Coast, and we hadn't been able to link up yet, but we both extended standing invitations if either of us was ever in the vicinity. I told her I was traveling to Washington, D.C., for the event, and my assistant bought her a plane ticket to come down. Jessa and I were getting along, and I wasn't sure how I would manage the Sarah situation. But if necessary, I would just be honest. It's not like Jessa didn't know I hooked up with other women.

I had a jam-packed schedule in the nation's capital. Jessa wanted to sleep in, so I asked Sarah to join me in the morning for a meeting with Senator Rand Paul from Kentucky. We played some liar's poker and hung out briefly. Afterward, Sarah and I climbed into a luxury Sprinter van for a three-hour drive south to Richmond, Virginia. A poker pal named Ron Devine owned a couple of NASCAR teams, and after losing to me in a poker game, he painted my face and my pet goats on one of the cars as my preferred method of payment. Ron met us at the main gate for the racetrack, gave us all access passes, and took us to his team area. I hadn't said anything to Sarah about the car's paint scheme, so when we approached it, she burst out laughing.

Drivers in the pit asked me for photographs, and I was happy to take them. I knew that the more attention I garnered, the more Sarah would want to fuck me. Not because she was a groupie, but just because it's human nature.

Clarence once explained a phenomenon he referred to as "fame brain." He'd been around a lot of actors and business leaders, and he noticed that attraction increased in proportion to the eagerness of others around a person. You may have heard the term preselection—basically, people who have met certain criteria are more trusted and thus

Sarah.

have more access. For example, if you're a college student at Yale, other college students will have accepted you for a variety of things just because you go to Yale. It's "you have gone through a process and are deemed worthy by others, so I accept that judgment to be true." People don't consciously think of this; we unconsciously, all the time make judgments about people's "value" based on preselection.

Fame brain is a very acute form of preselection. It's one thing to be admitted into an exclusive school club; it's another to have everyone everywhere recognize you and ask to take pictures with you. Girls/guys see this, and they immediately and unconsciously give you a lot of respect and have a desire to be near to, talk with, or have sex with you. How many times have you seen some charity enlist a clueless actor to speak on their behalf in Congress? They are using fame brain to their advantage. No matter who you are, you will be affected at some level.

Let's say that a woman named Jennifer lusts after David Beckham. She witnesses another woman flirting with Beckham, some guy wanting to shake his hand, and a CEO trying to strike a deal. Jennifer already had the hots for Beckham. Maybe she planned on being coy, waiting a while, making sure she thought he respected her as a person first. But after observing those other people fawn over him and knowing her time with him may be scarce, Jennifer's desire will increase until it becomes a momentary obsession. And if he knows how to play his role in this, she will pursue and throw down with him at the first possible opportunity.

I know because I experienced the same phenomenon. Women who would barely speak to me would now take my hand and lead me to a bedroom. They went from passive to aggressive real quick. My objective had been met. I was famous, and getting laid now took zero effort. I could hook up with virtually any woman I wanted.

We watched the race from pit row which was as close to the action as you could get. On the way back to the trailer, I made sure we walked by the crowd, knowing exactly what would happen. People shouted my name, shook my hand, and asked for pictures. I wasn't about to go against the science of preselection or fame brain. So I worked with it. And sure enough, Sarah's arm was around me before we even reached the trailer.

Some might view my strategy as overkill, and perhaps it is. But it's not simply about the act of getting laid. For me, the turn-on is when a woman is *really* into me, when she's ready to explode with lust just at the chance to be with me. I never cared if a woman had some exotic technique, was double-jointed, or could wrap her legs around her head. I'm not impressed with parlor tricks. It's the energy, the enthusiasm, and the passion that excites me. The more she wants it, the better our sex will be, and the more she'll want to please me. That yearning for deep desire is one reason why I never liked hookers. Paying for sex could, and would, make life easier, but I only enjoy it when women *want* me. It's probably rooted in insecurity from my childhood, from longing to be wanted or not getting enough attention, but it's led to so many unbelievable experiences that I've made peace with it.

Back at the hotel, Sarah and I went to our separate rooms because I was playing it cool. Walking down the hall, I realized her jacket was inside mine, so I went back to knock on her door. She answered wearing only a thong and fruit rollups on her huge tits. I'm a sucker for fruit rollups, and I was helpless under her fruity neon spell. After we fucked, I took a shower and hoped that Jessa wouldn't want sex the minute I walked in. If so, I figured I could probably delay that with a room service order, and then I'd be ready for a second round.

The actual White House Correspondents' Dinner itself was a bore. I had to wear a tuxedo and bowtie, which I hate, and stand in lines for the crazy security. Jessa looked great even though she wore a cheap white dress that looked like something her grandmother had sewn together using her curtains. She was so gorgeous that no one noticed. She wore five-inch heels, making her look six-two and me look short. But I expected nothing less.

It was crowded, and people kept coming over wanting to talk to me, so I took some Valium to make this miserable experience more tolerable. I snored and drooled on the table during President Obama's speech. Jessa woke me up by shaking me.

"You're snoring, you horse's ass!" she said quietly, trying not to laugh. All I wanted to do was get the fuck out of that place and get high in my hotel room. We left early to have sex and eat room service.

I got back to LA, and some liberal followers were upset that I'd gone to the NRA museum while I was in Washington, so I posted a pic of this hot girl feeding me grapes and said, "Focus on your job, it's a weekday you simple fucks."

danbilzerian
City of West Hollywood
View Insights
Promote
Liked by bulletslinger and 552,803 others
danbilzerian Lotta people talked shit about me supporting the #NRA, focus on your job, it's a weekday you simple fucks #Bilzerian16
View all 34,875 comments
April 28, 2015

CHAPTER 71

Texas Tim

I'd been hanging out with a former Miss New York pageant girl named Luciana, a skinny Columbian who was exactly my type—skinny with big tits, a beautiful face, and long legs. She was 5'7" but couldn't have weighed more than 110 pounds. She was the perfect girl to have around because she looked totally harmless, and all the girls thought she was gorgeous, so she got away with doing wild shit. Luciana would get naked and make everyone do shots. I remember watching her randomly go down on a girl in my kitchen once, totally unprovoked. The girl had a PhD in turning up.

She hit me up as soon as I got back from D.C. and said she wanted to come by with her girlfriend. I knew that meant a threesome, but I was kinda tired and told her I wanted to fuck her solo. She called me a pussy and said she wanted to bring her friend. So not wanting to be a pussy, I agreed.

She brought over a really well-known model with tens of millions of followers, and we had a threesome. I was kind of shocked she was down, because her boyfriend was really famous, but I shouldn't have been so surprised. It seemed like almost every girl I met cheated.

LIN OEDING

Director, Stunt Coordinator

Dan's Blue Jay house sat about as high in the Hollywood Hills as any house could, and because of that, the view was breathtaking. I had a girlfriend, but it was a hell of a place to be a fly on the wall. I'm not a professional bartender, but I do mix a pretty good vodka, cran cocktail, so I heard a lot of wild stories at the bar. Married women who were given a hall pass from their husbands to sorority girls who made flying to LA to party with a guy they only knew from the Internet sounds like some kind of foreign exchange trip. But crazier than all the stories I'd heard was what I witnessed.

I saw so many surprising things, and I'm not talking about orgies; the house wasn't some crazy sex dungeon like some might think. I'm more talking about the interactions and girls behaving in a way that I'd never previously experienced. One night, Dan was sitting on the couch across the room chatting with a woman. I was manning the bar when suddenly, I was startled by a voice.

"Hey! You're friends with Dan, right?" She sounded rushed, like it was some sort of emergency.

I spun around and saw an absolutely drop-dead gorgeous blonde leaning over the bar.

Before I could even get a word in, she continued, "Can you help me? I need to sleep with Dan!"

I was sure I'd heard her correctly and couldn't help but laugh. I texted Dan even though he was twenty feet away and said, This gorgeous blonde is insisting that she sleep with you lol.

He looked over and replied with one word only: Nah.

I gave her the bad news in as tactful a way as possible. I could tell just by looking at her that she'd probably never been told "No" by a guy in her life—and certainly not when the question was "Wanna have sex?"

She explained that she was in LA doing a photoshoot for a major brand and was flying out tomorrow morning, so she had to sleep with Dan—tonight! She was getting more frantic by the minute as she began thinking out loud, plotting desperate schemes to get Dan's attention, like some sort of perverted Wile E. Coyote.

"Text him and say its urgent," she pleaded with me. "Tell him I just want to have sex, nothing more! If he's too busy right now, ask if he would consider a raincheck if I come back later tonight?"

I pulled out my phone and relayed the message to Dan. We waited for his response in silence.

Moments later, I got another one-word reply: "Busy." I looked up from my phone and felt sorry for her as she was ready to sacrifice life and limb all for a night with him, and what did she have to show for it? A seat at the bar, alone, venting to the bartender. Had it been a guy in that seat, it would have been completely normal—if not expected and a bit creepy. But this Australian bombshell of a woman? That's some parallel universe shit only seen under Dan Bilzerian's roof.

Thankfully, this story has a happy ending. She said she was staying near the "W Hotel" and I'd mentioned that a buddy of mine, Steve, was having a party in that area. I felt a bit like a game show host offering a consolation prize, but she seemed happy to take Steve's contact information. What happened after that is Steve's story—one he loves to tell—which begins with "Dan Bilzerian and his absurdly high standards led to the best night of my life..."

A couple days later, I fired up the jet and went to Vegas because a billionaire Texan named Tim was in town. He did the wildest shit you could imagine. One time, he threw $200,000 worth of casino chips into a pool and told the women they could keep whatever they grabbed, but they had to dive in naked. People on fire don't strip down as quickly as those women did. Another time, Tim set up a glass phone booth in his hotel suite. He attached a leaf blower and fired in a bunch of $100 bills. The women could get in the booth and keep whatever they could hold, but they had to be completely naked. It was hilarious to watch. They tucked the bills in their armpits and between their legs, but it was a struggle because every time they would reach for more, some dollars would drop.

He also had some challenges that involved fully clothed adults. A model perusing the wine list announced how much she really liked good wine.

"You're a big wine connoisseur, huh? I'll give you $40,000 if you can tell the difference between red and white wine," Tim wagered. "But if you can't, you have to pack your shit and take a cab back to Los Angeles."

The girl feigned confidence as she put on the blindfold and promptly failed the test. Even just with a guess, she had a fifty-fifty chance of getting it correct. Tim didn't hesitate. He had the gorgeous model thrown out of his hotel room and sent home.

Another example was his trip with a limo full of women to Louis Vuitton. Tim told them they could have anything in the store, but they only had five minutes to get it to the counter. The girls went from classy to Jerry Springer in about point two seconds. They fought for bags and tripped as they sprinted to get their hauls to the checkout counter.

His disregard for money was like nothing I had ever seen before. He offered a woman $350,000 to let him fuck her in the ass. He bought 150 bottles of Dom Perignon at a club, got bored after five minutes, and left all the booze sitting there. The guy was an animal.

During this particular escapade in Las Vegas, I learned that Tim had rented every bungalow on the left side of an ultra-pool at the MGM Grand. He paid half a million dollars for the bar tab, but that wasn't the most expensive part of the day. It was his girlfriend's birthday, and Tim hired the Navy SEAL Leap Frogs parachute team to skydive into the pool with her attached to one of the divers.

Consider that for a moment.

You would need a waiver or approval from the City of Las Vegas to jump into a no-jump zone. You'd have to get clearance from McCarran International Airport, approval from the MGM Grand, and insurance in case something went wrong. Then you would have to obtain approval from the United States military to allow highly-trained, very expensive active duty soldiers to jump into a civilian pool for no reason other than for a woman's amusement.

That's some fucking juice.

Lots of people talk big about doing crazy shit. A few actually do it. But nobody did shit like Tim.

The SEALs did their job, professional and nonplussed as expected. They landed in the pool of the day club, folded up their chutes, and started drinking beer. I stood there in disbelief.

Later that night, we planned to head to the Floyd Mayweather and Manny Pacquiao fight, the "Battle of Greatness." Tim had done contests all week to select five women to attend the fight. He gave each woman a $500,000 necklace attached to a leash so he could stroll in with the ladies in tow. In the end, Tim didn't even show up.

Tim stayed in town for a few days, partying everywhere. One night, Noah a promoter buddy of mine, hit me up, saying that he and Tim were going to a club and asked if I wanted to join. I went over and it was like forty girls, a couple of Tim's friends, and the security at the table. Tim didn't show up, but his girlfriend was there. She was good friends with Samantha, and she also used to work at my poker games.

I was at the booth, sitting on top, and Tim's girlfriend was sitting between my legs on the bench cushion. After a couple glasses of champagne, she reached back and started rubbing my dick. I wasn't going to fuck her, she was just flirting, but one of the security guards saw it and informed Tim.

We left the club and headed back to Tim's villa. The security told me I wasn't allowed in the villa, presumably because of the dick-grabbing incident. But the next night, Noah said he talked to Tim, and he wasn't pissed. He said it was all good and invited me over.

There were 150 models and maybe only ten of Tim's people there. After a five minutes, I hooked up with a woman in the bathroom. She dropped to her knees and sucked my dick. But when I started to put on a condom to fuck her, she said no. I did my usual thing, which was be cool and leave. I found another girl, tumbled into a bedroom, and she sucked my dick on the bed. As soon as I grabbed a condom, she said no.

Exact same thing. Not wanting to deal with any more bullshit, I grabbed a girl I'd fucked in the past. When she pulled the same stunt, my head started to spin.

"Are these bitches allergic to latex all of a sudden, or what?"

In total, about four or five women did this. I got so pissed off that I left and went home to jerk off like a loser.

The next day, I debriefed with Noah.

"What the fuck was going on last night?"

He said he hadn't heard anything weird. Everyone had a good time.

"Two of these women had literally begged me to fuck them before. I'm so confused," I went on.

Noah let me go on and on until he couldn't contain himself anymore. He laughed hysterically for a solid minute before finally revealing that Tim had paid every single female at the party to *not* fuck me. I felt like I'd been trying to solve a puzzle or figure out a magic trick and now that I had the answer, it seemed so obvious. I couldn't help but laugh. It was genius.

CHAPTER 72

A Hurricane of Hedonism

Todd Phillips, the man responsible for *The Joker*, asked if I wanted to be in the movie *War Dogs*. The role would entail me beating the shit out of Jonah Hill and Miles Teller in the same Miami nightclub where that woman attacked my friend Christine.

Todd Phillips and Jonah Hill on the set of War Dogs.

Todd was a cool guy, always fun to hang out with, and very down to earth. He was the complete opposite of so many of the pretentious Hollywood douchebags I'd met. All in all, it was a good reason to visit South Florida.

I brought Luciana, who always brought fellow pageant girls into the mix. She loved to bring in other girls, and she was a huge instigator, but the best part was she was no drama. Women like her don't come around often; it's rare to find a hot girl like that who isn't a headache.

I always had good orgy etiquette. Fuck your girl first before her friends and give her the most attention. For this trip, Luciana invited Miss Florida, an innocent, recently single twenty-one-year-old who'd only slept with a handful of guys prior. We had a threesome the first night, spent the day on a yacht, and then went out on a fan boat in the Everglades that night.

Our guide brought a giant spotlight to shine the alligators. A normal motor would spook them, but the dull humming of the fan boat propellers mesmerized the reptiles. When we hit them with the floodlight, they'd freeze like a deer on the road. You could tell how big the gator was by how far apart its eyes were. I'd grown up in Florida and had played with gators my whole life. Ben Stevens got a cool video of me holding a six-foot alligator I'd grabbed, but upon review, my lawyer said it could be considered "molesting wildlife." I thought that would sound strange to have on my record, so I never posted the clip.

After a fun week in Miami, I returned to Los Angeles where a girl named Skye and her big-titted blond Canadian friend were waiting at my house for me. Skye had told her friend good things, and a threesome quickly ensued. We all ended up back at my house that night after the club with some random girls and Samantha. Skye and her friend were texting me to come fuck them in my guest room while I hooked up with a tall skinny blonde who later passed out in my bed. She woke up when I started fucking Samantha and ended up joining in. It's always interesting to witness the reaction of a woman waking up to you fucking a different girl. At first, they're confused. And you might think they'd get pissed off. But as long as the other girl is hot, they rarely seem to mind.

In the aftermath, around one in the afternoon, Jay Rich came into the room and just started laughing. He lifted his phone and took a picture without hesitation. I'd just gotten out of bed, and the room was demolished. It looked like a storm had blown through. Pillows and clothes were strewn about the floor. A stiletto heel was stuck in the side of my bed. Two naked girls were passed out face down while I looked at the mess half confused and half amused.

This candid picture was a perfect representation of what my life had become. A hurricane of sex and partying.

CHAPTER 73

You're Gonna Need a Bigger Boat

Tom Goldstien was hired to defend a Chinese billionaire held in Las Vegas on bookmaking charges. If Tom could get an acquittal, he would earn $10 million. But if he lost, he'd get nothing. After an intense eleven-month trial, he won. They were going to a poker game in London to celebrate and invited me to tag along on his client's G550.

I had no idea about the client. Didn't know the man, didn't know what he got up to. But Interpol evidently did, or thought they did, and they red-flagged his plane and grounded us in Montenegro. It turned out that they suspected Tom's client of being the head of the Triad crime syndicate. During our delay, we retired to the guy's $70 million-dollar castle, a gorgeous stone structure with terracotta tiles on the roof.

The authorities made it clear that Tom's client was not going to proceed to London anytime soon. Montenegro was nice, but after a week or two, I got bored and decided to link up with Clarence, who was on a yacht off the coast of Italy. I chartered a jet and asked Clarence how many girls he wanted me to bring.

“Bring as many as you want, the yacht is huge,” Clarence replied.

I called Nico, an Italian promoter I’d met in Cannes. “Do you have any hot girls in Italy?”

“Bro, I’m in Milan,” he laughed. “There is nothing *but* beautiful women here.”

“Grab all that you can and meet me at the port in Viareggio.”

“Seriously, give me a number.”

“Bring twenty women.”

“Okay, see you soon.”

Clarence was thrilled I was coming down, and he probably didn’t think that I would truly show up with that many women in tow. I had Luciana and Miss Florida meet me in Italy, and Nico pulled up with a fucking charter bus full of Italian models.

“You’re gonna need a bigger boat,” I told Clarence.

“Yeah, right,” he laughed.

But I was right. When the bus unloaded, he looked at me incredulously.

“Shit...I’m gonna need a bigger boat.”

Clarence actually had to charter a second yacht just to carry all the fucking women. We split the group up on the two vessels, and everyone grabbed a room. In Porto Azzurro, we went to a nightclub and just got bombarded. Those Italians went nuts, asking for photographs and selfies. I had to leave; it was just too much. Security surrounded us in a diamond formation to get us out of the craziness. On the way out, amid the mayhem, I saw two drop-dead gorgeous Italian women trying to get to me, so I pulled them into our group.

We finally made it to the van, and the two newcomers sat on either side of me.

A guy yelled at the door, “May I please make photo with you?”

I figured, *What’s one more?* so I leaned out and took the picture. He asked to join our party, and I said no.

“But that one, that one there, she is my girlfriend,” he stammered in broken English. I explained that the women were more than welcome to stay with him but he was not joining us. They looked at him, looked at me, and then turned their heads the other direction without stirring from their seats. That solved that.

We hadn't been on the road for more than a minute, and both the girls were sucking my dick. Clarence and his date were watching and laughing in the front seat, and the girls in the back were equally surprised at the absurdity of the situation. I had literally said zero words to those women. I was pretty certain they didn't even speak English. I just put the one girl's hand on my dick, and they did the rest.

At the port, I zipped up and got out of the van. The jilted boyfriend was there. He'd followed our convoy, which was a bit extreme, so I told security to have a word with him, and we boarded the yacht.

Security came back and explained that one of the women was his girlfriend and that they actually lived together. He said she had the keys to their house, and he couldn't go home without them.

"Just tell the girls to take off," I said. Security came back, giggling, enjoying their work as translators.

"The women, they...they say they will not leave without fucking you."

Clarence thought this was hysterical and started laughing like a hyena. I took the two girls to my room and fucked one in the ass while the other licked my nuts and vice versa. Both women got facials, and not one single word of English was ever spoken.

I showered, threw on some shorts, and went upstairs to eat. I found Clarence on the top deck in the Jacuzzi with a bunch of topless Italian models. This trip was off to a great start, and we hadn't even left port yet.

We went to Bonifacio, which was one of the most beautiful places I had ever seen. There were huge sheer cliffs hundreds of feet high with a big medieval citadel perched on top. We did some sightseeing and returned to the boat. I fucked Miss Florida before Luciana, which upset her a bit. Luciana told Florida to go fuck Clarence and to leave me to her.

Clarence had women lined up, and he was going down on them with the doors and windows wide open. He loved to eat pussy and didn't want any privacy. There were something like seven women on Clarence's bed when I entered with Luciana. It turned into a big orgy, and Clarence and I traded off. I started fucking Florida again; Luciana got jealous for the first time and fucked Clarence to make a point.

The boats sailed at night, and each day we awakened in a new port. While at sea, the women walked around the boat essentially in the nude. Clarence could only have sex once a day, but he constantly had women on his bed waiting to get eaten out like an all you can eat pussy buffet. The girls were super horny because the more sex you see and hear, the more it's on your mind. Clarence was coming off a tough divorce, and this debauchery was just what the doctor ordered.

There were twenty-four women rotating between the two boats; Nico was on the second boat, and Clarence and I were the only guys on the main yacht. I spent my days getting high, eating amazing food and going four to five rounds a day with beautiful women. I was having the time of my life.

CLARENCE WILSON *(NAME CHANGED)*

Hedge Fund Manager

Dan told me that more people came up to him than Mark Wahlberg as his plan unfolded, to which, internally, I was saying bullshit! But then I saw it firsthand with Dan in Italy. I was shocked, and the real craziness didn't start till later.

I witnessed a mob at a club surround our position, fighting to get into the small section we were sitting. It took a chain of over twenty bodyguards to escort us out, but then still somehow two girls managed to pile in the van we were leaving in, headed to the yacht. They immediately started tearing his pants down and blowing him in front of the five other people in the van as we drove back, nonchalantly playing it off as normal.

When we arrived, the one girl's boyfriend was hanging outside the yacht asking for the girlfriend to come back out. Not mad, just waiting. As if this was the famous "hall pass" he had to give. I witnessed the frenzy created and the competition firsthand to be with Dan. It was quite the spectacle, but it happened so often in so many different scenarios it would be boring to list them all.

No rock star could compete. You may be thinking these are just crazies, but I saw the most respectful and improbable fall prey to what I referred to as "fame brain." We truly are herd animals.

Dan was like the Eiffel Tower to hedonism. Ask anyone who has visited Paris—Did they go and see the Eiffel tower or at least take a picture with it the background? You'd be hard-pressed to find anyone who had visited and didn't at least take a picture. This was Dan; he was so famous, much like the Eiffel Tower, that you just had to see it and take a picture. Dan was Eiffel Tower of sex and partying.

You know the ride people stand in line for two hours at the theme park cause it's "the ride?" Dan is like the ride, and women were like, "There's no way I'm going to not fuck him."

CHAPTER 74

Presidential Tour

Before I met up with Clarence, I told my team that I was in Europe and asked them to set up some club appearances on my way back home. Ben Stevens lined-up some clubs on what he called the "Bilzerian '16 Presidential Campaign Tour." That's what my campaign in the summer of 2015 was. It was an excuse to get paid to drink and fuck girls. The first stop was at my version of a convention center or hotel ballroom: The Cabana Pool Bar in Toronto.

Samantha got naked as soon as we boarded the plane. I took an Ambien, told the pilots to give us some privacy, and got to work. We were flying in from Naples after spending the week on Clarence's yacht. I took Samantha because she never caused problems, we never fought about anything, and she was drop-dead gorgeous. Most of all, I liked that she was in medical school and had life aspirations other than modeling.

danbilzerian
St. John Bosco Catholic School
View Insights
Promote
Liked by bulletslinger and 553,305 others
danbilzerian Since I left my Jet in the U.S., my business manager said 125k for the one way was a waste, that turned out to be a lie
View all 26,985 comments
June 20, 2015
Samantha.

At Cabana, they had heavy security, big cardboard cutouts of my name, and a table with about twenty models and bottles waiting for us. Within fifteen minutes of arrival, I fucked a girl with an impeccable ass in a private bathroom. There was a shower, so I cleaned up, put my shorts back on, and went back to the table.

The club was wide open, and I was right in the center like a zoo animal on display. I didn't mind. I'd washed a couple 'ludes down with a Corona, so I was happy as a pig in shit. The setup was perfect. I had tons of girls at my table with dudes behind the ropes begging for pictures. Plus, I had Samantha standing next to me, looking bad as hell in an Italian bikini.

Cabana Club, Toronto.

The women couldn't help but be curious, and they had to come to me, which meant no effort. After a couple of hours hanging out, I invited the hottest girls back to my suite for an after-party. I fucked two girls in my bedroom while the rest hung out in the living room. After, I let some of the others into bed, where we smoked weed and ordered room service.

The next day, we loaded up in the jet and flew to Montreal. As soon as we landed, I went to George St. Pierre's gym and hit pads with his trainer. After, I got high, ordered room service, and had a relaxing night with Samantha at the hotel. Every now and then, I would look at my DMs. They were mostly flooded with guys wanting to hang out or asking for money. Only about 10 percent were messages from girls and of those, only about 10 percent were hot girls. It was like sifting a big river for gold, a lot of work for a small reward, but that night it was worth it.

Beachclub Montreal was a private island with a wakeboarding park on the right and a waterslide park on the left. They flew me in on a helicopter, and I told the pilot to forget landing—just hold a hover. As he did so, I dove out of the seat into the water.

Everyone went crazy, which was something I was getting used to. But I still wasn't accustomed to that much excitement just because of my presence. I never thought of myself as being special because I'm really not outstanding at anything traditional or quantifiable. I'm smart, but there are a million people more intelligent than me. I had no artistic talent; I couldn't sing, play an instrument, or act worth a shit. Looking back, it felt like I had a list of failures a mile long, hell I didn't even finish high school.

I tend to be hard on myself, probably because growing up the bar for excellence was set so unachievably high, but on that swim, I tried to be more objective. I looked at my failures and considered my accomplishments.

I wanted to be a Navy SEAL because I wanted to develop confidence and prove to my father and everyone else that I was tough. I made it to the last day of training, but I didn't play the game, so I failed. I did, however, succeed at my goals. I completed more days of training than almost any Navy SEAL, which gave me confidence, and finishing two winter hell weeks, proved by most standards, that I was a hard motherfucker.

I wanted to make a lot of money because growing up my dream was to have nice cars and cool toys like Ernie, but most importantly money represented freedom. I saw an opportunity to do this in poker, however I lacked discipline, so I failed. I went flat broke, but I got back up and played eighteen hours a day for thirty days straight until I had a bankroll and a plan. I cultivated a reputation that gained me entrance into the best games with the worst players. I worked at that strategy for thirteen years until I had more money than I knew what to do with. I now owned a jet and I had complete freedom to go or do whatever I wanted, whenever I wanted.

I wanted to get laid more because when I was younger, I got exactly zero attention from hot girls. I failed miserably for seven years straight until I learned how to get women to chase me. I utilized the power of competition, jealousy, scarcity, and ultimately the sledgehammer that was fame. The end result—I had so much sex that I had to start taking Cialis daily like a multivitamin, and even then, I still couldn't keep up with the demand.

I wanted to become famous because fame represented access, it was powerful, and I knew it would get me more pussy with even less effort. So I developed a strategy utilizing social media and digital press to become one of the most famous men in the world. After being mobbed by fans in every country and having women consistently throw themselves at me with reckless abandon; I knew I had accomplished my goal.

In BUD/S, I swam miles and miles. But I was more reflective and thought about more during that short hundred-yard swim at Beachclub Montreal than I had in all my previous swims put together. Every time I lifted my head for a quick breath, I heard the pounding music and cheering crowd. Through all the nonsense, I finally realized my talent. I had the ability to *setup* my life to get what I wanted. That was the only reason the partiers cheered for me. It doesn't sound as glamourous, but I'd much rather be good at that than at throwing a ball or playing a guitar.

When I went on stage with the DJ, the crowd went wild. They were having a blast just watching me party; it was a cool feeling and a complete 180 from my childhood. I'd come a long way since high school, and it made me happy knowing I created this reality myself.

Beachclub Montreal.

The helicopter picked up me, Samantha, and Rosie and took us straight to my plane. Rosie had lost her bikini and heads turned as she walked through the private airport topless. She'd been on the yacht with Samantha and I, but because of a passport issue, she had to fly commercial. Rosie was one of the coolest girls I've ever dated, she never got jealous or caused any problems; everyone loved Rosie.

Samantha and Rosie.

ROSIE ROFF

Model

Dan is the eye of the storm, calm and centered within a hurricane of excitement and chaos which manifests around him. Dan moves through life with complete ease, never pretending or overcompensating. He remains the same no matter how crazy or outrageous the situation. He is a beacon of stability, and there is truth in his character.

I've watched Dan swan dive off the top deck of our yacht in Italy; party in a room with twenty-five nude, beautiful, women; enjoy mushrooms peacefully on tropical beaches; play chess with Richard Branson on Necker Island; impulsively jump from a helicopter into the ocean in Bali; ride a glow-in-the-dark bicycle through the desert at Burning Man; and have a casual coffee at home with Lance Armstrong.

In a life of unadulterated hedonism and spontaneity, Dan's steadiness is magnetic. I've watched beautiful women around the world become instantly drawn to him. It's a harmonious balance of yin and yang. Order and chaos. I've always been unconventional, but I had never felt such hedonistic freedom as I did with Dan; it was pure spontaneity with no thought of anything except that moment in time. I treasure the memories and his friendship.

At my stop in New York City, I met up with a drop-dead gorgeous blonde who's DM I'd found while "sifting the river" in Montreal. She had some of the best tits I'd ever seen in my life, and we fucked straightaway at my hotel that afternoon. That night, she came to the club I was hosting. Her boyfriend showed up, and she sat in my lap in front of the dude. It can be brutal what women put these poor guys through. Men get the bad rap in dating, but I've seen women do *way* more fucked up shit, you just don't hear about it because they rarely get caught.

I brought a bunch of girls back to my hotel and hooked up with different ones in my bedroom while everyone else hung out in the living room like patients waiting on an appointment to see a doctor. Every night seemed to get crazier. The more shit I did, the more normal it started to seem.

The so-called campaign went splendidly. The clubs were happy, everyone had good times, and I felt on top of the world. I'd accomplished what I said I was going to do. I'd become world famous, and it only took me a year and a half. I was getting laid with zero effort, and with clubs forking over $75,000 an hour, I was even getting paid to do so.

At the club in NYC.

When I'd host those events, they'd always have a table full of models waiting. I always brought some, and then there were all the other girls in the club who'd come to the table to see what all the fuss was about. I was never a fan of nightclubs, but hosting was different. There is no better way to get laid than throwing a party, and hosting was the same as throwing a party but without the cost, headache, and cleanup.

Boston was the last appearance. It was the least prestigious booking of the tour but turned out to be the craziest. The models they provided were nowhere near as attractive as New York City and the Canadian cities, but they were wilder. They removed their dresses and pranced around in thongs with Bilzerian '16 bumper stickers on their tits.

After an hour, I grabbed some girls from the stage and headed down the hallway out of the club. A line of girls followed us out, and I picked and pointed at the ones I would let come after-party. When I was younger, this is exactly how I envisioned it would have been for rock stars backstage after their shows.

Back at the hotel room, there was Samantha, about ten cute women, and five hot ones. Samantha got into my bed, and I started fucking a girl next to her. Samantha fingered herself while watching us. When I finished, I took a shower and ordered room service. While I was waiting on the food, I banged another girl while she went down on Samantha. Some girl came in from the living room, crawled in the bed and sucked my dick to finish.

I went out to eat my food, and about twenty minutes later, Samantha came out and found me fucking another girl in the hallway of the suite while others stood around watching. Samantha was tired and wanted to go to bed in her separate room, but she discovered that her purse had been stolen in the bedlam. She phoned the front desk for an extra key, and when the bellman knocked on the door to deliver it, she stepped over me and the blonde going at it on the floor. The look on the employee's face was priceless because I didn't stop on account of him. Some dedicated fans were milling about in the hallway, and they got an eyeful as well.

I can only imagine what the White House would have looked like if I'd gotten elected, which was never going to happen. But I'm a determined motherfucker, so if I ever seriously set my mind to it...

danbilzerian
Las Vegas, Nevada

View Insights

Promote

Liked by **calebslife** and **503,977 others**

danbilzerian In an age of pussified political correctness, you have to respect people who remain unfiltered

View all 43,773 comments

December 16, 2015

CHAPTER 75

Jax

My buddy Jax and I were at a pool party when Meek Mill told me, "The hood loves you," which was one of the more surprising compliments I'd received. Growing up, I didn't get much respect, and I certainly didn't get any from guys in the hood. As a scrawny kid who didn't want to be scared of anything, I looked up to the gangsters who didn't take shit from anyone. I respected their lack of fear, and it felt good to get that respect back.

MEEK MILL

Rapper

Dan inspired us just by not following the standards of the so-called American lifestyle and actually made having money look like fun with his own way of

Chuck Liddell, Meek Mill, and Nicki Minaj.

living... In the hood, we don't ask, "What you do?" Well, the real hustlers don't. We just get inspired when we see winners!

Jax is Jackson Vroman, an almost seven-foot-tall power forward and center who'd been drafted by the Chicago Bulls but was playing in overseas leagues. He was the life of the party, an extremely popular, funny guy who never had a bad word to say about anyone unless it was to their face.

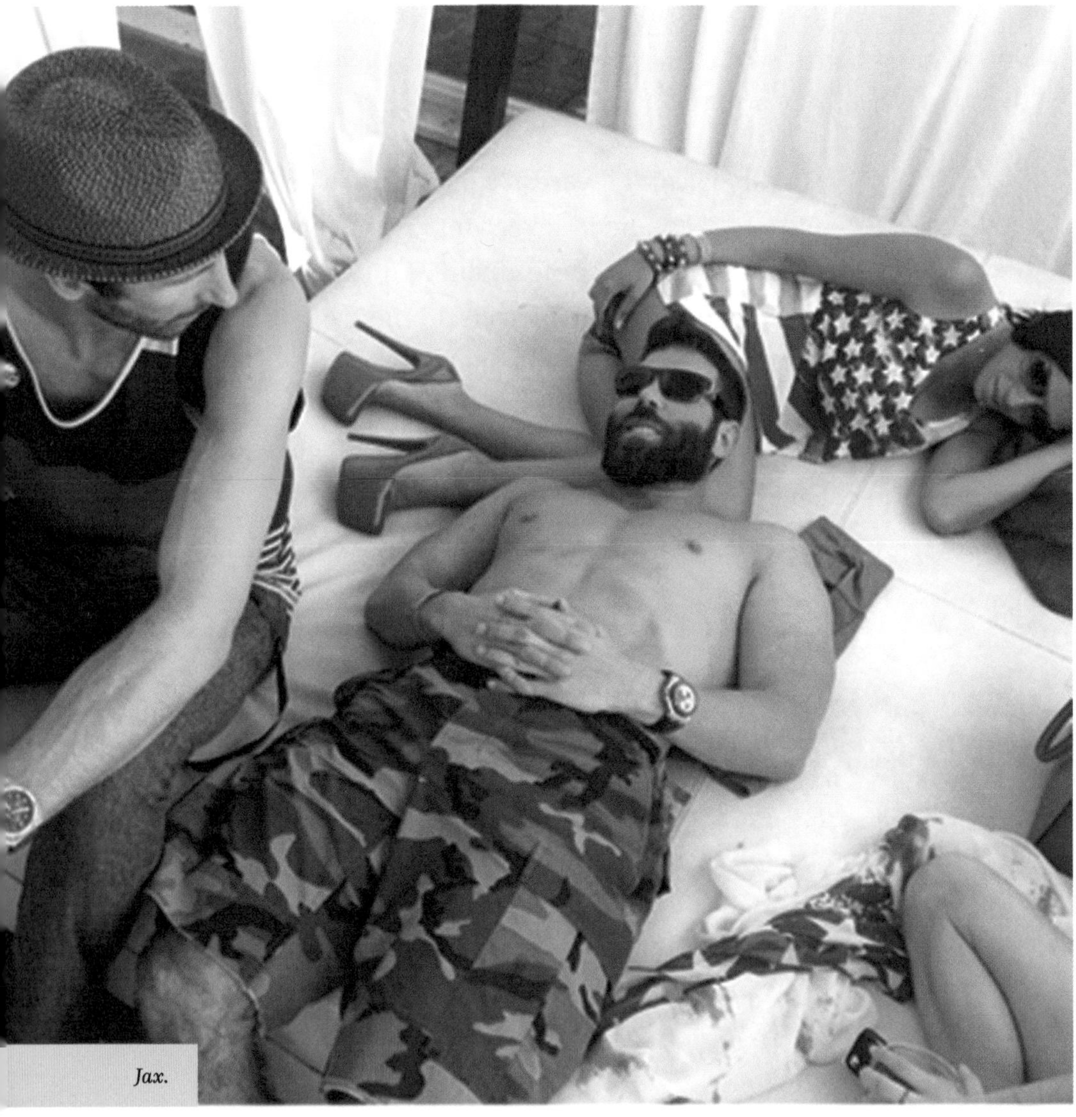

Jax.

We'd become close over the last couple years living in LA. As my notoriety grew, I left my house less and less, and we'd regularly get high on my bean bag chairs and talk about life, experiences, and girls. It seemed as if every hot woman in LA had slept with either him or me, so there was always lots to talk about.

He'd dragged me out of the house to celebrate his friend's birthday, but the pool party was kinda boring compared to the crazy shit I'd been doing anyway. So I left early.

That was the last time I saw Jax alive.

The next day, I received a frantic call that the giant was dead. I rushed over to his house. I beat the authorities there and walked inside. The few people in the house were sobbing, hugging each other, or just staring off into the distance in shock. I held out hope that somehow this was a mistake, someone fucked up, or maybe it was a sick prank. But then I saw him in the deep end of the pool.

Jax's eyes were open, forever staring up into the sky. His hair flowed around his face, and his long arms were outstretched. He was pale and almost translucent.

I've only cried a handful of times in my life, and that moment was one of them. It's horrible when anyone passes away, but Jax was so beloved. It was just heartbreakingly sad. Los Angeles was never the same after he died. Jax tied so many diverse sets of friends together, people who would not normally associate. Once that bond was gone, people went their separate ways.

Toxicology revealed ketamine, cocaine, and GHB in his system. Security camera footage showed him trying to stand from a beanbag but collapsing back into it. He finally got upright and stepped onto a lawn chair near the shallow end of the pool. He slipped, hit his head on the side, and fell into the water. That's what everyone thinks killed him. Official cause of death was accidental drowning.

But I think there was more to it.

Jax was incredibly generous when he was making good money. He bought everyone's drinks and rented nice houses. Jax spent every penny he made every season, which wasn't a lot compared to what players like LeBron James or Steph Curry make, but spending $700,000 in six months is a lot by anyone's standards.

Then he wasn't picked up.

With no contract and nothing in the bank, he struggled. A good friend named Stratton let Jax stay at his house and gave him some cash from time to time. I think it really ate at Jax that he had nothing coming in and couldn't reciprocate financially. He started getting more fucked up more often. He ended up in the hospital a few times, and we all told him to slow down. But when you're sober, you have no choice but to face reality. He wasn't ready to do that.

Financial ruin can be crippling. A few of my father's friends killed themselves because of money troubles. It's difficult to change your entire lifestyle, and it can seem like the end of the world—even though it's only the end of one chapter of your life and the beginning of a new one. Downsizing doesn't sound hard, but when you're accustomed to a certain level of social status and a high standard of living, it can be damn near impossible. Another peril of being rich is the higher up you go, the farther you have to fall.

I tried to think of something for Jax to do, but it was hard to come up with anything that would pay enough to sustain his standard of living. I wish I had an answer for him other than to just recalibrate to a more normal lifestyle.

I dedicated much of my life to accumulating wealth. Money can make life infinitely better in the short run. But as long as you have enough to survive on, it's not a solution to any *real* problems. In the military, I made $860 a month, got my ass kicked all day, and it was one of the happiest times of my life. I was working towards a goal, and the money was all relative.

In San Diego, on the rare instances when I had enough energy to go to the movies or out to dinner, that was a luxury. Those simple things brought me a disproportionate amount of joy. Conversely, when I bought half million-dollar cars or spent a normal person's lifetime income on one single week's vacation, it wasn't enough. Eventually, nothing that I purchased brought me lasting joy, yet still I couldn't stop doing it. It was more an addiction than a necessity.

I wish I had been able to communicate these thoughts to Jax at the time when he needed honesty and sincerity. But I was more caught up in the materialistic rat race than he was. I couldn't express these truths because Hollywood will make even the most levelheaded person think that nothing is ever enough.

I spoke at Jax's funeral. It was humbling.

"Jax had so many friends and everyone loved him." I paused for a minute, fighting away the tears, and I said, "I don't have many friends, but Jax was my friend."

CHAPTER 76

Caring Too Much

Draft Kings, the online fantasy sports betting site, paid me a million dollars to throw a party for ten of their winners.

The deal was I had to do a post on my social media saying I was going to throw the party, and they committed to give me another half million to cover the costs of the party. However, they'd gotten into some regulatory lawsuit a month after we signed the deal and had to stop all promotions. They said I could keep the million, and I didn't have to throw the party, but they weren't going to give me the half million.

I posted I was going to throw a party, and I do what I say, so the party had to go on. To ensure the ratio was good and the contestants had a good time, I'd told thirty-six Instagram models I was gonna pay them to go and post for the company, and I was going to honor that commitment as well. I hit up my buddy Bam, a former Marine who ran Wishes for Warriors, and told him to send me some combat-wounded amputee veterans. Then I called Clarence and asked him if he wanted to take the girls and the vets to Cabo and chop it. He had a blast on the yacht, so he didn't hesitate and said book it.

BRYAN "BAM" MARSHALL

Former Marine, Founder of Wishes For Warriors

So I'm sitting on the couch one day and I get a message from Dan: "Yo I want to send some vets with me to Mexico." I remember thinking, "Shit, this can go one of two ways...either give these guys a time of their life with Dan Bilzerian or...we are getting into major fucking trouble." Either way, I knew two awesome combat wounded guys that could use this trip.

A few weeks after, I get a call from one of the vets. "Bro! We made the cover of Playboy*!" I am like, "What the hell do you mean "We" made the cover of* Playboy*?" He says, "We as in me... and I am in a Wishes shirt!" I was laughing so hard I couldn't believe it. Out of all photos that could have been on this damn thing, it had to be the one where our veteran amputee's arm numb was on one of the chick's ass but it looked like a damn hot dog in a bun...all in a Wishes shirt! We were dying laughing and the guys said it was a trip of a lifetime!*

Dan's done so many badass things for vets during the time I've known him. From flying them out to all of his parties and taking them off-roading to large cash donations. Most of the time it goes well, but... one vet almost killed Dan's friend driving an ATV with a single prosthetic leg (thankfully nobody was injured). When Dan took some vets to Canada to party with him years back it cost one vet his relationship with his girlfriend. One guy made the cover of Playboy *and many others have gotten laid. It's not the story book tale most people have when doing charity, but his heart is always in the right place. Dan definitely lives life to the fullest and I respect anyone who wants to share that with veterans.*

I rented a huge compound with around twenty rooms, private beaches, and a main clubhouse area. My plane was down for maintenance so I chartered a G550 and filled it with the models, a couple vets, and Eve, a drop-dead gorgeous brunette I'd been wanting to fuck for years.

When we arrived, I asked Eve if she wanted to stay with me. She said if we were alone on the trip that she would, but she didn't want to be just one of the girls I hooked up with. I told her, "If we hook up, I won't hook up with any other girls on the trip," figuring that would surely seal the deal. She still said no. I said, "Ok, no worries." I was bummed—I really liked her—but figured it wasn't the end of the world. I mean, it wasn't like I was trapped on a deserted island with thirty-six large breasted models or anything.

While I was ordering a drink at the bar I observed Clarence talking to a hot, skinny, blue-eyed blonde with a big bubble ass. He was clearly in love with this girl, but she didn't seem very interested in him. He made mention of her muscular legs and then asked her if she played field hockey. I honestly have no idea where he even comes up with this shit.

He was overly aggressive with his approach, and it wasn't working, but he refused to take any hints. He then directly asked her if she'd hook up with him, and she said, "Absolutely not." He went to the girl next to her and tried the same approach sans the muscular legs comment. She gave a similar response, and down the bar he went until he had tried with every girl in the whole joint.

He came up to me visibly flustered saying, "I don't know why you invited me on this trip. These girls only want to fuck you. I don't even know what I'm here for."

"Stop with your temper tantrum, you big black baby. I literally don't know two-thirds of the girls here. Your approach is awful, and that is why they don't want to fuck you. You'd be much better off just pulling your dick out and saying nothing than the nonsense you are spitting at these girls. Be patient. We are here for five days, and you're asking girls for a verbal commitment to fuck you in the first five minutes. You need to chill the fuck out and have a drink."

I went over to the blonde field hockey girl and had a shot with her and her friend Skye, who I'd been hooking up with for a year. Field hockey was pretty flirty, and I couldn't watch Clarence flounder any longer, so I asked if they wanted to go smoke. They said yes, and we went to their room, smoked a pen, and I took turns fucking both of them.

I was covered in sweat, and I didn't feel like putting on my shirt, so I threw on my shorts and went straight to my room. I walked in the door, and there was Eve in lingerie brushing her teeth in my bathroom.

Shit.

I looked like I'd just ran the Boston marathon, so I headed directly to the shower. It was one of those open showers in with glass doors, and I still had the condom on my dick, so I detoured to the toilet. I was stressed out because I really liked this girl and didn't want to screw it up, but how on earth could I fuck her? I'd just gotten off two minutes ago, plus I'd been drinking, and I hadn't eaten in forever.

When I got out of the shower, she was waiting in my bed, smiling, looking at me with fuck me eyes. A shocking 180 from when we had arrived. Ignoring her at the bar and leaving with other girls had apparently done far better than my original nice guy nonsense. I tried to put it off as long as I could by brushing my teeth, but Eve didn't want to wait.

She started sucking my dick, and to my surprise, it got hard. I was so paranoid I wouldn't be able to go another round that I didn't even use a condom; I just bent her over and started fucking her. Things were fine, but I was still high from smoking with the girls, and I couldn't help but worry. I was so in my head about being able to perform that I gave myself anxiety. I kept thinking, *I hope I can keep my dick hard*, and strangely enough, she kept repeating, "Give me that hard dick," which made me think about it even more. I was so stressed out about it that my fears became reality, and my dick started going limp. Looking back, I don't know why I cared so much, but I really liked the girl, and I'd put the pussy on a pedestal.

Keeping your dick hard is all in your head; if you get stressed and worried about it, then your shit won't work. There is a scientific explanation like stress and anxiety trigger the fight or flight response, and your body isn't wired to have sex in those situations.

I took a shower and tried to give myself a pep talk, but, alas, I came out and did the same thing again. I was so irritated with myself that

I couldn't even sleep. I laid in bed thinking, *You fucking retard, look what you've done, and now you're trapped with her in your bed. A personal prison with a constant reminder of what a limp dick loser you are.* On top of that, I'd told Eve I wouldn't hook up with any other girls, which had the models on the verge of rioting by day four.

Clarence was not doing any better; even the girl he brought wasn't interested in banging him. He was really confused, so I sat down with him to dissect it, and I came to the same conclusion for him as I had for myself: He cared too much. Remember, nobody wants to give you something you need, and he needed sex. I also explained how terrible his approach was and told him that he needed to establish himself as a guy who wasn't needy. "Remember there are more than thirty drunk, horny girls that haven't had sex this whole time, and you're the only guy other than the vets who can fuck them." Or so we thought...

Cabo.

We later found out it had gotten so bad that my security guard had been pulled into a room to have sex, and one girl allegedly fucked my chef in the bushes. With this setup, you could literally sit there, not say one single word, and still get laid. I mean, just ask my security guard. And Clarence had not had sex once. Impressive really.

Clarence and I chartered what was supposed to be a sailing yacht, but it ended up looking more like a dilapidated pirate ship. He finally took my advice, got drunk, and stopped giving a shit. The girls had gone days without sex, I was on a self-imposed monogamous lockdown, and everyone was drunk. A Colombian brunette named Julia asked Clarence to go to one of the rooms, and they started hooking up, but she was so sloppy, he said, "Let's do this when you're more sober." She called him a "pussy faggot" and shamed him into fucking her.

I took Eve below deck. I had nothing left to worry about; it's not like I could have worse sex with her, so I didn't think twice about screwing it up. I didn't care, and we had amazing sex, she came a bunch, and finally, I could relax.

After the boat, we took our bus to a bowling alley that we'd rented out. Everyone was drunk, and there were girls half-naked, taking pictures in the lanes, and hooking up with each other in the bathroom. Clarence took this girl Presly upstairs and fucked her out in the open. The staff was horrified and asked us to leave, but not before Clarence and I had our bowling match.

Clarence was with Julia and began bragging about how good he was at bowling. He said he wanted to bet twenty-five grand on the match. Before making any bets, I try and assess the outcome, so I asked what he usually bowled. He said he usually bowled a 170. This had me nervous because I sucked at bowling and could maybe hit a 130 on a good day. It was Clarence and Julia versus me and Eve. Eve was winking at me like *we got this*. I remembered her bowling regularly with Jax, so I figured she'd be good and Julia was slurring, so I accepted the bet.

I wasn't too concerned since I was still up twenty-five thousand from a Fruit Ninja bet we'd made the day prior. Upon arrival in Mexico, Clarence ordered his assistant to buy thousands of dollars of fruit, a ninja outfit, and somehow smuggle Japanese katana swords across the border. “I want to play Fruit Ninja on the beach,” he said. Clarence is such a ridiculous human being. Needless to say, we threw pieces of fruit at each other and bet on who could slice the most without missing. I got a bloody lip after taking a lemon to the mouth and I almost sliced my finger clean off, but I won.

Fruit Ninja.

We started bowling, and after rolling six balls in the third frame, Clarence had not knocked down one pin. My girl accidentally dropped the ball on one of her rolls, and after six throws, she had only hit seven pins. It was like dumb and dumber; I'd never seen worse bowling in my life. Clarence ended up rolling a 76, and with Julia's score, I think they barely broke 100. I rolled one of the best games of my life and scored around 130 just like I said I would.

Clarence leapt up from his seat and said, "You hustled me!"

"Are you out of your fucking mind, you said you were going to roll a 170, and you rolled a 76. My girl can't even keep the ball in her hand. This is absurd!"

Clarence started laughing. I mean, what's he gonna say? He's the only guy I know who overexaggerates his abilities when making a bet. That fucking guy had never rolled a 170 in his life. I had him send the fifty thousand to the Wishes for Warriors charity and told him to put "atrocious bowling" in the memo on the check.

When we got back to the compound, Clarence had a threesome with Presly and the girl he'd originally brought on the trip. I was proud as a peacock strutting around my bedroom and mentioned something about our great sex to Eve.

She said, "We had sex on the boat?"

I was furious. After three days of bad sex, she was so drunk she didn't remember the Peter North performance I finally put on. I was done!

Eve went to bed, and I went to the bar. I started talking to Lauren, a college girl from ASU who had one of the best asses I'd ever seen. She was the hottest girl on the trip aside from Eve and definitely the sexiest. We talked for a bit and ended up going to her bathroom to get high because her roommate was sleeping and my room was out of the question. After a few hits of her weed pen, we pretty quickly got to fucking. Fifteen minutes later, I was tired of having her ride me on the shitter, so I picked her up and carried her to the couch next to her bed.

She started panicking because her roommate was sleeping six feet away. They'd just met on this trip, and Lauren didn't wanna make a bad impression. I thought it'd be funny, so I scooped her up, and started fucking her right on top of Presley. Presley woke up confused and then after about thirty seconds unexpectedly asked me to fuck her. Lauren was just happy she wasn't mad and said, "I wanna watch."

I'd love to tell you I put on some great show, but I'd been at it for a while, and I lasted about nine pumps before unloading on Presley's face. Presley was probably thoroughly unimpressed, thinking, *That's what I got woken up for?* But that's how it went down. I put on my shit, got Lauren's number, and went back to my room to shower.

CHAPTER 77

Bike Bet

Rick Salomon considered taking the $600,000 bike bet, but he called a friend who was a world record holder, and he advised against it.

I kept pinging it around in my mind, and it seemed doable. But I wasn't in good cardio shape, and I hadn't ridden a bicycle in eighteen years. Hell, I didn't even own a bicycle.

I woke up the following day and couldn't get the bet out of my head. I called a cycling buddy who said I could definitely do it with six months of training; it could be theoretically possible but unlikely with three or four months of training; and it would be physically impossible with one month or less.

In my head, I heard the words of Jim Carrey from *Dumb and Dumber*: "So you're telling me there's a chance."

That was enough for me.

I phoned Clarence and told him I'd take the bet for $600,000 with six months of prep time. We went back and forth before agreeing to the terms and ended on: Ride a bicycle from my driveway in Las Vegas to my driveway in Los Angeles in less than forty-eight hours with six *weeks* to train.

Clarence had been in a mood at my house that night: He'd bet my brother $300,000 that he couldn't go forty-eight hours without saying the word "the." My brother accepted the bet and refused to speak to anyone until Clarence bought out for $150,000 an hour later. Then he turned his attention to Rick, and the great bike bet was born.

The beauty of bets is they settle arguments real quick by making both parties put their money where their mouth is. The best guy to bet with is a rich guy with a big ego because they will defend their points by betting on them rather than accept that they could be wrong. Like negotiations, poker, or sales, the person who cares about the money the most usually ends up with it. When it came to money and gambling, I learned a long time ago to check my ego at the door; I was okay with people thinking I was an idiot or a sucker as long as I ended up with the money.

This bet was different. This time I was the guy betting with my ego. I wasn't sure about my chances of winning, but the more everyone said I couldn't do it, the more it made me want to prove them wrong. *You've pushed your body way further than what these people could even comprehend. These motherfuckers don't know you, they don't know what you're capable of* my ego screamed in my ear.

To test my endurance and evaluate my chances, I went to the gym and got on a stationary bike. After forty-five minutes, I was torched. I only covered ten miles in perfect conditions, and the actual ride for the bet was over three hundred miles in varying terrain with the wind and the rain. *Shit.* And with that, my ego had left the chat.

"I have to ride three hundred miles in two days, so I need something fast and comfortable," I said to a hipster working at the bike shop.

"How many centuries have you done?"

"What the fuck is a century?"

"A century is a one hundred-mile ride."

"I haven't ridden a bike in almost two decades, and I've never ridden more than five miles."

He started laughing. "There's no way. It's physically impossible."

"Well, I'm gonna do it. Just give me two of the best bikes and all the shit to go with them. And I need a good coach, too, if you know anyone."

The kid went nuts with that. I dropped $30,000 in a couple of hours at the bike shop and got a cycling coach named Nate.

I went home and put my new bicycle on a stationary stand designed to simulate the resistance of the road. After fifty minutes, I was covered in sweat, my legs burned, and my ass felt like I had been sitting on a medieval torture device. I began to wonder if the guy at the bike shop was right.

My coach Nate did a lactic acid threshold test and told me the results weren't good. Once my heart rate went above 125, I'd start to produce lactic acid and fatigue quickly. So I had to train at a low heart rate and condition my legs and my ass. Those years of juicing and lifting weights were of no use here.

In addition to fanatically training, my whole team kicked into gear trying to find any advantage, no matter how trivial, to improve my chances. Support vehicles were allowed in front as well as in the rear. The lead vehicle would provide a useful draft against the wind. My assistant researched the best routes. I wanted to avoid highways, and my team figured out if we got permits to film, I could pay for a police escort out of Las Vegas and into LA.

Then Joe Rogan texted me.

"Hey, is it okay if I give your number to Lance Armstrong? He wants to help."

Fuck yeah it was okay. Spandex wearing cyclist snobs looked down on Lance for using steroids, but I was not such a purist. Obviously. I'm a *whatever it takes to win* type of guy, and Lance did just that. I couldn't wait to get him on the phone.

"What's the optimal drug regiment for this type of training?" was the first question that I asked the guy who won seven consecutive Tour de France events. He didn't want to go anywhere near that subject. When he tactfully redirected the conversation, I figured he was just averse to talking steroids on the phone.

I discussed different types of bikes along with the benefits and dangers of vehicle drafting. He said, "Recumbent bikes (bikes that places the rider in a reclining position) are for pussies." I laughed, but I didn't care. I'd wear a pink leotard if it helped my chances; I just wanted to win.

He went on to say that he thought I could succeed. Of the hundreds of experts I talked to, Lance was the only person who believed it was possible.

Lance was super sharp, and in ten minutes, he diagnosed something that took my doctors years to figure out. I mentioned a high red blood cell count, and he said it was from sleep apnea. He was right; I'd wake up frequently while sleeping because I would stop breathing. This would put me in a hypoxic state and signal my body to produce more red blood cells, similar to someone living at altitude. And while it was bad because it interfered with my recovery, it was positive in the sense that I had a good oxygen supply when training.

GPS technology had become so advanced that all my training data was immediately shared remotely with my coach. He saw everything from my speed and distance to my pedal rate and power output. Based on that information, he adjusted my rides and recovery intervals. On my third ride, I got up to fifty miles per hour going downhill. But every training session was a risk. A single injury and I'd lose the bet, so I had to be careful.

After a month of training, Lance came to visit with his two sons. He said they were fans of mine, which I found hilarious. Their father was one of the best athletes in the world, yet they idolized me. I showed them my gunroom and took them to shoot machine guns in the desert. Then Lance

Lance Armstrong.

and I went for a bike ride, where he gave some pointers. I really just wanted the cyclist drug cocktail, but he refused to talk about it.

After Rogan texted me, I watched Lance's documentary. I thought it was sad. He beat cancer, was on top of the world, and got busted for using the same drugs every other cyclist used. While we rode around, I could still see pieces of a cocky champion in him, but the scandal had really beaten him down.

Clarence asked Lance how long it would take him to do the three hundred-mile ride. Lance said he could easily do it in a day, and Clarence offered to bet him he couldn't. Lance told me he could do it no problem but was worried about negative press, so he declined. It was hundreds of thousands of dollars that Lance could have easily won but opted out of because of the possible public perception.

Lance, to his credit, wouldn't even take money from me for his coaching. He just asked that I donate $25,000 to his wife's charity if I won the Vegas-to-LA wager. He seemed so scared of negative press attention. That was strange to me, and I told him so.

"Tell them all to go fuck their mothers," I advised. "Own your shit. You juiced, and so did everyone else in the sport. Tell them to suck dick. You're not sorry."

That was always my response to bad press or critics. No apologies. Own who you are. Unfortunately, what Lance was fighting was too powerful to be stopped, way bigger than anything I'd experienced, so he was on the defensive. The media is out of control. They love to tear people down and then—when they're down, kick them until they can't move. Then later, they might feel sorry for the person and lift them up a little so they can tear them down again. Most journalists were never popular; they probably got bullied as kids, so when they're presented the opportunity to take down celebrities while hiding safely behind a computer screen, they do so with glee because it makes them feel powerful. It's their *Revenge of the Nerds* moment.

I didn't adjust my drug regimen. I kept doing my standard hormone replacement therapy: 100 milligrams of test every four days and one IU of HGH every day. I completely stopped all weightlifting, put in three to five hours of riding a day, and worked up to two fifty-mile treks in a day. I practiced vehicle drafting and communicating with the chase car. I rode in the rain and at night with forty mile per hour winds. There was no stopping once I took off to LA, so I had to be prepared for any kind of conditions; the weather can change a lot in forty-eight hours.

There was a ton of side action being wagered. Clarence had around $2 million total, and Rick was betting big against me also. I told both of them I was going to do it, but they didn't believe me. Rick even thought there was a decent chance I would die. So I offered to bet my G4 against $250,000 cash from him. He agreed to pay if I did the ride in under forty-eight hours, and he got the plane if I died during the race. Towards the end, I bet another $250,000 to offset the expenses that kept piling up. By race day, I had over a million on the line.

I'd paid for police escorts out of Vegas and into LA. I had eleven squad cars with their lights on blocking the Las Vegas Blvd intersection. You would've thought the president of the United States was coming, but alas, it was just an asshole in spandex on a lowrider bicycle.

I was drafting off the support van and making good time in the flats as I approached the first big hill. I lost my police escort when I crossed the state line, and the sun began to set as I started the ascent. There was a total of around thirteen thousand feet of climb on the ride, which is about half the way up Mount Everest.

By the time I reached the peak, it was pitch-black, and I was freezing. The winds were screaming as I opened the door of the support RV. I knew there was going to be a long, really high-speed downhill section coming up in the complete darkness, so I went in to regroup.

"Damn, it got cold fast," I said to my coach.

"Yeah, it's thirty-one degrees, you're not gonna last in that T-shirt," he replied.

I threw on a ski jacket and started the descent. I was doing about thirty-five miles per hour, and things seemed to be going well when out of nowhere I had a blowout. My front tire burst. I immediately leaned as far back as I could and rode the rear brake hard. My heart was racing as I came to a stop—that could have been bad.

I switched bikes and got back on the saddle.

By the time the sun came up, I was ahead of schedule. I'd finished the hardest climb and descent, so the people betting against me were starting to get worried.

Meanwhile, Clarence had a tour bus following me filled with hot girls trying to seduce me. He offered any of them $50,000 if they had sex with me, but sex was the last thing on my mind.

About seventy miles from my Los Angeles home, I got on the road bike, put my head down and started charging. For the whole ride I'd been going at a moderate heart rate to conserve the fuel in my tank, but now I looked at it like a race. My heart rate was maxed and I was hauling ass doing 40-50 mph on the downhill section coming into the city. My coach told me to slow down, not wanting me to blow up before the finish, but I wasn't hearing it. I got a massive second wind knowing the end was in sight; they call it "Smelling the barn." I finished the three hundred-and nine-mile ride in just under thirty-two hours with sixteen hours to spare.

I learned a few things doing this bet. First, cyclists are pussies. These fitness queens massively overestimate the difficulty of their sport (except Lance—he never doubted me). Second, I learned the importance of target heart rate training and lactic acid threshold knowledge. In layman's terms, if you keep your heart rate low, you can go forever, but once you let it get into the lactic acid threshold, you burn the fuel in your tank fast. Third, I learned biking is way easier than running or swimming and is a great way to add lots of volume to your regiment without overtraining.

But more important than what I learned is what I proved. My bike ride was chronicled in news outlets around the world, and everyone saw that I succeeded.

Let that be a lesson to you: If you're in a situation where you think something is near impossible, just remember your body is capable of ten times more than your mind thinks possible, and cyclists are pussies.

CHAPTER 78

No Sex

I finally broke up with Victoria for good in an effort to win $600,000.

We had been fighting, separating, and getting back together for ages. She was amazing, and it wasn't fair to her that I hadn't cut it off for good. She was too loyal to leave me, and it was hard for me to give her up because the sex was so damn good even after three years.

On a flight to Shanghai, a week after the bike bet was over, I told Clarence that we were done. For real this time. He thought I was full of shit. He'd never been a big fan of my relationship with Victoria, partly because she'd been an impediment to me having girls around, which was an impediment to him getting laid, and partly because he knew I wasn't making her happy but mostly because she hated him.

"I'll bet you $600,000 that you can't go one year without having sex with Victoria."

This would be much harder than the bike bet. But I knew it was the right thing to do. It would be the only way I could let her go. As much as I loved her and the sex, I wasn't going to effectively pay $1.2 million to fuck her.

Victoria went ballistic when she heard about the wager. And she certainly did not make it easy. She'd always been amazing at dirty talk, and she would text me things that made me consider actually buying out of the bet with Clarence. I even jerked off to some of the texts and videos she sent, and I hadn't masturbated in years.

It was painful for both of us, but breaking up for good turned out to be the best thing that ever happened to her. She started dating a guy around our tenth or eleventh month without sex, and they eventually got married. I gave Victoria $60,000 from the bet, and I let her keep my cat. She's a good girl and deserved to be happy.

CHAPTER 79

Wishes Ranch

After training for the bike bet and not focusing on pussy, I noticed I was more relaxed and happier without the constant distractions. I really wanted to go deeper into the minimal effort lifestyle.

I was sick of LA and poker, so I decided to get rid of my place there. It made sense when I was running poker games and throwing parties, but I didn't feel like dealing with either. I wanted to spend more time traveling and hanging with my guy friends, off-roading and wakeboarding in Vegas.

Vegas.

After a couple weeks in Bali and Japan, I spent three weeks in Europe on a couple's trip with Lauren and Clarence and his girl. Full disclosure, we brought five other girls and were not monogamous, but we mostly hung out with our main girls. We rode bikes in France, partied with Chris Brown in Milan, and spent nine days on a yacht off the Amalfi Coast.

Rosie and Lauren in Capri.

Out at sea.

After that, I wanted to just wing it. So I called my pilots and told them to stand by as we looked at a map debating where we should go. First, we flew to Prague, then Venice, and our last stop was a few days in Iceland.

Pompeii.

Positano.

Lauren in Venice.

Icelandic glacier.

Lauren flew home from New York, and I hosted some clubs on my way back to Vegas. After a week at home, I flew to Minnesota with Lauren, and hung out with my family for a week. I wake-surfed and water-skied during the day and played cards with the family at night. It was nice for me to step out of my crazy life for a bit and regain some life perspective. When you live in a tornado, it can actually be more interesting to experience a moment of calm.

Sleeping with tons of women hurts your soul, and not in a religious way. It draws on your energy, your life force. Being pulled in so many directions and having so many relationships isn't easy; it can really be draining. Finding hot girls to fuck is pretty easy, but finding hot girls who are cool to hang out with for more than a day is a bit more challenging. Hanging with dumb girls is fine for an hour or so, but they'll drive you crazy if you get trapped with them. I was super picky when it came to seriously dating a girl, so losing Victoria was a serious blow, but it was the right thing for her, so I didn't regret it.

In the midst of my introspection, I decided I needed more guy time, so I hit up my friend Bam. He founded the charity Wishes for Warriors to help combat-wounded veterans, and he'd sent me the amputee guys for Cabo and my previous parties. His guys were all super cool, so I suggested we do a veteran trip and told him to cherry-pick some good guys. We planned a trip to Wyoming to shoot guns, off-road, and do man shit.

I rented a big ranch, and my assistant and chef hauled out all my guns, ATVs, and an endless supply of beer. We sat on the back porch and shot clay pigeons with machine guns while listening to country music. I felt like I was back in the military. Everyone had good stories, and the vets were stoked to be there.

After a couple days, I flew a girl named Alyssa out because it was difficult to go any duration without getting it in. Alyssa was a tall, head-turning half-black girl with green eyes and a perfect body. She was a really cool, down to earth twenty-one-year-old who grew up in Texas, and her dad was a cop. She'd met me in New York after the yacht and I figured this trip would be perfect because she enjoyed shooting guns and off-roading. Things with her were good, but having a hot girl with huge tits bouncing around the cabin threw off the dynamic, so I sent her home after a few days.

It messed with the guys' heads because now they were thinking about pussy. Bam's business partner Carl invited out a cute blonde girl that he'd been talking to online for months. She met us at the lake for a few hours of wakeboarding and then headed home. The girl lived a couple hours away but agreed to come out to the ranch later that night with a girlfriend. When she arrived, I didn't waste time with the typical nonsense small talk that most guys have with girls.

"What's the sluttiest thing you've ever done?" I asked the blonde's friend. She said she fucked her best friend's boyfriend, which isn't really that bad. Not compared to the crazy shit I'd seen women do.

Then I asked Carl's blonde the same question. She dodged and told me to answer first. Wasn't hard for me to shock the small-town locals. Then blondie shared something that was vanilla by my standards but sufficient to ensure she couldn't play the good girl card with Carl. It was all setup. My work was done, so I smoked a bowl and went to bed.

But for ages, I could hear Carl and the blonde talking, nothing more.

Hurry up and fuck that girl, I texted him from the bedroom directly below his. *It's almost four in the morning. She's ready to go, bro.*

Dude, she's a fucking tease. Lets me get all the way and then stops. Fuck my life.

That's brutal.

Fucking friend just fucked it all up.

I stomped upstairs to see what was up with the friend and stop her from cockblocking. The friend said that the blonde didn't want to fuck Carl, and she kept sending her texts asking to be saved. Then she handed me her phone to prove she was telling the truth.

"Why in the hell would she drive an hour and a half at midnight to see him? Why would she go to his bedroom if she didn't want to fuck?"

The friend got a little squirrely. Then she confided, "She does want to fuck."

"Good, then tell her to stop bullshitting," I said.

"She wants to fuck you."

This caught me totally off guard. I'd barely acknowledged, looked at, or said a word to this girl all day.

What kind of trollop drives out to a guy's ranch and then last minute decides to bang his friend instead? I wondered. The friend must have texted her because, moments later, Carl's blonde walked into the kitchen, and I confronted her with the news. She looked sheepishly at the ground and then back up at me.

"I'll fuck you if you fuck Carl after."

She said no.

"I'm not going to fuck you unless you at least suck his dick. This whole situation is messed up."

She didn't answer.

I left and went downstairs to my room. But she followed and shut the door after walking in. We started hooking up, and I could tell she didn't want anything conventional. I was choking her and told her she had to agree to suck Carl's dick after. She was smiling and clearly into kinky shit, so I slapped her and told her to say, "Yes, Daddy," or leave. She squealed, "Yes, Daddy!" So I fucked her and then triumphantly marched her to Carl's bedroom.

"This girl is ready to suck your dick now."

Thinking I'd solved the problem, I turned and walked back out. He didn't want to hook up with her at that point, called her a whore, and kicked her out of his room. She came back downstairs a couple minutes later; I fucked her again and went to sleep.

Carl was better looking than me. He's a tall, cool guy, and everyone respects him. But he fell victim to the most common trap. He communicated interest too early and got stuck in bed with a girl who wasn't ready to fuck him. This put her in the driver's seat, and when she pumped the breaks, instead of stopping, he kept trying. With each failed attempt, her interest in him decreased until she ultimately wanted something else. Just like in sales, you don't take the buyer to the register before they're ready to buy the product. Also, if you act desperate and push the sale, it'll make the buyer wanna run.

Maybe I should've said no, maybe I'm a dirtbag, but it seemed clear that she wasn't gonna bang him, so I at least teed up a guaranteed blowjob. I'm also kind of a sex addict, and you don't put an alcoholic in a bar and expect him to come out sober.

Sex addict or not, I am definitely no Don Juan. But I understand psychology, and I don't make the mistakes that most guys do. Trigger attraction and always be willing to walk. The person willing to walk has the power. To be clear, I wasn't gaming this girl; I showed no interest because I had no interest.

The secret to having power with women is not needing them. There are a couple ways to accomplish this. One is to have multiple options, but the best way is to be happy alone. Being happy by yourself is an invaluable trait, and if you don't have tons of options with women, it will surely give you more. Girls want to be around guys who radiate confidence and don't need them for their happiness.

When you get your happiness from within, you'll most likely end up with a better woman and much better relationship. She'll trust you more and live up to higher expectations if she knows you have the confidence to walk and don't *need* her to be happy.

I invited Lauren out to the ranch, but she said she was busy with school and a move. It seemed she only wanted to see me when an exotic locale was involved, which hurt because I liked hanging out with her. I unfortunately didn't have that happiness from within, I didn't like being alone, so I needed the options. Between Lauren's rejection and the blonde making me think about sex again, my short-lived mellowing out period ended, and like a junkie who just fell off the wagon, I was back at it again.

Even though I'd rented the ranch for three weeks, after eight days of only fucking two girls, I cracked. I told the boys to stay as long as they wanted, left the guns and the Can-Ams for them, and headed to the plane. Jay Rich met me at the airport with six girls, I had invited two more, and we all flew to Cabo together. Three girls is the minimum for a trip because then when you hookup with one, the other two girls can hang out, and it's not awkward. Eight works also.

I posted a pic, and all of a sudden Lauren's schedule freed up; it was like one of those gold digger pranks on YouTube when they find out the guy has a nice car and all of a sudden want to hang out. I told her to piss off.

Todd Phillips had asked me to post something about *War Dogs*, and I told him no problem, send me a screener. He said legal wouldn't allow him to give the screener to friends. I apologized and said I couldn't vouch for something I hadn't seen. A month later, the studio reached out, paid me $60,000 and sent me the screener in Cabo. We all got high, and everyone watched me beat the shit out of Jonah Hill. I chartered a yacht, lifted weights, smoked weed, hooked up with most of the girls, and left Cabo. The end.

CHAPTER 80

Harem

Always say "It's good to see you" when you meet a woman.

After Cabo, I backslid hard. I'd started to like Lauren, and to get my mind off of her, I fell right back into the old lifestyle. It was common for me to have a house full of girls and be sleeping with almost all of them. New girls would hit me up, and girls I was dating would bring friends. It was like a revolving door of repeats and new girls coming and going every couple days.

Jay Rich brought a bunch of women to my Vegas house, and I mistakenly said "Nice to meet you" to a woman I had fucked multiple times previously. He pulled me aside and expressed concern that things were getting out of hand. This wasn't the first time it had happened. I'd been going hard for so long that it was all becoming a blur.

I had a rotation of over fifty women at the time. I never cut anyone who was hot and cool, so sometimes these women would be around for years. The key was variety, and I could mix and match old and new.

Contrary to popular belief, I didn't pay any of them. I couldn't keep up with what I had, and that made it competitive. Paying them would have been counterproductive; it actually would've made them like me less and expect more from me. I know this sounds counterintuitive, but over the years, I'd consistently noticed that a high percentage of the time when I'd do something nice for a girl or buy them something, they'd actually treat me worse.

My theory is models usually don't think that highly of themselves since they know their value is solely based on looks and it's fleeting, so the better you treat them, the more their respect for you diminishes. Plus, they've probably had tons of suckers kiss their ass and shower them with gifts in the past, so there's a subconscious correlation between doing nice things and being a chump.

As women got jealous or started seriously dating someone, they'd drop out and new ones would join. I didn't try and control them, and I never told them they couldn't see other guys.

My harem was like a snowball; the longer it went down the mountain, the bigger it became. As the women got more and more beautiful, it made others even more curious: *What is so great about him? He has four hot women all over him. I want to know why.* The more women wanted me and the more competitive it became, the easier it was to attract new ones. Conversely, when there were less women, the girls had higher expectations, became more attached, and, as a result, didn't last as long.

Now there were so many it didn't matter if they dropped off and they knew that, so they focused more on what they could do for me and less on what they wanted from me. The stronger the competition, the more the girls wanted to win, and winning for the girl was getting me to like her. That's the type of dynamic that you want to create when dating: Make the girl work for your approval. Not the other way around.

PART 5

Finding the Limits of Excess

CHAPTER 81

Nina

I hosted a pool party at Marquee Day Club with Floyd Mayweather and about forty girls. I had the three-story bungalow hotel room attached to the day club. There couldn't have been a better *setup*.

One of the women at my table was Nina, a tall, thin, stunningly gorgeous brunette from Norway with long legs and big tits. She had just won Miss Globe and was one of the most beautiful women I'd ever seen in my life. I don't think she knew who I was, but there was so much commotion around me—people wanting pictures, guys trying to say hello, and girls trying to get my attention—that I'm sure Nina had to be curious. I gave her my phone to put her number in when a girl named Sofia came up to me and started flirting.

Sofia was a college girl with huge real boobs that Jay Rich had found on Instagram, and we'd flown her out for the party. I asked her if she wanted to smoke, and off we went to my bungalow. We started kissing, but she stopped and asked about the weed. I said, "Oh, I don't know where it is," and walked out of the room. Evidently, she really did want to smoke.

Either that or she wanted to play hard to get and not seem too easy. Whatever the case, I didn't care. I just walked out to find another one.

I hung out with Floyd and French Montana at the pool and introduced them to some girls, then found one to fuck myself, followed by another. After a few hours, I brought all the girls back to my house. Sofia kept coming over to talk, and we ended up fucking in my closet while her best friend sat in my room. I suppose after watching me fuck a few other girls, she realized I wasn't gonna chase.

French Montana.

Afterward, along with the fifteen other girls staying at my house, we put on the movie *Spring Breakers* in the theater room. Most of the girls were in bikinis or underwear; one girl was dressed like a cheerleader. Jay Rich thought it was a good opportunity to do my first Facebook Live, and hundreds of thousands of people online got a look behind the curtain. Sofia and a couple other girls laid on me, petting my chest and beard. It all seemed normal to me, but the guys watching and commenting thought it was crazy. Jay went around to the guest rooms; girls were in night gowns or lingerie walking around the house. He showed me the video later, and it looked like the Playboy Mansion used to. Eventually, we migrated upstairs, and I had a sevensome with some of the girls.

Sofia (smiling, to my right) in my theater.

The following day, we took machine guns into the desert and blew up thirty pumpkins for Halloween. Then we went to the casino. As I strolled through with fifteen women in lingerie costumes, people went nuts.

This was the end of 2016, and I was a legitimate celebrity at that point. Critics try to downplay it and say, "Instagram famous." But this wasn't Instagram. This was real life; in every city and every foreign country I'd been. I'd been around a lot of celebrities and hadn't seen anyone generate that type of hysteria.

Fame is a weird thing. It can be debilitating if you like being out in public. Once the first person comes over and asks for a photo, then everyone else just lines up. Sometimes people will ask for a picture, and they don't even know who you are. Those are the only ones I reject. What kind of sheep do you have to be to want a picture with a human being simply because you saw other people taking photos of them?

After the party with Floyd, I flew to LA with T-Pain, Francesca Farago, and her blonde friend Crystal. T-Pain had just released a song called "Dan Bilzerian," where he rapped "I got ten Brazilians like I'm Dan Brazarraan." He said my name wrong, but T-Pain is a legend, and I was honored nonetheless.

While we were out at a club in LA, I sat there with Francesca and Crystal on my lap watching T-Pain on the mic singing a song about me. I remember thinking, *Damn, I really made it, they're writing songs about me.* After the club, I went back to the penthouse apartment a friend was letting me use and had a threesome with the girls in the living room.

T-Pain (far left) and Francesca Farago (to my immediate left).

FRANCESCA FARAGO

Model, Star of Netflix series *Too Hot to Handle*

I met Dan working at a beach club in Montreal, Canada. His grand entrance for the day was a dive into the lake from a helicopter. I remember him having so many beautiful girls all over him, and I've still, to this day, never seen anything like it. Every girl wanted to be Dan's #1 girl, and you needed to do something to stand out because he had so many options. My tactic was anal sex and it worked!

He took me on his private plane to a beautiful island. We went scuba diving with turtles, did mushrooms, and had so many beautiful yacht days. While with him on our little adventure, he actually flew another girl out to the island, strictly to have sex with. Normally that would've bothered me, but because it was Dan, I thought it was amazing. No one else could've pulled that shit off!

Since becoming his friend I've introduced him to my entire group of friends, and even though this was years ago, I have very vivid flashbacks of all of us naked on his plane or hooking up in a limo; there were really no clothes around Dan. I've been around many celebrities before, but the power Dan holds is unlike any other. Everyone's quite literally running around naked vying for his attention. All trying to be his #1 girl even if it's just for a night. And I can say from experience, being his #1 girl—even for a night—is life changing.

Nina and cat.

Nina joined me in Las Vegas a week later with a hot blonde friend. She was super cool, always smiled, and never complained about anything. She even paid for her flight to see me, which is something models never do. I didn't know how it was going to go with her, so I had Crystal stay with me in case Nina didn't want to fuck for some reason. But that didn't turn out to be the case.

I took her to Aoki's brain cancer charity event, and everyone broke their necks when she walked by. We shot machine guns in the desert and then went to Top Golf. The girls had never shot a gun or swung a golf club, so they were stoked, and my cousin Nick ended up hooking up with Nina's friend.

I spent a week with Nina before she had to return to Norway, and she was all class—super appreciative of everything and expected nothing in return. If her English had been better, I would have seriously dated her. On top of everything, she was sweet to the other girls and was cool with me fucking them. They broke the mold when they made Nina.

Crystal was pissed because I hadn't been hooking up with her. I told her that if she sucked my cousin Nick's dick, then I would fuck her. She thought I was kidding, but I said I was tired.

"Wake the kid up and do him a solid," I urged. "I'll rally and fuck you."

Nick was the little boy who had been my wingman those teenage summers in Minnesota. He happened to be visiting me and said he thought Crystal was one of the hottest girls he'd ever seen, so I figured he'd be stoked. Besides, fucking her wouldn't exactly be a chore, no matter how tired I was. We went back and forth about it, and finally she agreed. Crystal opened his door at two in the morning and crept in to wake him up. He was pleasantly surprised, waking up to his dream girl sucking his dick. I certainly paid him back—with interest—for helping me get laid all those summers ago.

CHAPTER 82

Crypto

I hadn't been playing much poker, but back in 2014, I was paid over a million dollars in Bitcoin from my Macau ponies. Back then, it was around $700 a coin, and I'd forgotten about it. Now that it was around $2,100 a coin, the news began to cover it, and all of the different types of coins were going up, so I bought some Ethereum, Ripple, and a few others. My coin accounts would go up and down hundreds of thousands and sometimes millions of dollars in a day.

I kept piling in until Bitcoin reached around $17,900 a coin, and Clarence was panicking, trying to sell his coins. He said something that really stuck with me: "If you aren't a buyer at $17,900, then you should be a seller," he advised.

Bitcoin went up to $19,500, and I sold all my crypto as it started to fall. I cashed out at $16,500 a coin and was happy with the insane profit. It was fun to gamble every day and have the big swings, but it was better to put a ton of money in the bank. I kept a couple of million in coins just for the sweat but took the big money out.

This was a big deal for me and a totally unexpected windfall of money that I only had to pay capital gains on. I'd pretty much stopped playing poker at this point because AG had quit me and the smaller games weren't worth the time. I had enough money to do whatever I wanted, so I decided to focus on doing things that made me happy, what I thought would make me happy anyway...

CHAPTER 83

Stampede

I met Ron and his Canadian nightclub owner friend Will in Panama for stem cells. These guys went hard. They'd go to the local clubs and bring hookers back to the hotel. I don't mean one or two prostitutes. I'm talking like fifteen or twenty of them. They needed multiple elevator trips to get all these whores to their room.

On the way up, Will grabbed a federal cop from the lobby, brought him up to the room, and had one of the girls fuck him on a chair while he was still in uniform. Will lined ten hookers up against his hotel window and went down the line fucking them all like a sewing machine. Hookers were never my thing, but I couldn't pass up the opportunity to have a threesome with two hot biological sisters. I was banging them together on the floor while Ron was getting his dick sucked in the bed.

Mel Gibson was down there too, and we met up with him and the head doctor of the clinic the next night for dinner. I'd watched most of his movies and was interested to meet the man. He was a lot different than other celebs I'd met; he came in by himself with no security, which surprised me. He also clearly didn't give a fuck about being politically correct at all and made some comments at dinner that really made me laugh. He was unfiltered and seemed like a no bullshit guy. So when he

Mel Gibson.

told me stem cells got his ninety-something-year-old father out of his wheelchair, I knew he was telling the truth.

Mel had been roasted in the media for popping off to some cop about Jews, and everyone went crazy. I'm part Jewish, and it didn't bother me. He told everyone to get fucked and made a half a billion dollars on his *Passion of the Christ* movie, and I respected that. Kinda like when I heard Denzel Washington bought all the black guys on set jackets and didn't get the white guys anything; I thought that was funny. I never got offended by shit like that. I could care less what your beliefs are as long as you're honest and upfront about it; everyone is entitled to their opinion.

My Florida public school was divided growing up, so I get it. I used to resent blacks for arbitrarily punching and jumping white kids in school on what they called "cracker day." In the military, I stopped caring about race because it didn't feel like it was blacks against whites; we were all on the same team. After traveling as much as I have, I realized that there's no shortage of shitheads and good people, and I've found no correlation with race. I laugh when people are proud to be Mexican, black, white, Jewish, whatever—I don't take pride in or identify with any race, location, or religion.

You should take pride in what you have accomplished, what you've built, and who you are as a person, not where you were born, what color your skin is, or anything else that you have no control over. That said, it took me some time to figure this out, so I don't dislike people who are racist. In fact, if they are open about it, I respect their authenticity. I just look at them as being less advanced.

Will saw people coming up to me constantly, and he asked how much he'd have to pay me to host his club in Calgary during Stampede (Canadian Rodeo). He kept talking about how amazing this rodeo/festival Stampede was, so I figured I'd check it out.

"Give me $60K to cover the jet fuel, and I'll cruise up," I said.

"Done."

I got up there, and he had two hundred women lined up for a hot girl contest. My DMs were blowing up with hot girls that heard I was hosting, and there was no shortage at the venue either. Will was right; this place was pretty sick. I did the meet and greet and went to my table.

An hour later, Ron and I got into an argument about his cowboy hat. He'd loaned it to me and now wanted it back after I'd been wearing it for an hour, and my hair looked like matted shit. I had to take pics all night, so I said, "If you take the hat, I'm going to fuck your girl."

Sure enough, a few minutes after he reclaimed his hat, I had the random club girl he was talking to sucking my dick in a public bathroom stall, hat head and all. He pounded on the door and yelled for us to stop.

"Give me the hat, and I'll give you the girl!" I yelled. And he begrudgingly tossed the Stetson over the stall.

I unlocked the door, walked out, grabbed a hot, big titty brunette I'd been talking to, led her back into the bathroom, and fucked her in that same stall. It sounds absurd, but that's the way it went down; ask Ron. Being famous and becoming a sex addict is like owning a bar and becoming an alcoholic.

A bunch of people ended up at my hotel room after the club. Ron walked in the bathroom unannounced as I was fucking two girls in the shower. He'd seen me bang enough girls that he wasn't fazed.

"Hey, man, what time do you wanna go to the shooting range tomorrow?" he casually asked as I pumped away.

"I dunno, probably around one. I'll text you when I get up."

After I finished, I sent the girls away and ordered room service. One of the bottle girls from the club showed up and fucked me before the food arrived. It was like this every time I hosted a nightclub. I just ate Cialis, smoked weed, and fucked all night. It never got old because the women were always different, but something was missing.

CHAPTER 84

Sofia

After going balls to the wall for four years, I needed a break.

I'd *set up* my life so I was in complete control and had no chance of being hurt. I also had pretty much no chance of finding a decent girlfriend either. By having a bunch of girls constantly around, I was never available or susceptible to attachment. It was a power play and a defense mechanism all in one. I got to live out my childhood fantasy and fuck tons of hot girls while never having the headache or the risk of caring. The ego boosting sex and crazy adventure was amazing, but after doing it for four years, I needed a break.

Sofia, the girl I met at the Marquee pool party, happened to catch me at just the right time. Things started very casually, but progressed quickly. She was athletic and quickly learned how to wake surf and drive the off-road vehicles. Pretty soon she was holding her own, keeping up with my buddies and me blasting down the Vegas trails at over 90 mph. She was smart, and we got along well, but most importantly, she had huge tits. Her sarcastic personality grew on me, and after a few months, Sofia and I were living together.

Sofia.

I'd been looking to spend more time with my guy friends and it was much easier with a girlfriend. Before my buddies would come around and they wouldn't know what to do with themselves, constantly distracted by the girls walking around wearing barely anything. I can't blame them, it was quite the distraction, but it messed up the dynamics nonetheless. Now I was able to have a guys' night at the house, and my friends who were married were finally allowed to hang out.

Things started off so good...

CHAPTER 85

Hawaii

We were flying in from Bora Bora after a week of surfing and exploring Tahiti. Everyone sat around the table in the back of the plane and played low-stakes poker while listening to Stick Figure and discussing what we should do in Hawaii.

It was a couple's trip, and I'd brought Sofia. We had to stop for fuel, so we figured why not check out Hawaii before returning to Vegas? I'd rented a wood-carved Asian-themed house that was inland on a couple of lakes. It looked like the temples in Shanghai set in the jungle. And the lush green backyard was full of birds and wild geese.

My buddy "All-American Dave" had lived on this island before, so he knew his way around. The first thing we did was surf at a mellow sand bottom spot with the girls. Then we went on a hike up the coastline that ended in a waterfall by the ocean.

On the drive home, we stopped to pick up some fresh coconuts from a local stand. I was pretty fucking thirsty after the three-hour hike, and the coconut water really hit the spot. Back at the house, my chef had prepared us a massive feast. I'd never felt so relaxed, sitting on the couch, watching *Big Wednesday*, a classic surf movie, while passing a joint around.

I slept like a baby that night and woke up feeling good. We had breakfast, loaded up the boards, and went surfing again at the same spot. After a couple hours, Dave took us to a really bomb fresh fish taco restaurant. Next door, there was a bohemian store that sold high-end art, handcrafted trinkets, surfboards, and pretty much everything in between. I went in looking for weed and left with Golden Teacher psychedelic mushrooms.

The next day, we went to a secluded beach and did the mushrooms. I didn't wear a shirt, sunblock, or shoes almost the entire trip. We left the cell phones in the SUV and headed down to the beach with only a water bottle. It felt nice to not need anything. It was hot, and the ocean was there to cool you off if you wanted, but there was no need for towels or shoes.

The mushrooms kicked in on the hike down to the beach, the colors became much more vibrant, and I became more connected to the earth. We got to the beach, and everything and everyone looked more beautiful. The landscape on this island was already insane as it was, but with the mushrooms, it was indescribable. I ran to the ocean and dove in. The water was warm, and the waves were about four to five feet, so enough to have fun but not big enough to fuck you up. I got in about seven feet of water and held my breath. The waves would come, pick me up, and set me back down. I felt weightless like a jellyfish.

Dave was bodysurfing, and everyone else was hanging out on the beach, absorbing the sun's energy. After an hour of breath holding in the ocean, I went for a run to warm up. Everything had a shimmer to it, the water, the three hundred-foot rock walls, even the mist from the ocean spray on the rocks. And the lighthouse at the end of the beach on the top of the cliff looked like something out of an oil painting.

I felt distinctly relaxed and happy; there was no stress or worry. Everyone was smiling, and after about four hours, we decided to go get some Mexican food. I lit a joint in the car and put on some reggae music. As we drove down the cliffside highway with the bright blue ocean on the right, and the lush green mountains on the left, I remember thinking that I'd just had one of the best days of my life, and it cost no money. A hippie in a van could have had the exact same day, and there was something really cool about that.

The next day, the realtor who rented me the house offered to take us up the coast and show us the more remote parts of the island. They took two boats, and he let me drive a Wave Runner. On the way there, we drove into some massive caves and snorkeled with giant sea turtles.

The ride ended on an isolated beach only accessible by water. They anchored the boats, and we all swam in. The beach was surrounded by sheer rock walls that went up hundreds of feet and to the left was a big arching cave that lead to another enclosed beach with a sixty foot waterfall in the back. Everyone had lunch on the beach, and we agreed that this place was a perfect spot to shroom.

All American Dave on the far left.

The last day we packed up, went surfing, and then took a helicopter tour of the island that ended at my plane. Everything was loaded up when we got there, so we smoked a joint, hopped on the jet and took off to Vegas.

We played cards on the way back, and the time went by fast. The way the plane was set up, it felt more like hanging in a living room than traveling. I was happy, I'd had one of the best trips of my life, and I was only with one girl. There were no headaches, no distractions, and for once, my dick wasn't running the show. I finally figured out the secret to mushrooms was to be in nature, and I knew I was going to live in Hawaii someday.

CHAPTER 86

Hurricane Harvey

I bet two million dollars on Floyd and felt pretty good about it, especially since he'd let me watch him train.

My buddy Mike and I watched the Floyd Mayweather–Connor McGregor fight at my house in Vegas. I knew he was in good shape, but I'm not gonna lie, I was sweating in the first three rounds. After Floyd won, I turned the channel and news coverage of Hurricane Harvey came on. Houston was flooded, and thousands of people needed rescue.

"Wanna fly out there and help?" I asked Mike.

Mike was a bit of a hermit and didn't like to leave the house.

Floyd Mayweather.

But he was also a devout Christian and knew it was the right thing to do. A friend of Clarence's in Houston offered his house to serve as our base camp. We flew down the next day.

I didn't really have any kind of plan but I had faith that I'd figure something out. A friend of a friend had a helicopter and was flying in supplies, so we went with him for the first day. It was worse than I'd expected. Houston was completely underwater. Only the tops of houses were visible and it reminded me of Venice, Italy.

Houses flooded in Houston.

The second day, we flew to a small airport where all the government agencies refueled. It was hard to do anything if you weren't in uniform, so I told a DEA agent that I was a cop in New Mexico and asked if I could help out. He told me to wear my badge and sent me to help load people onto a C-130 for evacuation. I carried suitcases for old ladies and made sure everyone from gangbangers to church grandmas got up the back ramp of the military aircraft.

Carrying peoples' bags wasn't why I flew down there; I wanted to do something more impactful, so I hit up my buddy Ron. He owned a firearms company, and he worked with the police, so I figured he might have some insight.

"Come by tomorrow," Ron told me. "I'll talk to the PD. I've got a deuce and a half you can drive, and you can run it all day, pulling people out."

The deuce was a six-wheeled military troop transport vehicle equipped with a snorkel above the cab that allowed it to drive in up to twelve feet of water. We picked up two local cops and drove them into the flooded neighborhoods so they could respond to distress calls. The water was six feet deep in some areas, and I had to cut a couple fallen trees with a chainsaw to make it through.

Driving through Houston.

It was summer in Texas, and the deuce didn't have air conditioning. With the humidity, it felt like we were in a bathroom after the shower had been left on for twenty minutes. I felt bad for the cops wearing full uniforms and body armor, but they didn't seem to mind; they had good attitudes and were appreciative of the help.

The following day, we found a neighborhood so flooded that I accidentally ran over a car because the water was three feet above the roof. Residents were using kayaks and inflatable rafts to evacuate their homes. Mike and I made runs all day, hauling out dozens of people at a time. They were very thankful, and it felt good. After five days, we flew home, exhausted.

A couple of weeks later, I linked up with Taylor Hammond, a kid I'd met years prior through the Robin Hood Project. I hadn't seen him in a while, and I wanted to hang out with him since he was struggling, and his parents didn't know how long he had left. We hung out for a couple days doing the kinda stuff I did when I was his age (Mexican dynamite and machine guns), and he made me feel a lot better. Hanging around people like him forces you to improve.

Taylor was living in poverty with leukemia, constant pain, terminal cancer, and God knows what else wrong, but he was always smiling and walking around with a better attitude than me. Most kids find things to bitch about, but not Taylor—he had a list a mile long, but he never complained about anything. I remember him always being happy, which made me happy. Taylor had a great perspective and that made all the difference.

Taylor Hammond.

Having a good perspective was never one of my strong suits. I never felt like anything was good enough, probably because growing up I never felt like I was good enough. Finding lasting happiness was always difficult, but I did figure out that making other people happy does make me happy. I believe everyone is connected, and when you help others, you're also helping yourself. It's much better to focus on happiness than pleasure as you will soon see the perils of my pleasure seeking.

CHAPTER 87

Route 91 Shooting

Jake Owen invited me to his concert in Las Vegas. It'll be fun, he said.

Jake walked on stage barefoot with a big smile, and the crowd went crazy. It was strange watching him sing in front of all those people; he'd come a long way since our Little League days in Tampa. His singing was really good, but I was even more impressed with his stage presence. Knowing him only as a shy kid, I was surprised how comfortable he was in front of that massive crowd. It was like he didn't have a care in the world.

JAKE OWEN
Country Singer

I remember sitting in the back of the Escalade, scrolling through my phone while waiting on wherever it was we were going next. My manager was sitting next to me doing the same. I'll never forget him asking me, "Have you heard of this Dan Bilzerian dude?"

I told him, "The only time I've ever heard the name Bilzerian was when I was a kid in Tampa, Florida, playing Little League baseball. Paul Bilzerian was my coach, and his son Dan was on my team. We were pretty damn good. Why do you ask?"

He proceeded to show me this dude on Instagram that looked like Zeus, firing guns with fine-ass women all around him. Although I hadn't seen him in twenty-five years, I said, "Holy shit, that's definitely him." I immediately sent Dan a message from my Instagram account and said I'd love to connect next time next time I'm out around Vegas or Cali.

Fast forward to a Sunday night, October 1st, 2017. I was playing the Route 91 Country Music festival in Las Vegas with my buddy Jason Aldean. Seemed like the perfect time to reach out to Dan and invite him out. After my show, we hung out on the bus for a bit and laughed about old times.

Aldean had just started playing his set. I mentioned to Dan and his buddy we should go watch the show from the side stage. We did just that and hadn't been on stage for more than a few songs when amid our mid-yelling conversation, I heard the first few pops. My first thought was pyrotechnics or a light blowing out.

Dan looked at me and said, "I know that sound...that's gun shots."

The music kept playing, and everything seemed fine for another twenty seconds, and then all hell broke loose. It sounded like a machine gun. Nonstop gunfire. I had no idea where it was coming from, and for some reason, we all ran off the left side of stage. I remember running through the crowd of people. Everyone panicked, running for their lives or clinging to someone they came with who was already shot. Dan was insisting he was going to find a gun, gunfire still ringing out. I saw my buses in the parking lot across the street and made a run for it. That's where Dan and I split.

I don't talk about that night much. I've kind of tucked it away in my mind in a place where I don't like to visit. I'll never forget it, though. One minute, we were all partying and loving life. The next minute, people were losing their lives. I know Dan has been in crazy situations in his life, but I'm pretty damn sure he'll always remember the night he decided to come see his buddy Jake at a country music concert.

Jake had taken our gang to the side of the stage to watch Jason Aldean play. After a couple songs, there were audio problems, and I heard what sounded like electronics crackling. Twenty seconds later, the music stopped completely, and I knew right then the *cracks* were bullets flying by us. I'd heard this familiar sound seventeen years ago in the military when I was downrange behind a berm changing targets. It wasn't the sound of a gunshot; at distance, the gunshot is heard long after the bullet arrives. This was a distinct whip crack noise caused by a bullet breaking the sound barrier, and you hear it when a supersonic bullet travels by you.

There was panic, and then people started to run. With the music off, I could now hear the heavy machine gun fire clearly.

Shit, I need to find a gun. Where is it coming from? You stupid fuck! Why didn't you bring your gun? were the first thoughts in my head as I ran.

My buddy Brendon, who was a professional surf photographer, was running behind me, and his first instinct was to record on his cellphone. I heard bullets hit the ground around me, and people were running and screaming. It was chaos.

As we approached the back of the venue, I saw a parked police car with flashing lights and made a beeline for it. The car was empty, and I didn't see any cops in the vicinity, so I searched it for a weapon. I immediately saw a duty shotgun locked upright in a harness between the seats. The keys to the squad car along with fifty others dangled from the ignition. I tried key after key, but nothing would unlock the shotgun.

Frustrated, I dropped the keys on the seat and went looking for the cop the vehicle belonged to.

At first, everyone assumed that there were multiple shooters moving through the crowded festival, mowing people down. The gunfire kept coming in long, fully automatic volleys, echoing through the streets and buildings, but nobody could tell where it was coming from.

I ran over to a girl lying on the ground surrounded by friends. She had been shot in the head, and it didn't look good. I didn't check to see if she was alive; I just told them to bring her to the squad car. Figuring I'd borrow the car and bring her to the hospital. But when I got back to the vehicle, the keys were gone.

Gunfire erupted again, and I took off running through an empty lot toward the Mandalay Bay. While I was running, I whipped out my phone and threw up an Instagram story saying that a girl had been shot in the head. I wanted people to know an active shooter situation was happening at the concert I'd been posting about. My stories were getting around eight million views at the time, so it was the best way to generate awareness.

As I approached the hotel, the gunfire intensified, so I crouched down near a small concrete lane divider. "Hey, the security is boning out!" Brendon yelled as a two security guards and a police officer ran toward us. The cop was carrying an M4 carbine and as soon as he reached our barricade, I told him, "I'm a cop!" and held up my police ID.

"Go, go!" he yelled.

"I need a gun," I said.

"Get the fuck away from me," he said. "I don't know who you are."

"I'm a cop. I just showed you my creds."

"That's fine, I don't know who you are. Keep moving! Let's go," he said as he turned and ran away.

The gunfire was increasing, and my chances of finding a gun seemed to be nonexistent, so we doubled back. Some guy in a van yelled my name and asked if we wanted a ride. I thanked him and got in. On the way out, we picked up a couple of injured girls and headed to the hospital. On the ride, I called my New Mexico police chief.

"Can I grab a gun, wear my plate carrier, and go back?"

"Definitely not, Dan," he ordered. "You can carry concealed, but under no circumstances should you go back with a visible weapon. You'll be shot by the police."

I hadn't even considered that possibility. It suddenly dawned on me that if I'd gotten that shotgun unlocked, I might very well have been shot by the cops myself. Looking back, I probably shouldn't have asked that cop for a spare gun either, but I was a cop and people were being murdered, so it seemed like the thing to do.

After the hospital, the driver dropped Brendon and me off at my house. I ran upstairs, grabbed a pistol, and headed back. While I was driving, Chief called me and said his friend's daughter was at the show and needed to be taken out. I had him send a pin of her location, but the police had barricaded off the roads, so I couldn't drive to her. I parked as close as I could and called him as I was jogging back.

The shooting seemed to have stopped, but I still had no idea where it had been coming from, and that was nerve-wracking. As I neared the concert area, I saw bloody bodies on the ground. A few cops drew down on me; it was all a panic. The police didn't know who the gunmen were, and there were reports of multiple shooters over the police radio.

Las Vegas Blvd.

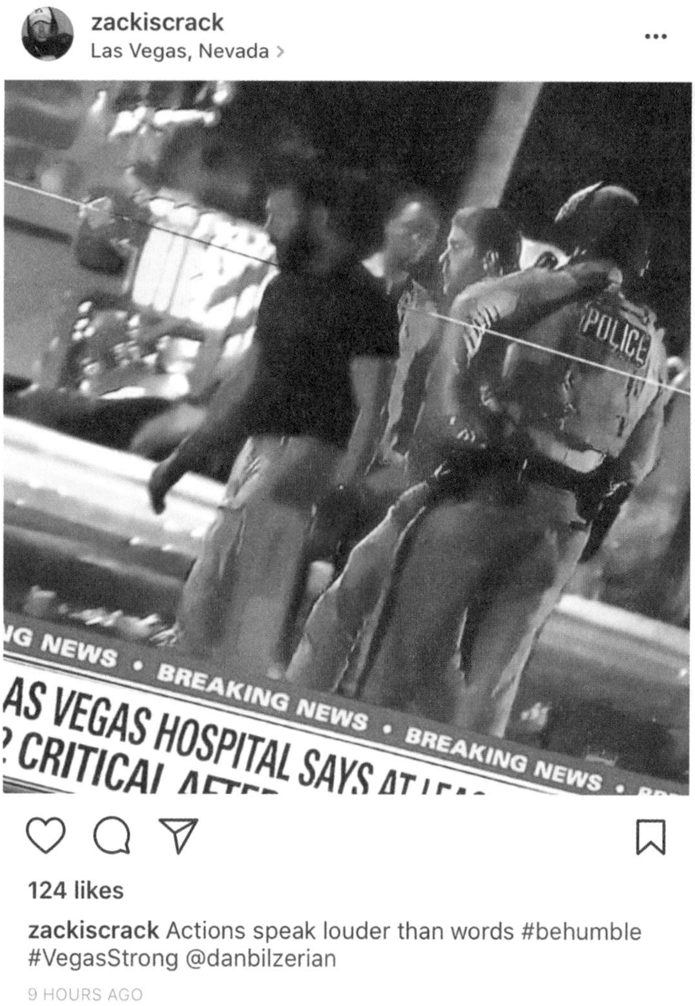

I made my way to the congregation of police cars on Las Vegas Boulevard. There was a dead body in the middle of the street, and the police were hunkered down behind their vehicles. I linked up with some first responders, and we walked around looking for people who were injured. The whole situation was fucked up; cell phones on the bodies rang nonstop as people across the nation tried to reach their friends and loved ones. It was brutal.

After a couple of hours, it didn't seem like there was much more I could do, so I went home. On the drive back, everyone was texting and calling me. I wasn't in the mood to answer the same questions over and over, so I posted a story saying I was fine and put my phone away. When I got back to the house, I saw Brendon on the couch, and he was pretty shaken up. He showed me the video he'd recorded, and we watched the news trying to figure out what in the fuck happened. We talked and replayed the nights events for a while before going to bed.

The next day, news outlets asked to interview me, but I told them to piss off. I wanted nothing to do with the press. The hospitals were packed, and the staff was working overtime. They were asking for blood, water, and food donations. I didn't think anyone wanted my hormone-infested blood, so I jumped in my five-ton six-wheel military truck and went to Costco. I bought ten thousand pounds of bottled water and delivered it to a drop point for contributions for the hospitals. Then I met up with Jessa at a local Mexican restaurant that wanted to donate a ton of food. We loaded it up and brought it to the drop point as well.

When I got home, I received a text from the Chief telling me Dakota Meyer, a Marine Medal of Honor recipient, was blogging that I was a coward for running away from the shooter. I thought Chief was fucking with me, but sure enough, this fat idiot was online blogging about how I shouldn't have run away and that I should've stayed and helped people. Dakota was one of my followers, and he saw the Instagram story I posted while running *towards* the Mandalay. Unfortunately, he wasn't very bright and interpreted that as fleeing.

I was livid. I went from feeling good about the donations to pure anger. Instead of helping, this asshole was online, blogging about what a hero he was and what he would have done if he was there. I mean what a tool, using a mass shooting as an opportunity to try and make a name for himself. Notwithstanding, I didn't run away; I actually ran directly towards the shooter.

I was confused because getting the Medal of Honor was supposed to be a huge deal, and usually a recipient is a stand-up guy, so I looked into it. The articles I read said the Marine wrote his own report on the events to receive the Medal of Honor, and the video from the soldiers' helmet cams contradicted his report. Another article said he was hospitalized after an eighteen-year-old beat him up in a bar and that he was fired from his last job for being mentally unstable and having a drinking problem. After getting more information, this idiot's desperate cries for attention started to make more sense. I wasn't going to think twice about him using my name to get views, but then the press got involved.

The same reporters that I'd told to piss off when they wanted to do a hero story on me now were actually calling me a coward. These journalists who would have been the first to start crying in that situation were now saying I ran away, which was false. But even if I had, criticizing an unarmed man for running during the deadliest mass shooting in United States history is absurd. And the message the media was conveying to all the survivors is that they were cowards for running from machine gun fire, which is really fucked up. I knew these motherfuckers were dumb, but this shocked me.

Then military guys started posting comments and talking shit. It was really brutal because, thanks to Brendon, I had a video of the entire shooting that clearly showed me staying in the heart of it for seven of the nine minutes it was going on. My police chief didn't want me to post it because he was worried it would bring a lot of heat on the program. So just like Miami, I had to read all this bullshit and do nothing.

One of the problems with being a celebrity is that the media can just print lies, and you have no real recourse. Denzel Washington once told a reporter, "If you don't read the newspaper, you're uninformed; if you do read it, you're misinformed. We live in a society where it's just first. Who cares? Get it out there. We don't care who it hurts, we don't care who we destroy, we don't care if it's true. Just say it, sell it. Anything you practice, you'll get good at—including BS."

I went to some hospitals and dropped off food, but it didn't make me happy, I was too angry. The whole thing really messed me up; I went from wanting to help people to not wanting anything to do with them. Brendon wasn't doing any better, so I suggested we get the fuck out of there.

CHAPTER 88

Shaun and the Halfpipe

I flew to Fiji with Brendon to surf and get away from the bullshit. After a couple weeks there, we figured we'd check out New Zealand since it wasn't too far away, and I'd never been. We went paragliding, hiking, and on some high-speed jet boats through fjords.

With social media, everyone knows where you are whether you know them or not. Snowboarder Shaun White knew my pal Steve Aoki, so when he saw me post from New Zealand after the shooting, he asked for my number. He texted and said he was practicing for the Olympics at a half pipe on a nearby mountain and asked if I wanted to come watch. When I got the text from Shaun, I told my assistant to find a helicopter.

Brendon, a few girls, and I flew over to meet Shaun. His team gave me a snowmobile and I met him at the half pipe.

Shaun started out with something simple, and then went for a crazy double or triple flip 1080. He flew into the stratosphere, spinning to the point where I had no idea how he knew which direction was up

Shaun White.

anymore. And evidently, he didn't. Instead of landing on his board, he dropped directly on his face.

The impact of the sharp lip of the half pipe split his face from his mouth to his forehead. I watched in shock as he slid down the side until he crunched up like a scorpion at the bottom. Coaches and medical staff rushed over, and I stood on the top of the pipe, thinking, *What the fuck did I just watch?* I'd just met this extreme sports legend thirty minutes earlier, and now he'd possibly died in front of my eyes. A pool of blood stained the snow as they carted him off to the medical center at the base of the hill. They told me Shaun would live but that he had to be flown to a hospital immediately.

"Take my helicopter," I told them. "It's right there."

But for some reason, they made him wait over an hour for one to fly in from the hospital. He was in a lot of pain, and they told everyone to leave. We went back to the half pipe, wondering if Shaun would be able to snowboard again. I felt somewhat guilty, wondering if me being there had distracted him or thrown him off.

Shaun was hurt pretty badly, but he recovered and went on to win the gold medal in the Korea Olympics, landing the exact same trick that almost taken his head off. Talk about fucking balls.

SHAUN WHITE

Three-Time Olympic Gold Medalist Snowboarder, Fifteen-Time X Game Gold Medalist

I met Dan in New Zealand in 2017. He helicoptered in to watch me try a new trick. I had been planning on doing that trick for some time, and I love a crowd to motivate me, so I figured that day would be the day to nail this trick and go jet boating with Dan and his crew to celebrate pulling it off. Next thing I knew, I was covered in blood, trying to piece together what had just happened. I remember Dan throwing an army rag down on the floor of the pipe, shouting to put some pressure on it...meaning my face. I did what he said but couldn't help think, This guy just carries army rags around with him???

I haven't seen my face yet...Dan took one look at me and said "Don't worry, I've seen worse. You have money...doctors back in LA will have you looking normal before you know it."

After all the tests were run at the hospital, it was determined that I had suffered massive pulmonary lung contusions, I got sixty-two stitches in my face, and I had a slight concussion. I spent the next week in the hospital where they pumped blood out of my lungs before I was allowed to fly home.

As miserable as I was, I did have a good laugh when Dan told his millions of followers on Instagram to DM me nudes to cheer me up in the hospital.

Fast forward, Dan and I are still friends because of this wild experience, and I appreciate him keeping his cool during such a dramatic event in my life.

CHAPTER 89

Sam, the Final Chapter

I was down in Central America for another round of stem cell treatments when I received word that my crazy, funny, outlandish friend Sam Magid was found dead in his home. I hadn't seen him in almost a year, but we'd texted and spoken on the phone frequently about an animated series I was producing about my crazy life. I'd sunk over a million dollars into the project, and a third of the stories were about Sam.

He'd done his own version called *Painman* and printed the logo on golf balls. Those were the projectiles that he usually cajoled naked ladies into sending forth into the neighborhood. The house that was the most frequent target turned out to be owned by Cher. She sent demand letters to Sam's house, but for some strange reason, they were all addressed to me. He paid the bills but never clarified that it wasn't me doing the late-night driving.

One time, she sent a couple of lackeys over to rough us up and collect the damages.

“Did you hit this ball into a house across the way?” They held out a golf ball with Sam’s face on it.

“Yes.”

“It’s $20,000 for the repairs.” No way the costs were that much. They just threw out a number.

“Okay, give me a minute.” Sam ducked into the house and returned with $80,000 in cash. “This should cover this one, and the next couple as well.”

They were thoroughly confused but impressed. They gave their numbers to Sam and said to call if he ever needed anything. They had come to beat him up and left, offering favors. That was Sam.

I thought of that story for some reason when I heard the news. He was so lovably fucked up, and his death was inevitable. Though he was so open and shameless with his money and lifestyle, there was one thing he rarely shared: that he had a rare autoimmune disease called granulomatosis with polyangiitis. And that’s why he lived like there was no tomorrow. There really wasn’t one.

When doctors told him that he had two to ten years left, Sam liquidated all his stock positions and moved to Hollywood to be a rock star. He did precisely what I would have done if I had hundreds of millions of dollars and as little as two years left to live. Sam made it eight years, which, considering his drug use, was nothing short of a miracle. He bought a sick bachelor pad, fucked tons of girls, and partied his ass off. Sam was a legend in Los Angeles. He partied with the best and worst of them, banging Lindsay Lohan and getting high with Charlie Sheen.

His family asked me to speak at the funeral because I was his best friend. I tried to keep it together, but it was impossible to stand over his casket and tell stories without getting emotional. His freakish ability to frustrate and terrify me meant that I constantly wanted to kill him. But in truth, I would have done almost anything to save him.

CHAPTER 90

Ignite

I went from zero to 100.

In November of 2016, marijuana became legal for recreational use in Nevada. The minute I saw the news, I knew I wanted to do something in that space. Cannabis felt like a natural fit since I was getting high every day and I wasn't afraid of the negative connotations. Plus I was tired of playing poker; I didn't like that for me to win someone else had to lose. I wanted to build a business where I could provide value and not deal with the stresses of gambling.

After a year of flying around looking at grows, meeting with partners, and a road show to raise money, I launched a cannabis business called Ignite with commitments for $10 million to do a reverse takeover with a Canadian public shell company. In January 2018, we had our launch party in Vancouver.

Ignite launch party in Vancouver with Sofia.

During that past year, things had changed a lot. I'd been working hard on setting up Ignite, and that required a lot of focus. Sofia and I had been monogamously dating for almost a year, and my time was being spent working, traveling and hanging with my guy friends. When I wasn't working, it was couples ski trips to Aspen, the Galapagos islands with my aunt and uncle, and surfing in Hawaii anytime I could.

I'd had an amazing year free of partying and female distractions. I was happy, but I was getting restless and I wanted to make Ignite a success. It was time to climb another mountain. I was famous, but the clock was ticking. I knew I wouldn't be relevant forever, and if I was going to do something with it, the time was now.

Fame had robbed me of a lot of freedom and all of my privacy. It was isolating and very limiting; I couldn't even walk the streets in obscure foreign countries without getting bombarded. Sporting events, concerts, and festivals were no longer an option without security. The relevancy would go away, but the recognizability wouldn't, and I knew that, if in five years I was still having to take pictures in fucking parking lots and I'd never monetized it, I would regret it.

The first thing I needed to do was get *set up* in my city. So I searched for a property that was bigger than my reputation and found it: a sprawling Vegas compound that had been listed for $25 million.

New Vegas house.

I bought the house in June of 2018. The seller wanted to move it, and I paid all cash, so I got a good deal. The home was 41,500 square feet spread over five acres. There were four gates onto the property, and the garage held sixteen cars and had ports for two RVs. The living quarters had seven bedrooms, fourteen bathrooms, a regulation indoor basketball court, a batting cage, golf simulator, a pool with an industrial water slide, twenty-foot high dive, and outdoor air-conditioning. There were six fireplaces and two imported Italian wood-fired pizza ovens. The master had a custom-made ten-foot bed and a shower that could comfortably hold thirty people. I hoped it was big enough.

I bought a Rolls Royce Cullinan for $450,000, a Bentley Continental GT for $300,000, and the new Ferrari 812 Superfast for $475,000. I bought them all cash, then invested $500,000 on home automation. I threw down $500,000 on a loft and airbag, and $675,000 on an off-road truck.

All cash. No leases. No credit. No half stepping. Anything worth doing was worth doing right.

CHAPTER 91

The Ignite House

The world had changed in the intervening years.

Hollywood had begun taking cues from whatever self-righteous hashtag was trending on social media, which brought the label "toxic masculinity" into the mainstream as if acting like a man was now some sort of disease. It seemed like the crusade to emasculate men was spilling into everything; even razor companies had joined the fray, airing a commercial *during the Superbowl* that lectured men on the inherent dangers of manliness. The more brands castrated themselves, the more the marketplace was flooded with neutered products, the more I was going to stand out.

I wasn't going to Tweet apologies for offending people or feign regret for sleeping with a bunch of women. Not a fucking chance. I was gonna put it right in their faces with billboards on Sunset Boulevard that would cause accidents. It was risky. I knew it would cause outrage, especially in California, but my following was built on authenticity and not being a sheep. So I did what I'd been doing my whole life and continued to swim upstream. The plan was to build a counterculture brand the world would recognize—and I was going to do it in record time.

I knew what the Playboy Mansion had done for the *Playboy* brand. The mansion was listed as their most valuable asset when I'd previously offered to buy the company. They were arrogant and their inflated valuation was way too high, so I decided to let their brand die and create a better version of it.

I needed to reestablish myself in Los Angeles, and I was going to be loud about it. I knew what it took to stand out in that city of rich suckers, so I looked at every property in Los Angeles listed for $50 million or above. One house stuck out like a sore thumb. It took up a city block on the side of a mountain in Bel Air and looked like a beached ocean liner. It was four stories and 31,000 square feet of marble, granite, and glass. Twelve bedrooms, twenty-six bathrooms, nine wet bars, a movie theater, a bowling alley, and a twelve-car garage with rotating turntables. The master bedroom alone was 5,500 square feet. That monstrosity was a big fuck you to everyone in Los Angeles.

Ignite house.

I knew this was the house, no question.

It had originally listed for $110 million, then the price dropped to $90 million, which was still a lot of fucking money. We came to terms where I paid $5 million for a three-year option to buy it and $2.4 million per year in rent. I went out and raised $30 million for Ignite in less than twenty-four hours and locked up the Ignite house. It was game time.

There was a tennis court on the roof, but I was more of a meathead than a country club guy. So I bought an LA Fitness gym, shut it down, and had a crane lift all the equipment onto the court. I put a slip and slide in the backyard, installed a cryotherapy machine in my bathroom, and bought a custom-made ten-by-ten alligator skin bed. Just the essentials, you know.

Jordan Belfort, the inspiration for *Wolf of Wall Street*, came over to the house to discuss talking about Ignite on his podcast. He was pretty animated and exactly what I expected given what I had seen of him in interviews. We talked Quaaludes, and he begged me to give him one; I told him I only had a few left and didn't want to part with any of them. He then offered $5,000 for one pill, but I declined. We had a lot in common, a couple of adults that still thought like college kids.

JORDAN BELFORT

Wolf of Wall Street

What was supposed to be a quick thirty-minute business meeting to discuss the possibility of doing a podcast together ended up lasting for over three and a half hours and culminated with Dan and me hitting golf balls off a makeshift driving range that he'd had retrofitted to one of his house's countless outdoor decks.

"You think that neighbor will get pissed If I shank this seven-iron into the window of his Rolls Royce?" I asked Dan.

"Fuck him if he can't take a joke," Dan replied quickly. "Besides, my neighbors are gonna hate me anyways, a broken car window is the least of their worries."

I nodded in agreement, marveling at how effective this type of twisted logic could be at rationalizing even the most extreme forms of unneighborly conduct. I had used this sort of twisted logic myself in my younger and wilder days to rationalize a laundry list of socially unacceptable behaviors—everything from landing a helicopter in the backyard of my estate at two in the morning to turning a blind eye to the presence of a van full of hookers in the lower level of the Stratton Oakmont parking garage.

The housewarming party consisted of 485 women and about 40 men, including Chris Brown, Tyga, Shaun White, French Montana, and Marshmello to DJ.

A buddy showed up with some G, and we went shot for shot until I said, "Fuck it," and drank right out of the water bottle. I blacked out for the first time in almost two decades and hit my head on the side of the dining room table. Security carried me down to my room and left me on the bed. I woke up covered in my own piss and puke like a freshman in a fraternity.

I looked at my phone and had ninety-three text messages, mostly from women.

"You fucking asshole! I can't believe you ditched me."

"Are you fucking that girl?"

"Are you coming back out?"

"Why are you with that bitch?"

It was really funny because this was the only party I can remember where I didn't get laid. Jay Rich made a great video, and thankfully I got a quick pic with Marshmello, so there was something to post letting people know I was back. Everyone said it was the party of the year, so it was a total success—other than my face. I had smashed my nose on the table and had no skin left on the tip.

I went out to the pool to survey the damage and the view beyond. The Jacuzzi was full of hot girls in Ignite bikinis drinking champagne. Coincidentally, Eminem's "Without Me" came on the sound system: "Guess who's back, back again!"

CHAPTER 92

Back in LA

I'd cut off my harem, so I had to rebuild my stable. Initially I thought it would take some work, but after the first party the floodgates opened. Word traveled fast.

Sofia and I broke up the day I locked up the Ignite house in LA. Toward the end, our relationship was barely hanging on by a thread because of trust issues. For instance, she accused me of cheating while I was playing poker at the Aria. I hadn't left the table, but she insisted that a girl had DMed her saying she saw me with Lauren (the girl from Cabo). I told her she was full of shit and asked for a screenshot of the DM. Sofia went silent until she produced an obviously photoshopped conversation. She literally made up the entire incident in her head and lied about it because she was stalking Lauren on Snapchat and saw she was in the city. I broke up with her then and numerous other times because I had no patience for her Colombian craziness.

She didn't trust me, and her insecurity ate her alive. Granted, I've got a lot of baggage, but considering I'd fucked two girls hours before having sex with her on the day we met, what the hell did she expect? The Ignite house was just the straw that broke the camel's back. To be fair, it was more of a telephone pole than a straw, but it was for the best. We wouldn't've lasted a day after I moved into the Ignite house.

Everything happened so fast. I went from being a low key minimalist living in nice 9,400 sq foot $4 million-dollar home in a quiet golf course neighborhood to living in two of the biggest, most expensive houses in the world. I went from not caring about social media to relying on it to build my brand. I went from not partying at all to throwing the best parties in LA, and I went from monogamy to buying economy size boxes of condoms on a biweekly basis.

This was not a slow turn up, I came out of the gates firing. Ignite raised another seventy million, and we were sponsoring everyone, hiring influencers, athletes and models. There were models, photoshoots, and castings at the house every few days. I would be in business meetings, working out in the gym, or getting high. Because they didn't see me, girls would get curious and go looking for me, some would even ask employees how they could hook up with me. There were girls staying at the house all the time, and on numerous occasions I found girls I'd never even met waiting in my room or in my bed naked. It was like being the only guy living in a sorority house. Things were nuts before, but this was a whole different level of crazy. My DMs were flooded, and A-list celebrities were showing up asking to hang out by the pool.

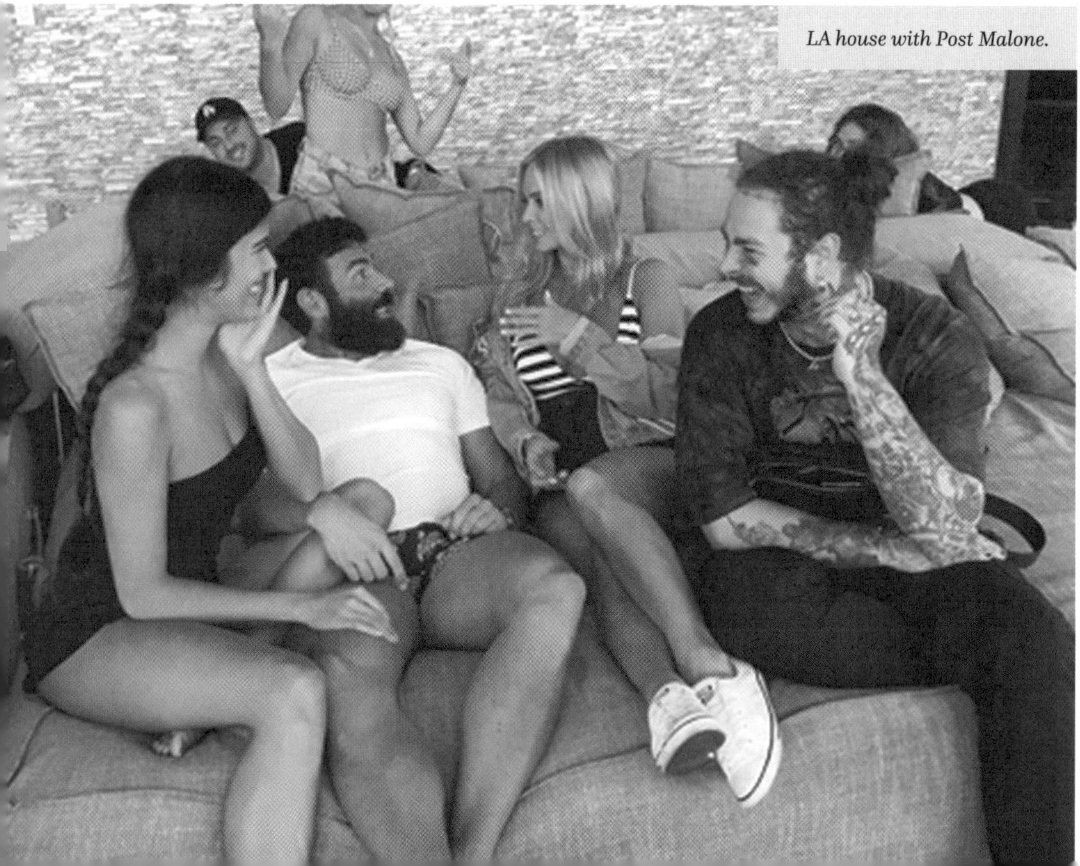

LA house with Post Malone.

Vegas house.

SWAE LEE

Rapper

Living in LA and being a significant influence on the LA party scene, word starts to travel. I had some parties at my house in Woodland Hills, and I'd always hear about girls either getting ready to go to or leave Dan's. Somehow the stars aligned, and I learned exactly who that Dan was, and it's something the normal person would think a real-life Project X or Hugh Hefner would look like in modern day...Girls are like life A&Rs, and they love to be around fun and good vibes. I think Dan's lifestyle requires spending half your time on private jets, and it's one not easy to achieve. Wherever he's at in the world, I know it's looking like the Playboy Mansion/living room, and he's sitting cool, calm, and collected.

When I first moved to LA in 2012, I was living like I had hundreds of millions in the bank. Now I actually had hundreds of millions, but I was living like I had billions.

CHAPTER 93

International Incident

Three months after moving into the Ignite house, my father insisted I become an Armenian citizen.

Disillusioned by the way he'd been treated by the United States judicial system, my father had moved to St. Kitts and gotten my brother and I citizenship down there. He'd renounced his US citizenship and acquired Armenian citizenship as well and wanted my brother Adam and me to become Armenian citizens. He held meetings with high-ranking government officials, and they agreed, but first Adam and I would need to actually travel to Yerevan, the capital of Armenia.

I grabbed a couple girls, fired up the jet, took an Ambien, had sex, and passed out for pretty much the rest of the ride. A ton of paparazzi were camped out at the airport, but the last thing I wanted to do after a long flight was be photographed, so we hurried through the airport and went to the hotel. There are only three million Armenians in the country, and it felt like every single one of them knew me. We were mobbed everywhere.

Dad had a full schedule for us. First, we completed the paperwork, met with some government officials, and then received our passports. The military set up a day of shooting, but evidently didn't think it was important to disclose that it would take place in a disputed territory. Every gun in their military armory was laid out and ready. Pistols, machine guns, sniper rifles, grenade launchers—you name it. All the way up to tanks. I shot everything, and my brother and the girls also got off some rounds. Finally, they gave me a rocket launcher and instructed me fire it into the side of a mountain.

The following day, Azerbaijan issued an international warrant for my arrest. According to them, that mountain was attached to Azerbaijan, and they didn't appreciate me firing a rocket into it.

I wasn't far from Thailand, where my buddy Tarzan and Jay Rich were already shooting a music video for Ashanti. So I figured I'd hang with them and then just fly my plane the rest of the way around the world for the first time.

The next day, I arrived at Sri Panwa, a really high-end resort in Phuket owned by a rich Asian named Wan. He was friends with Jay and a gracious host, allowing me to stay in a $17 million villa for free. I wanted to give his resort a shout-out on social media, but I worried that Azerbaijanis would show up with ski masks and AK-47s and extradite me to their country to rot in prison. This wasn't a totally sarcastic concern as the incident was getting international press, and I was now a pawn in their land dispute.

View Insights
Promote
Liked by billperkins and 2,425,585 others
danbilzerian @ignite won the @hightimesmagazine
cannabis cup for best CBD pen, see

Meanwhile, all this high-profile activity, the good and the bad, had only served to help my brand awareness. The Ignite vape pen won the Best CBD Vape Pen category at the High Times Cannabis Cup. They sent the trophy to my villa in Phuket, and we set up a quick photo with a curvaceous model. In front of the infinity pool, she bent over at the waist, nude, while I perched the hardware right above her ass. It quickly became one of my most liked posts.

Ignite had really pushed me to lean back into social media as it was the best way on the planet to promote a cannabis company. My Instagram stories were getting between seven and twelve million views, and my posts were getting between thirty and sixty-five million impressions each. I got a half a billion impressions on Instagram alone in one week. Not everyone could follow me because of wives or jobs, but everyone was watching.

Former UFC fighter Mike Swick operated a first class Muay Thai gym and let us train and use all the equipment. It was cool to be in a ring in the middle of the jungle where this particular fighting discipline had originated in the eighteenth century.

That night, Mike took us to a local fight and then to a "ping-pong show." I'd heard stories about ping-pong shows for decades. They were legendary among sailors. The wealthy Wan arranged police escorts for us, while Mike arranged heavily tattooed mafia enforcers. The meet up was slightly awkward, but not a single soul would fuck with us.

As we settled into the show, an older, unattractive Thai lady came on stage. She lit a cigarette and inserted it into her vagina. That was followed up with multiple cigarettes, blowing out smoke rings on the "exhale." Then she squatted over a bowl of water and dropped three full-size fish out of her pussy. They plopped into the water and swam around in the bowl. She then inserted a tube and shot darts out her pussy at balloons around the room. It sounded like gunshots when they popped. Then a live bird went in and out of her orifice.

The climax of the show, if she was still capable of climaxing through that beaten-up thing, was a string of metal nails and actual razorblades that she pulled out of her vagina. There was nothing sexy about it at all, but in terms of training and discipline, it was impressive.

We packed a lot into the week in Thailand. We went to the Phi Phi Islands where they filmed the DiCaprio movie *The Beach*, and I drove one of those crazy Thai fishing boats with a twelve-foot shaft on the motor. Tarzan caught a six-foot monitor lizard with his bare hands, we got in a snake pit with king cobras, and Wan flew in a world-renowned Japanese sushi chef for $25,000 for a day.

That night, everyone ate weed brownies and met up at the sushi bar. Wan grabbed a brownie from the Tupperware container and offered it to the old chef. In Japanese culture, it's considered to be poor manners to decline an offer, so the chef grabbed the brownie and ate it. This old man had no idea what he was getting into, and it took all my self-control to not bust out laughing.

Fifteen minutes later, Wan held out the container of brownies as a joke. Before we knew it, the old chef had grabbed another. Wan tried to convince him not to eat it, but it was too late. We all started laughing, knowing you can't overdose on weed, but that he was gonna be on another planet in about forty-five minutes.

The chef did his omakase menu where he made what he wanted based on what he thought were the best ingredients. The fish had all been caught maybe an hour prior, so it was physically impossible to be any fresher. Still to this day, it was the best sushi I have ever eaten, and the chef was a beast; he maintained his composure and never let on once that he was high as a giraffe's pussy.

Nina, the next level gorgeous girl I'd met at the Marquee Day Club, messaged me while I was in Thailand right after breaking up with her boyfriend of a couple years. I hadn't seen her since they got together, but even still, she said he'd become obsessed with me. At first, he thought it was cool that we dated but after a while became jealous and eventually broke all of her furniture. I found I have a strange effect on guys who date women I've been with.

Once, a husband gave his wife a hall pass to fly out and fuck me. Everything was fine until she returned home. Then he wanted to know everything. He peppered her with questions until he became so jealous that they ended up getting a divorce. I probably messed up a lot of relationships, and after this incident, I made it a rule to only fuck single girls. I believe that when you have more power, there is a higher level of responsibility that comes with that. An exception was if the girl was cheating on the guy anyway; then it was open season. For example...

Hanna was the quintessential hot blonde. She was 5'9" with blue eyes, natural DDs, a bubble ass, and a small waist. She slid in my DMs and agreed to meet me in Hawaii on my way back from Thailand. When I got to the house, I found her drinking in the Jacuzzi. I was pleasantly surprised to see she looked better in person than in her online pictures.

She asked me to join her in the hot tub. We talked, and she told me that she'd watched all of my interviews on YouTube. This seemed to be the layup of all layups, and I considered just taking off my shorts to avoid wasting anymore time.

I said, "Let's rinse off," and two minutes later, we were naked in my shower. We started kissing, and then we moved to the bed. This is where it got weird; she wouldn't suck my dick or fuck me. Normally I'd tell her to leave, but we were on an island in the middle of the Pacific

Hanna.

Ocean, and she'd DMed *me* and asked *me* to fly her out. I was really confused, so I asked her why.

She danced around the question before finally saying, "I am probably never going to have sex with you."

Now I was really curious. After more prodding, she finally admitted that she had a boyfriend and said she really liked him. I could respect that, but I was obviously wondering why on earth she was in Hawaii naked in my bed, so I dug a little deeper.

"How many guys have you cheated on him with?" I probed.

"Three."

I didn't expect that, but this was certainly getting more interesting. She went on to tell me some crazy stories about how it was all threesomes with her female roommate who was a sex addict and that it was only guys her roommate really wanted but couldn't get without her. This was getting better by the minute.

"The old roommate charity threesome excuse, huh?" I said jokingly.

She wasn't very bright and didn't get the joke, which was fine because right then Leslie, a shorter but similar looking blue-eyed blonde with big natural tits text me from the living room.

Wyd.

Getting high in my room, wanna fuck? I replied.

Be right there, she said.

She walked in wearing some tiny shorts and a crop top that barely covered her nipples. When she saw Hanna butt-ass naked in bed, she looked a little disappointed and said in her Texas accent, "I don't know if I have the energy for a threesome right now."

"Nah, Hanna is leaving," I replied.

Hanna was a bit shocked; I don't think she'd ever been kicked out of bed before. Leslie started sucking my dick while Hanna walked around the room flustered, retrieving her clothes. She darted into the bathroom to get her bathing suit, and I was fully fucking Leslie by the time she came out. Hanna went to the kitchen where my boys were sitting around the table playing cards.

"Can you guys believe Dan just kicked me out of his room to fuck another girl?"

They didn't flinch, and Frank said, "Yep."

After I showered, I saw a text from Hanna that read, *I'll never say never* with a kissing face emoji. Clearly referencing her "I am probably never going to have sex with you" line.

U just wanna fuck me now b/c you aren't supposed to, I replied.

Hahaha we'll see ;)

About ten minutes later, Hanna came in the kitchen wearing a see-through robe and sat on my lap. I'd told my buddies what happened, and when she came out wearing that, they just smirked like, *I've seen this movie before.*

We obviously ended up fucking, but what was interesting about the situation is something I've actually had happen to me a few times. When I fucked another girl in front of Hanna, I proved unequivocally that she is replaceable. She had my attention, and now it's gone. This triggers something. It makes her want to be *wanted* again. I can almost guarantee, had I done what most guys would do and cater to Hanna, I probably would not have fucked her on that trip.

As strange as this sounds, most of the girls I really liked, but was having a hard time fucking, happened immediately after I gave up hope and behaved like I didn't care. Fucking another girl in front of a girl you are pursuing is probably the pinnacle of not giving a fuck, and that's why it was so effective. It sounds crazy, but it works like a charm.

CHAPTER 94

Holidays

My life was fully turned up, I was having sex with at least two to three different girls every day, and I was having parties and after-parties for every occasion I could think of.

Alesso, the Swedish DJ, was performing at Hollywood Palladium, and he wanted to do an after-party at my place. In exchange, he offered to DJ my next party for free.

"Done deal," I said.

His after-party was mostly girls and required no real effort on my end. I had an orgy with nine girls and just me. Full disclosure, I only fucked six of them.

Alesso's guy texted me at four in the morning to see if they could keep going. *Sure*, I responded, *but kick the guys out.*

An hour later, he texted to say they were in my guest room with thirty women and wanted to know what I was doing. My response was a selfie from my tub with six naked girls: Katie, Hanna, Amanda, and a few others. That snap turned out to be my most liked picture on Instagram.

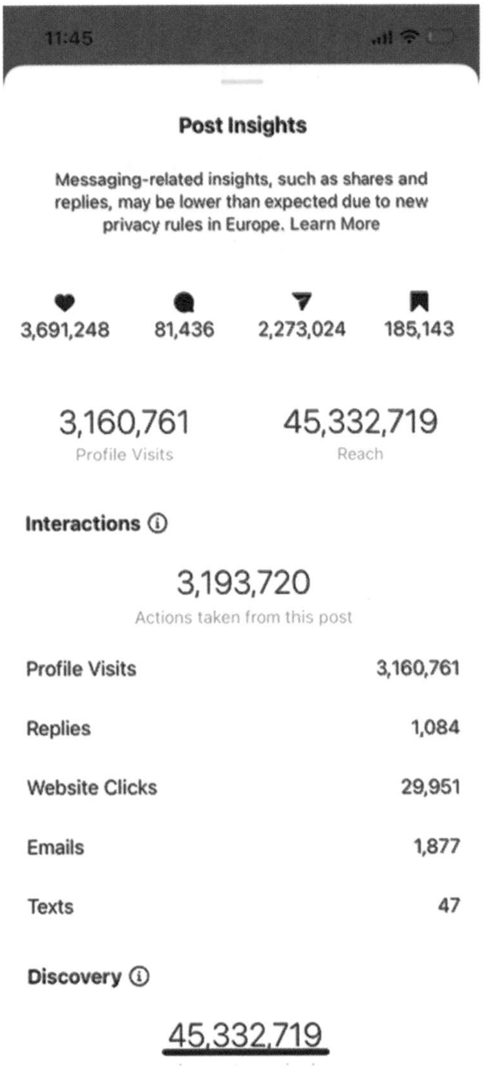

ALESSO

DJ

Some of the craziest nights I've DJed has been at Dan's parties. Halloween 2019 was something else! At one point, there were so many girls in the booth that I fell behind the stage in the middle of my set (true story lol).

For Halloween, I threw my best holiday party to date. Alesso Djed as promised, and the place was packed with beautiful women and celebrities. The VIP list was long: Diddy, Maluma, YG, The Chainsmokers, Jason Derulo, Steve Aoki, Tyga, Machine Gun Kelly, and Ludacris, to name a few. There were more, but some wanted to remain anonymous. I can tell you that one celebrity, who shall remain nameless, buttfucked two women in the VIP section raw dog. A battalion of almost seventy security guards with shotguns and assault rifles kept the place locked down. It was like the Fort Knox of fucking.

Alesso.

MALLY MALL

Grammy-Winning Artist

The best way to describe Dan's parties—over the TOP. Wolf of Wall Street on steroids. I'm talking 15:1 ratio of women to men, super models—runway-style Victoria Secret type. Right away from the military security with AR-15s to greet you out front, then the oversized mansion which took up the whole hill by itself. With what seemed like twelve to fifteen levels of different vibes going on. Five-star food being catered. Seven bars, the best hospitality you can imagine.

The roof top was fire. I remember being there with my brother FRENCH Montana, SWAE Lee, Usher, and so many celebs. Hanging, drinking, smoking, scoping out all the baddies or actually getting scooped out by all the baddies. Then inside, it was packed like a Black Friday shopping mall full of bitches. Performances by the best artists, the bars, all of it was like something out of a movie! Basically, every party he has is the best party you ever went to.

Aoki, MGK, Maluma, and Drew Taggart of The Chainsmokers.

Katie, Hanna, and hens.

I had shut out Hollywood agents, managers, and sugar daddies, so they all began to dislike me. But regardless of their opinions, no one could say that I didn't throw the best parties in LA.

Instead of spending Christmas in Minnesota that year, my family joined me in Vegas. The house was perfect for the get-together; we played volleyball in the basketball court. I took them off-roading, and we shot some guns in the desert. It was good to see them, to reconnect with my past, and be treated like a normal person.

My new Rolls Royce SUV arrived that holiday season, and I took Dad for a ride. Neither of us could figure out half the buttons, and it felt like a couple kids going for a joyride in their parent's car. I had grown much closer to my father, and he had chilled out a lot after I left the house and my brother had his kids. He was a great granddad. He couldn't get enough time with my brothers' boys, and I think that made my brother's relationship with him better as well.

The truth of it is my dad wasn't an asshole; he just wasn't a normally social guy. He didn't drink with his buddies, he never chased women, and he spent almost his entire life working; that was just who he was—a workaholic. As a man with possibly the most addictive personality on the planet, I began to understand my dad's motivation better as I fought my own addictions. I guess it's all perspective, and who am I to judge a man for working too much when my sex addiction was borderline crippling?

The day my family flew out, I airlifted a ton of girls in. The sentimental family bonding was nice, but I was a degenerate and needed to get back to it. I had to charter a bus to fit the sixteen women I took out for New Year's Eve.

To save time and avoid any confusion, I used my video guy Jay as an opening act to explain the situation.

"Dan is never going to try and hook up with you," he'd instruct them. "If you want to get with him, you need to be proactive. He likes submissive women that are into him. If he doesn't get the vibe that you're into him, he won't fuck you. Don't matter how hot you are."

This saved me a lot of headache because it was true. I didn't want to hook up with a girl who wasn't seriously interested, and it informed the girls who were, that they would have to pursue me. It's always better when a woman approaches you, and you can push them off a bit until you feel like it.

The vast majority of my sex life involved getting high, fucking, showering, eating, and then repeat. I put in a ton of volume because I just really liked getting high and having sex. Some people like cooking or playing golf or drinking fine wine. My hobbies just happened to be more fun.

Or so I thought until I went to Antigua.

CHAPTER 95

Private Islands

Every single night cost $85,000. We had a five-night stay booked. But Clarence was paying, and he didn't sweat budgets when it came to his birthday.

Of all the places I have visited in my life, Richard Branson's Necker Island in the British Virgin Islands is the most amazing. The ocean was clear and warm like bath water. The sand was snow white, and the air hovered constantly at eighty degrees.

The main hangout area was on top of a mountain with a 360-degree view of the multicolored—almost fluorescent—ocean and surrounding islands. The whole island was stocked with exotic and endangered animals, eight hundred-pound Galapagos tortoises, lemurs, flamingos, and more. He had wakeboarding boats, paddle boards, kayaks, kiteboards and sailboats. If there was a toy or amenity you could think of, Branson had it.

Clarence had never done mushrooms but agreed to try them with me for his 50th birthday. We went to a quiet beach and ate a few together. I grabbed a mask and snorkel and went for a swim. It was fucking amazing. The sand and coral on the bottom were moving like a kaleidoscope. The fish were brighter, and every stroke felt like it was propelling me ten feet.

I held my breath and swam to the bottom to hang with a massive sea turtle, and I felt I could stay there forever. One of the keys to breath holding is being calm, and I was as calm as a cucumber. When I surfaced, I saw six naked girls jumping on the inflatable trampoline. The water was shimmering, their big tits were bouncing everywhere, and Branson was kiteboarding in the background.

I would say it was like a scene out of a movie, but no movie ever looked as good as this. Then I looked to the beach, and Clarence was running around naked, swinging his black dick around and laughing. The scene was over.

The day we were leaving, I challenged Branson to a game of chess and beat him. When I asked if he wanted a rematch, he said he only wanted to play speed chess with a short timer, so we played that, and he beat me. I appreciated that he was like me: he couldn't stand to lose, so he set up a game where the odds of winning were more in his favor. His whole island was a setup, and he had everyone he wanted to meet coming to him and paying for the privilege of doing it. It was pretty genius.

Richard Branson.

Soon afterward, inspired by Branson, I rented another private island in the Bahamas for $65,000 a night. I brought fourteen women down there, and it was a good 50:50 ratio of new girls and ones I had hooked up with previously.

These trips were as much about marketing Ignite and building the brand as they were about having fun. I still had a good time, but I was quickly learning that being an entrepreneur was a lot more work and less fun than being a rich playboy who just partied and fucked girls. It looked similar: the photographers would shoot the girls all day and would schedule stuff like swimming with the sharks, volleyball, the pig island, and more. At night, we had big group dinners, and the girls were allowed to drink and party if they wanted. But there was a purpose.

Things were also different now because of the social media element. I was tagging girls I was dating, and their accounts were growing like weeds. In the past before being an influencer was a career, things were more organic, but now girls would aggressively seek to have sex with me in hopes of getting posted on my page. Another thing I saw was that the girls on a trip would develop their own pecking order based on the size of their social media following. Since they all wanted to be famous, the one who had the biggest following usually ran the herd; the leader holding possible Instagram tags over the other girls' heads like a dangling carrot.

The whole thing was a bit ridiculous so on that trip, to take some of the pressure off, I started the @Ignitesmodels account. Before the getaway was over, that model account had more followers than most of the girls individually, and I figured it would be a good way to help our girls grow without me having to post them directly on my account.

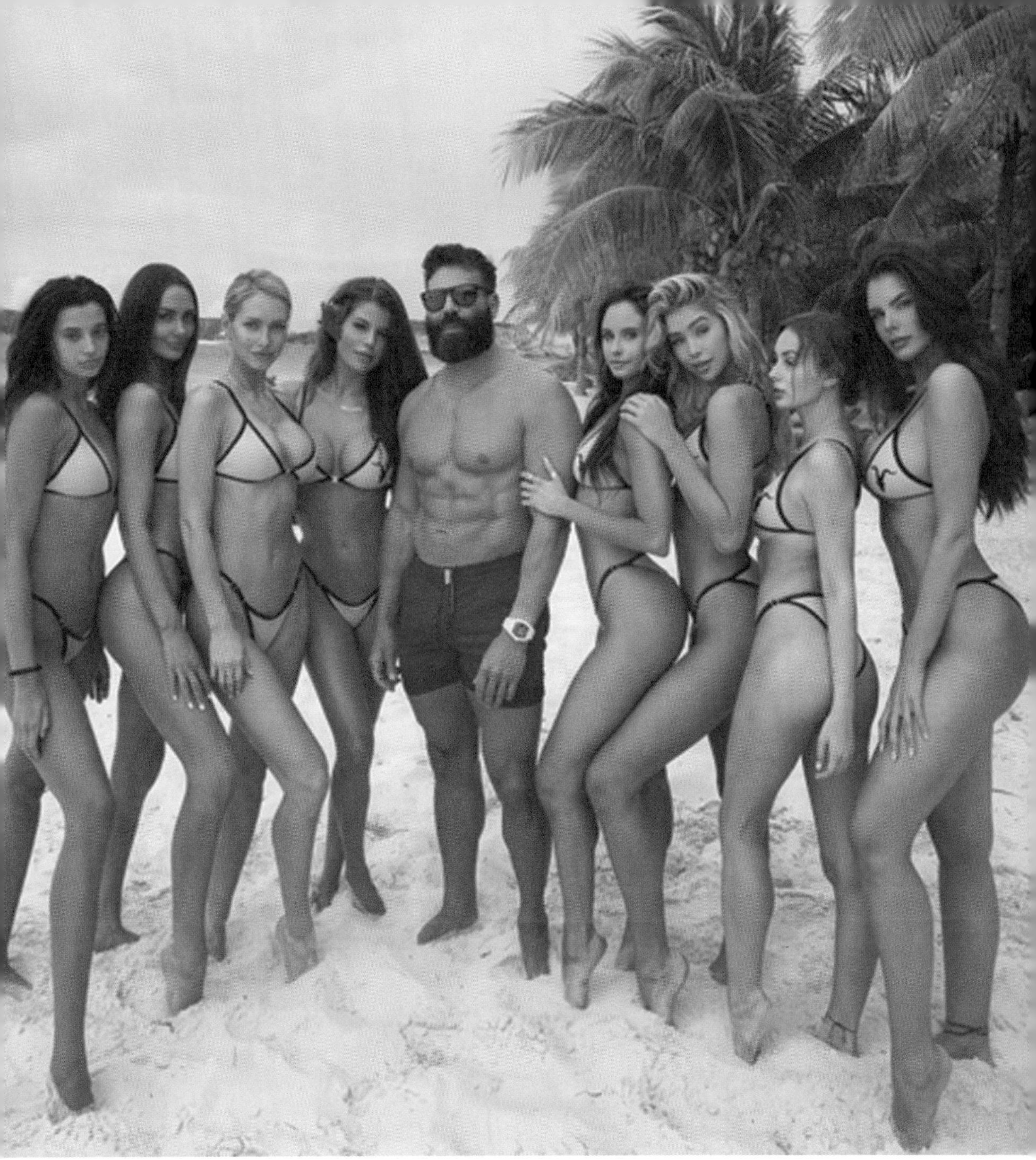

Next, I set up an Ignite trip to Antigua with eighteen women, my buddy Lin, and some photographers. The trips had to focus on documenting the lifestyle because it was helping so much with the promotion of Ignite. @Ignite had already gotten millions of followers and become bigger than all of our competitors' social media accounts put together, and I was just getting started.

CHAPTER 96

A Message from the Universe

"The devil doesn't come dressed in a red cape and pointy horns. He comes as everything you've ever wished for."

TUCKER MAX

It was raining in Antigua, and the only place that had blue skies was Turks and Caicos. I told the pilots to fire up the bird, and I had my assistant rent a house for the day. When we got there, I ate some mushrooms and headed to the beach.

I learned a lesson that day. More is not always better. There were too many women, and it fucked up my trip. I was being pulled in so many directions, it wasn't fun. So I got on a paddleboard and headed directly out to sea.

I like to be on my own sometimes when I'm shrooming. It's when I learn the most. I'm alone with my thoughts, and I can find answers to my questions. My life had turned into a circus, and sure, it was a guy fantasy to be around tons of beautiful women. But I only had one dick, and this was too much.

The content was great, and in the past, more was better, so I kept upping the bar to experiment with how far I could push the limits of this lifestyle. I'd gotten to the point of extreme excess, and it was in every aspect of my life. The cars, the houses, the vacations, and the girls.

Before, when I got a better car, bigger house, or more girls, it brought me some joy, but now I was numb to it. I missed doing surf trips with my buddies and not being a slave to my dick.

I paddled out to sea thinking, *Where do I go from here, and when am I going to stop?*

The answer came to me.

You've had too many almosts in your life. You almost graduated high school, you almost graduated BUD/S, and you almost graduated college. You've done too much work to not bring this to the finish line, Finish the fucking job.

I had a publicly traded company, and I wanted to make myself and my shareholders a bunch of money. The foundation was built, the road was paved, and to stop now would mean everything I did up to this point was a waste. I was a lot of things, but I wasn't a quitter.

I had questions about why girls were acting crazy in certain situations. The answer was, I'd *set up* a ridiculous environment, and it would be illogical to expect people to behave normally within it. The whole thing was nuts, but I'd concocted it, much like Frankenstein's monster, now I had to live with it. So I figured I'd try and enjoy the circus I'd created and make Ignite an international brand worth more than me.

CHAPTER 97

Happiness vs. Pleasure

Before the Turks and Caicos trip was even over, I started booking an over-the-top European tour. First stop would be London, then Venice, then a superyacht on the Amalfi coast, and I would end in my favorite place: Iceland.

We got to London, and the Ignite marketing team had rented an entire hotel to throw our UK CBD launch party. I did some interviews, went to a CBD convention, and then to a nightclub. Everyone took pictures and made a big spectacle of me being there, which was good for the launch.

On our second day in London, we had our hotel party. I came down late because I had an interview and needed a nap. I went to the party and took a girl up to my room pretty quickly. I had another girl texting me to come by, and after I fucked and showered, the next one showed up. It was an awkward come and go at the same time, but I didn't care at this point. I had a seemingly never-ending stream of girls. After that girl left, my photographer texted me a pic of a tall Victoria's Secret model-looking girl she said really wanted to bang me.

Send her up.

So I did a triple-header, all back to back. I ordered room service, then the first one came back for a second helping. I had gotten so used to condoms that I didn't even notice wearing them. I had forgotten what sex without latex protection even felt like. The secret is to always wear them no matter what because the moment you stop, it's really hard to go back. Then you never have to worry about anything, and it doesn't matter if the girls bang other guys.

When we got to Venice I spent time with the two main girls I was dating—Desiree, a beautiful half-Asian girl and Leidy, who was a gorgeous, fiery Cuban. From there, we jumped on my plane and flew to Naples where we boarded the three hundred-foot yacht, though that's not technically accurate. This thing was so massive that it was actually classified as a cruise liner. We had to moor with the cruise ships because the standard yacht slips weren't big enough.

There were forty-two staterooms and multiple boats that would crane off the top deck into the water, including a full-size wakeboarding boat, a tender, and WaveRunners. The boat had everything from a gym and salon with laser machines to a disco club and a movie room. We had twenty-seven models, Clarence and his three girls, Jay Rich and his girl, a girl photographer, plus my two assistants.

I was really looking forward to the trip because I'd had such good times in the past on yachts. Even though I learned my lesson about too many women in Antigua, I wasn't fully realizing the implications yet, and I was about to get smacked in the face with it.

I'd previously hooked up with almost every girl on the boat, and they quickly became catty. Des and Leidy went from hooking up to hating each other. I always thought more was better, and the scarcity model was good, but I'd made a tactical error in taking it to this extreme. This was *way* too many options/obligations, they were almost all veterans, and I was trapped on a cruise liner with them.

I realize that it's pretty ridiculous thing to complain about being trapped on a $300 million boat with a bunch of models cutting throats to bang me. But I was miserable. I was suffering from something worse than Jax's dilemma: I kept shifting my lifestyle upward, but nothing was ever enough.

I don't think I fucked Des or Leidy one time the whole cruise, and that just made them more pissed off. The girl that hit me up the most was Genni, a twenty-year-old college girl with big natural tits. She texted me for dick constantly. One night, I turned down a foursome with her to crash early because I was tired. She was ashore with Jay and the rest of the girls and ended up fucking a waiter bareback outside a club and videotaped it. I was about to go to sleep when I got a text from Jay sharing the sordid tale.

I texted Genni back: *I heard you fucked a waiter lol.* She swore to God that she didn't hook up with anyone. Then she got Leidy to lie to me about it, so it was confusing. I felt like I was playing a game of Clue, and I really wanted to figure out what happened. Jay's story seemed less probable than their version, and he had been drinking heavily this trip, which made him less reliable. It took three hours, but I finally got the full story. Once we had the exact details and eyewitnesses, Genni admitted to it.

Turns out that the guy was a fan of mine, and he had found her through the @ignitesmodels page and DMed her. They met up at the club, and he took her out back and banged her with no condom while she recorded it. Then she went inside and showed the girls the video. Hilarious. Sounded like some shit I would do, and I was proud of the guy. That was a pretty strong move. I don't know if I ever banged a girl outside of a club before. I thought her videotaping the whole thing selfie style was the funniest part. The only thing I was pissed about was that she'd lied to me and fucked up my sleep schedule. So we had her pack her shit and dropped her off at some pier. One more time I was glad I always used condoms.

The girls ate mushrooms after the club and ran around the boat naked until the sun came up. Jay flew a drone to get video of them all dancing on a nice wooden table, but they broke it and collapsed into a lump on the deck. Leidy asked to fly the drone, and Jay agreed if she was certain she knew how to operate it. She assured him she did. Jay showed me the video of her taking the controls and flying the drone right into him. In the video, I saw the drone jolt towards them. She ducked, and his eyes got real big as it went right into his belly. Jay showed me his bloody arm and the cut on his gut.

Pro tip: Don't let girls on mushrooms fly drones.

Wan from Thailand joined us on the boat around one in the afternoon. He was with his girlfriend and the guy who started Lyft or Uber, but they weren't ready for this. Our boat was almost twice the size of theirs, and everyone had been partying for twenty-four hours, so it looked like a Mötley Crüe hotel room after a show. Naked women were fully passed out, baking in the sun. Those still awake were drinking and snorting Lyrica. I think Wan's girl was severely traumatized by what she witnessed.

Lyrica was sold in Italy without a prescription and was similar to Quaaludes. It makes you happy and feel a little drunk, but you'd slur your speech a little bit if you took too much. I only took it once because when I woke up the next morning; I still felt a little wobbly, and I don't like hangovers. But Clarence and the girls loved it. I've said it before and people usually don't believe me, but I always felt like I was the normal person surrounded by crazy people.

Even though I thought this would be the trip to end all trips, I didn't have much fun. The setup was wrong. I was so focused on doing everything bigger and better than before that I'd missed what was most important. That was enjoying each day and doing things that made me happy. Sometimes with social media, you can get so caught up in showing everyone you're having a good time that you forget to actually have one.

There was an article in *Vice* where the writer decided he'd do everything I did for a week. "Dan Bilzerian isn't real in the traditional sense," he wrote. "He's more like an advertisement for bachelorhood. Dan is a poster boy for what life could be if us guys stopped being afraid and started working out."

After doing a low-rent version of everything I did for a week, the writer concluded, "Dan epitomizes the eternal search for more. Everything he does is massive and bombastic and covered in cocaine-powered pussy. He is America in the flesh. [But] after a week of Dan's life, I realized it's not even that great."

He went on: "Sure, private jets are nice, but they're just pipes with wings. Laying in a small pile of strippers was nice, but they're just people. In the end, the whole thing was like planning a big trip to Europe, just to arrive and go *yep, that's an old church. What else*. But Dan can't stop. He's an Instagram celebrity, and he's stuck on this big meaningless, exhausting, eternally ungratifying treadmill."

It's cute that he thought he was living like me. He was probably a loser journalist banging sixes on a budget that wouldn't cover a bar tab. But his theory wasn't far off. I was doing what I always said I never wanted to do, which was documenting more than living, imitating myself instead of being myself, regressing as a person instead of growing.

I had gotten so obsessed with building the Ignite brand, making noise, giving people a show, and flexing on anyone who had talked shit that I was losing my soul in the process. I'd truly reached the limits of excess and found that there was no happiness there.

People think money can buy happiness, but it can only buy pleasure. Those are very different things.

Happiness comes from doing things you love, having meaningful relationships, helping people, working towards a goal, and being at peace with yourself. Ultimately, though, happiness is a state of mind, not something that you need to feed, and it can last a lifetime if you keep your mind right.

Pleasure, on the other hand, needs to be fed. It comes from hedonism, sex, money, partying, and self-indulgence. It is addictive and functions *exactly* like a drug. You get an intense high that quickly flees. The more you do it, the more you need to do it to get that same high—and after a while, you don't even get high anymore. But you have to do it just to not feel like shit.

I had fully maxed out these highs for so long I couldn't feel pleasure anymore, let alone happiness. The latest Ferrari I bought didn't even give me pleasure for twenty-four hours. I had fucked so many women I was numb to it. I used to feel like I accomplished something when these things happened but not anymore.

Having objectives like money, pussy, and power will never lead to happiness. Because no matter how much you have, you always want more. It's like trying to fill a black hole. You can't fill a black hole. These things are infinite and endless traps.

When I first started gambling, I thought a million dollars was a good goal. Then I was sure that $5 million would be plenty, then $10 million. And it kept escalating. Same with women. How many girls did I need to fuck to feel like I'd succeeded and could stop? There were times when I didn't even want to have sex, but I would fuck girls just because it was wired into my brain that I was supposed to. Like a billionaire who sees a hundred-dollar bill on the street—he doesn't need to, but he's always going to bend down and pick it up.

I had so much more fun shrooming, surfing, and hiking with my friends in Hawaii than I had on this vacation. I've found the things I have enjoyed the most in my life didn't cost much money.

I can tell you the hedonistic narrative I've preached before, that money is freedom, and it's fun to drive fast cars and fuck hot girls. It's nice to get respect, to be able to tell people to get fucked, and not have a boss. All those things are true, but I'm one of the few people who can actually vouch for it not being a goal that in it of itself will bring long-term lasting happiness.

I left the boat with Leidy and Des and instantly felt happier without the harem. As soon as we arrived at the hotel in Iceland, I hooked up with Des and then Leidy. The girls were happy, and I felt much more relaxed. We ordered a bunch of food, smoked weed, and went to a volcanic hot spring.

Leidy and Des.

Two women was nice; more is not always better. After the boat and the Ignite UK launch, I decided as we ended the trip in the beautiful and surreal landscape of Iceland that was it. My plan to go bigger was over; I'd finally hit the ceiling. That said, I still had a company to run, and the show must go on.

CLARENCE WILSON (NAME CHANGED)

Hedge Fund Manager

Once the fame genie was out of the bottle, it was extremely hard to contain. In the beginning, Dan relished in his newfound power. The ability to not have to compete for sex (for a sex addict) was liberating. At first, he was happy to always have a hot girl wanting to sleep with him anywhere he was in the world. But then it was a burden; he was the pony everyone wanted to ride in the circus of his life for "whatevers." He tried to have fun with it, the ring master that he is, but often he was overwhelmed and overrun.

I can't count the number of times he would tell some large breasted girl to smack my head with her tits to wake me up at 2:00 a.m. and have sex with me or some other person first before he would consider having sex with them. And sure enough, they would try (wait in this line to ride the ride).

A man has only so much energy, and eventually, Dan couldn't physically satisfy the demand. He created a prison, not able to enjoy normal outdoor activities without getting mobbed by people wanting a picture or trying to strike up conversation. In many ways aside from what you may think, it was miserable and limiting. We often just hung out at home, hiding out playing chess or arguing philosophy and politics.

He did try to have relationships, but his sexual addiction and the relentless sexual pony ride eventually took its toll on every relationship. At first, they were all about the craziness, but after a while, they couldn't take it. How could they? Dan couldn't take it; even with all the steroids and Cialis a man could possibly take, it was still too much.

Dan taught me in a matter of months that my dream of being famous was a nightmare in disguise. What I once would have given my net worth for, I now would avoid like the plague because he can't turn it off.

There are brief periods of time where he goes underground, cuts off all women and hangers-on, and we can be human and play chess and pontificate. But much like the ring in Lord of the Rings, fame whispers to him, and he puts his ringmaster hat on, and the circus is in full swing again. Ring masters don't retire young, I guess.

The worst part of all this experiment gone wildly successful, so much that it hurts, is that it obscures many of the great qualities and traits that Dan does have. He is generous, compassionate, caring, of high integrity, and has a lot of don't quit grit. Yes, he has many controversial takes and some bad programming, but it is not out of malice. Most of all, Dan is a learner always trying to be a little better when the circus doesn't have its grip on him.

I'm very much looking forward to the second act of this circus. This is going to be the part where he has figured out how to make maximum positive impact on the world and use his fame to that end. It's been in the works, and if he's at all one-tenth as successful as the first act, it will be a great benefit to all. Fingers crossed!

CHAPTER 98

The Final Party... For Now

I'd had sex with three girls before the party even started, and I'd fuck five more before the night was over.

It was October, 2019 and it was time for Ignite's second Halloween party. Seventy ex-military security guards roamed the property armed with AR-15s and shotguns. I'd hired tons of extra promoters and door girls to make sure everything ran smoothly. Shuttles were flowing to the house packed with models.

The party started at ten, but I told all the girls they had to be at the house before nine if they didn't want to shuttle.

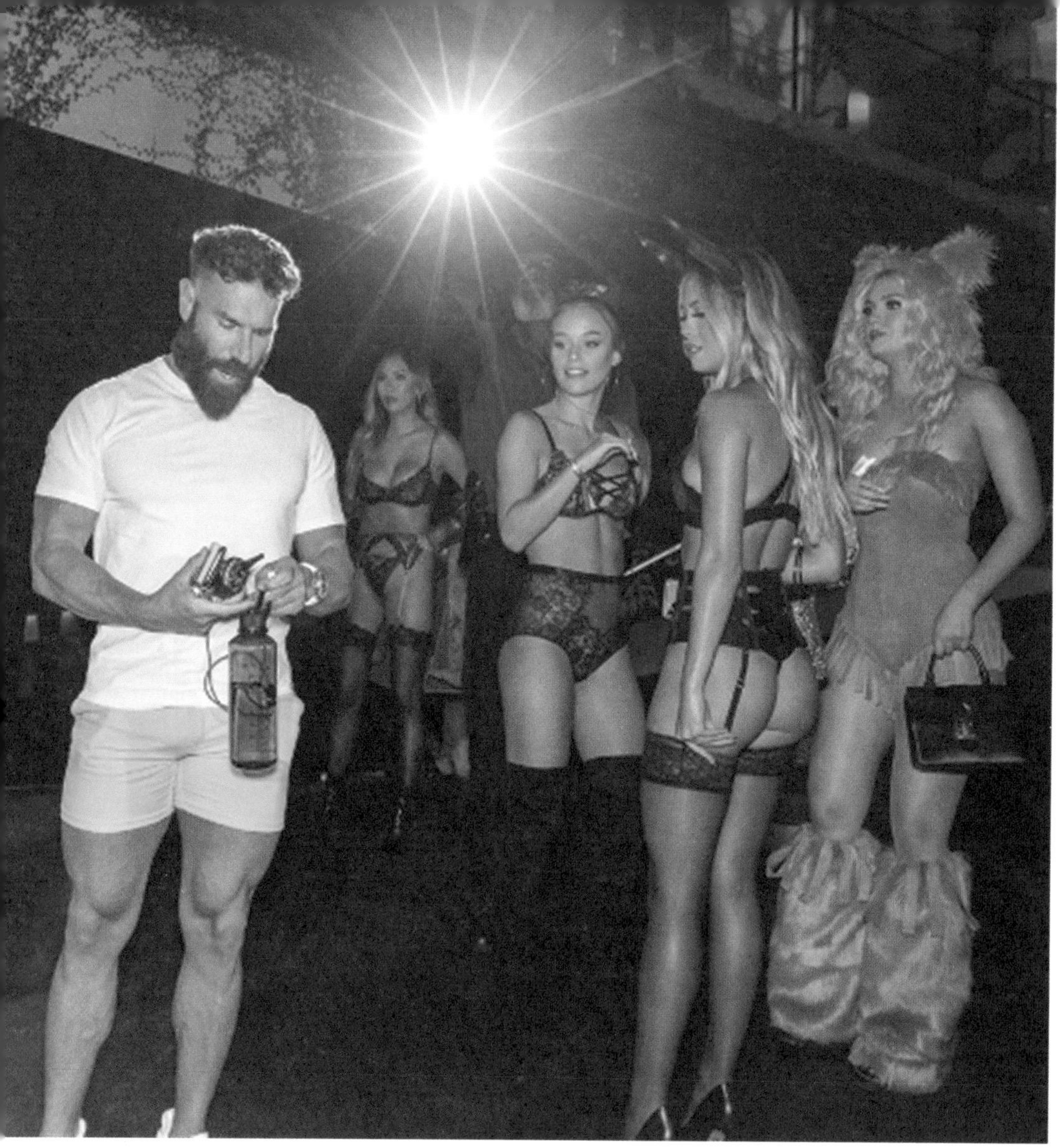

There were over 1,600 women in the house before the party even started. I had flown out four random followers who'd commented on my last pic. They wisely showed up two hours early and were loving life. By the time ten rolled around, the house was slammed, and it was 95 percent gorgeous women wearing lingerie at the most. I had the forty women I was dating and other random hot ones in my sectioned-off VIP room reserved for A-list celebrities.

As I walked through the house with my heads of security parting the way, all eyes seemed to be focused on me. Some of the girls I was dating proudly strutted by my side while a string of others followed closely behind. I didn't spend a lot of time out and about at my parties, but when I did, it caused quite the commotion. Heads turned and iPhone lights shined as people filmed and snapped pictures.

There were always girls following me and the trail seemed to grow until I got to my bedroom or an area that required a special wrist band. Once special access was required the girls became more aggressive, grabbing arms or other limbs trying to get my attention.

Throwing great parties sounds cool, but it's a pain in the ass. There is a ton of pressure to do it correctly and I pissed off way more guys than I made happy because of the strict guest list that I kept. My phone was flooded with text messages and there were a million things going on, but I took solace in the fact that at any given moment if a girl caught my eye, I could get laid as quickly as I could find a bedroom or bathroom. When I was younger I never dreamed of being this desired and it felt good knowing I could sleep with almost any woman I saw.

There were around three thousand people there, and it was pretty much all women, artists, athletes, and celebrities of some sort. Just about everyone I spoke to said it was the best party that had ever been thrown, hands down. People have always wanted to see me fail since I was a kid. So I relished the fuck-you moments of life, and this rager was one of them.

I made my way to the fourth-floor day bed in the VIP area, and it immediately turned into a giant dog pile with me and twenty girls. I texted my chef that I was ready for breakfast and asked security to get me a couple beers. The food was going to take thirty minutes, so I decided to take a lap. I headed towards the DJ booth where Diplo, Carnage, and Alesso were all spinning together. I stood behind them and looked at the crowd; it was just a sea of hot women. Locating a Y chromosome in that ocean was like playing a game of *Where's Waldo*.

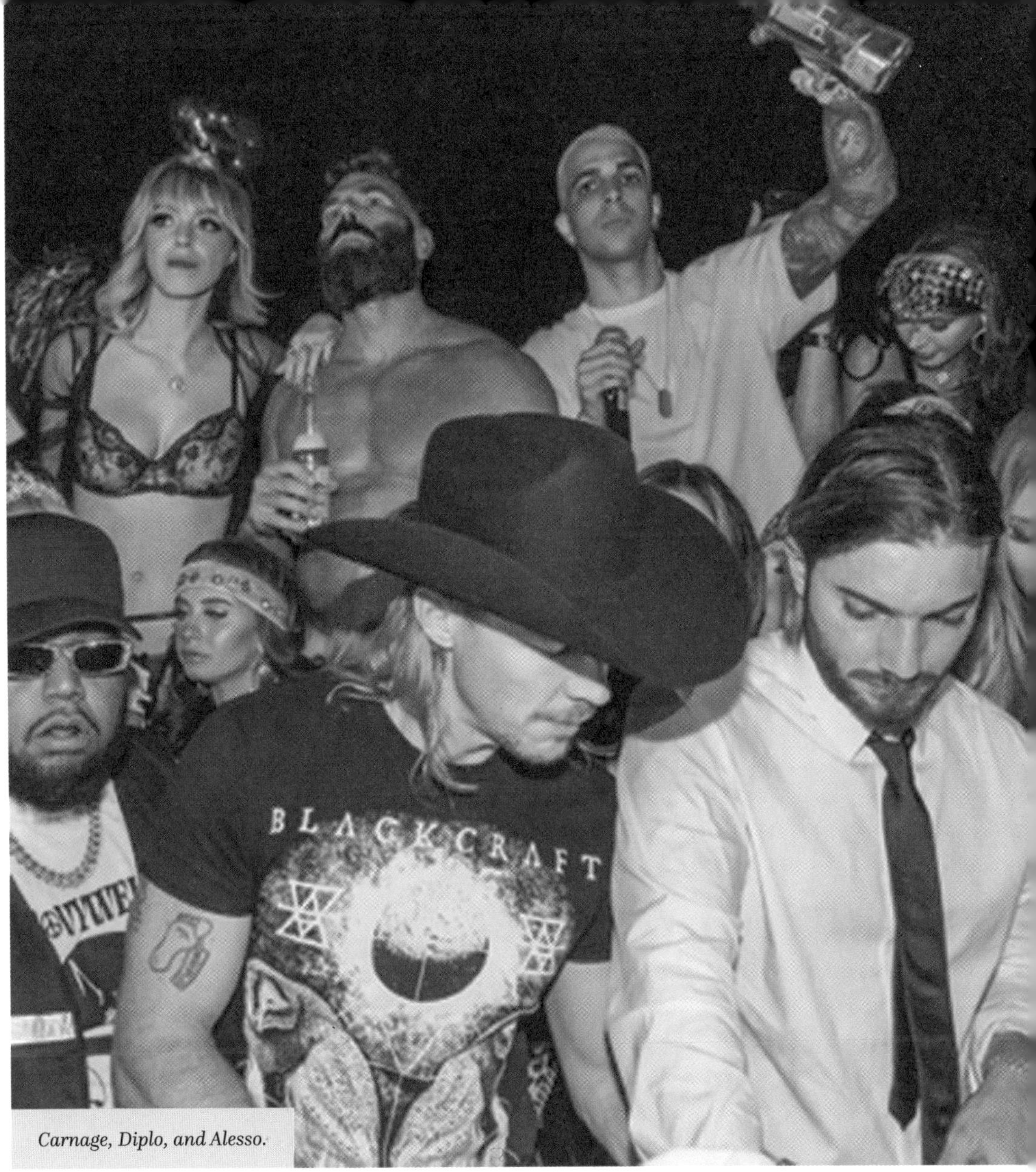

Carnage, Diplo, and Alesso.

My breakfast was waiting when we got back. I sat on the bed and ate while girls crawled over each other to scratch my back and rub my legs. People standing around the bed filmed with their cellphones. I could see the surprise in their faces, shocked that this was real. This wasn't planned or orchestrated in any way; it was just a natural spectacle that occurred because of the environment that I'd created. I sat there thinking about it, knowing I'd done what I'd set out to do. I'd accomplished all of my hedonistic goals. This was the top of the mountain.

I soaked it all in and smiled.

It was the perfect setup.

Epilogue

In all likelihood, Oprah will not have me on to cry about my inspirational story. My tale isn't the usual feel-good transformation that makes for clearly defined self-help books. I am the guy who doesn't conform to social norms, who doesn't follow the rules—a sort of antihero at best.

But I did overcome, and I did it my way.

And you can too.

You simply have to decide what you want, and then set up your life so you can acquire it. You pay now, or you pay later in life, and setup is all about paying your dues early so you don't have to later. Everything I've accomplished in my life has been achieved through setup and perseverance.

There isn't a magical incantation I can give you unless it is this: Do not give up. Success is a matter of willpower. I suffered through physical pain, humiliation, and failure but all of that helped me; I used it as the fuel for my drive. With a strong will and an agile mind, you can overcome almost any limitation.

Look for the angles. Devise a good setup. It doesn't matter what your goals are. You might be a one-woman type of guy, a one-guy type of guy, or a ten-guys type of woman. You might be a sex fiend, a work fiend, or a philanthropy fiend. Regardless, establishing an effective life setup will allow you to accomplish your goals, and in the long run saves untold time and effort.

You don't need what society tells you to succeed. You don't need a college degree to get rich. You don't have to be good looking to attract tons of women. And you don't need any talent to be famous. Life is a game, and like any game, you must have a good strategy to win. The implementation of that strategy is called the setup, and it paves the road to success.

Before you figure out a way to hack life and rig the system to accomplish your objectives, just make sure your goals are the right goals. Because as the old saying goes, be careful what you wish for. You might just get it.

Acknowledgments

Thank you to David Goggins for motivating me to write the book at the perfect time. To Naren Aryal for helping me self-publish, so I didn't have to give 85 percent of my money to a traditional shithead publishing house. To Neil Strauss for the first edit. To Rob Judge for putting up with my late night calls and helping me with my never ending editing process. To Wayne Marquez for suggesting I add vignettes; they add a great perspective and color to the story. To everyone who wrote vignettes, thank you for taking the time and doing such a great job. To my mother and father for helping me with dates, timelines, and pictures. To everyone I gave early copies to for your feedback and critiques.